OVERDRIVE

A Personal Documentary

OVERDRIVE

A PERSONAL DOCUMENTARY

William F. Buckley, Jr.

Little, Brown & Company

Boston   Toronto

FIRST PAPERBACK EDITION

Published by arrangement with
Doubleday and Company, Inc.

Selections from this book first appeared in *The New Yorker*.

Grateful acknowledgment is made to the following for permission to reprint their copyrighted material:

Excerpt from "In Memory of W. B. Yeats," from *The English Auden: Poems, Essays, and Dramatic Writings, 1927–
1939*, by W. H. Auden, edited by Edward Mendelson, re-
printed by kind permission of Random House, Inc.

Excerpt from "God and Boys at Millbrook" by William F.
Buckley from October 4, 1981, *New York Times Magazine*,
copyright © 1981 by The New York Times Company. Re-
printed by permission.

Lyrics excerpt from "Hair," copyright © 1966, 1967, 1968
James Rado, Jerome Ragni, Galt MacDermot, Nat Shapiro,
United Artists Music Company, Inc. All rights controlled
and administered by UNITED ARTIST MUSIC. All rights
reserved. Used by permission.

*Published simultaneously in Canada
by Little, Brown & Company (Canada) Limited*

PRINTED IN THE UNITED STATES OF AMERICA

FOR
Shirleykins

ACKNOWLEDGMENTS

A portion of the book was first published in *The New Yorker*. The reminiscence on Millbrook School was first published in the New York *Times Sunday Magazine*. Kate Medina of Doubleday, with whom I had not previously worked, helped me enormously with suggestions major and minor. So did Samuel Vaughan, as ever with that distinctive touch, light and substantive. Anyone inclined to blame them for the shortcomings of this book can have copies of their criticism. Sophie Wilkins read the manuscript, and returned me a cornucopia of wonderful suggestions. My brother Reid made comments extraordinarily useful, as did my son Christopher, who in his marginal notes did not even fight back about his mustache. I am grateful also to Charles Wallen, Thomas Wendel, and Steve Umin. Dorothy McCartney, head of research for *National Review*, has, as usual, made an honest man of me. I should add that David Green of *The New Yorker* is the most thoroughgoing and resourceful researcher in history. I cannot imagine why those who wonder what is the meaning of the Aztec calendar stone don't simply ask Mr. Green? Susan Stark did the manuscript with the help of our Z-89 word processor (using HDOS's PIE and TEXT, as per the instructions of Hugh Kenner). Frances Bronson did the general editorial supervision. Chaucy Bennetts did a superb job of copy editing, among other things reminding me that "irradiates" is a transitive verb. Inasmuch as I belong to Mr. Theodore Bernstein's school, which favors dropping the accusative form of the pronoun "who" (except after a preposition), the liberties I take in this matter are my own responsibility. Joseph Isola did his fine job of proofreading. To them all, my thanks.

overdrive *n* [*over* + *drive*]: an automotive transmission gear which transmits to the propeller shaft a speed greater than engine speed.

INTRODUCTORY EPILOGUE

(What follows is an essay on the critical reaction to the publication of the hardcover edition of Overdrive. *It can be read before reading the book. Or after reading the book. Or not at all!)*

When Ray Roberts, who is my editor in this paperback edition of *Overdrive*, asked if I would write an introduction to it I agreed right away to do so. I did this because I thought the reviews of it worth going over with some thought, hoping that such a study would interest readers, and knowing that it would interest me. There are over a hundred of these (*Overdrive* was handled intensively by the critical press) and they say something about the book but also about the culture in which they cropped up.

I begin, in search of focus, with a chronology. I reveal in the text of *Overdrive* when exactly it occurred to me (quite suddenly) to write this book, a journal of that particular week in my life. I had done such a book ten years earlier. It was here and there suggested by some critics that I had dreamed up a way to discharge an obligation to my publisher. Not so. In fact, the contrary is the case because when I decided to write this book I needed to get my publisher's agreement to postpone a commitment I had already made. I decided that I wished to write *this* book.

So I did: during the two months (in February and March), in Switzerland, when I have the time substantially to devote myself to book writing. It took me as many weeks to complete, almost exactly, as any of my other books, including my novels. It was suggested by one critic (you will see) that I more or less dictated scraps of this & that into a machine, presumably while skiing. Other critics, however (you will also see), did not challenge that the book was written with care.

When I returned to New York, the manuscript complete except for the fine-tuning I do in July, I sent a letter to the editor of the *New Yorker*, Mr. William Shawn. I told him I thought it unlikely he would want to see my new book, given that I used exactly the same formula I had used ten years before in writing *Cruising Speed*, which the *New Yorker* had excerpted. Mr. Shawn replied that he would like to read *Overdrive*, which he subsequently bought.

It happened that the task of editing *Cruising Speed*'s excerpts fell to Mr. Shawn, if it can be said that anything at the *New Yorker* "falls" to Mr. Shawn. In any event, I had the extraordinary experience of working with him, he going over every sentence. When we lunched together one day I remember that a substantial part of our meeting was concerned with my habit of placing commas in unconventional places. This finally drew from Mr. Shawn, over the telephone, what I take it must be the sharpest kind of reproach the gentleman ever permits himself: "I am afraid, Mr. Buckley, that you do not really know the proper use of the comma." If St. Peter had declared me unfit to enter the Kingdom of God, I could not have felt more searingly the reproach, delivered in Mr. Shawn's inimitable (meiotic) manner. I hardly intend to suggest that he is otherwise permissive, though he sticks firmly, after the *New Yorker* makes the first-draft selection, to his determination to let authors whose works are being excerpted signify what they wish included, what excluded. Merely that he is meticulous. "I want *you* to be pleased with what we publish," he said to me. I have had a wonderful relationship with the *New Yorker*, having submitted five book manuscripts to Mr. Shawn, and received five acceptances.

I did not again work directly with Mr. Shawn. My next editor, William Whitworth, also demanding, and thorough, and civil, is now the editor of the *Atlantic Monthly*. The succeeding editor was Patrick Crow, a genial, surefooted, relaxed and amusing man who does not for a moment attempt to conceal that Mr. Shawn is *the* editor of the *New Yorker*, who reviews every controversial decision made during the many hours spent between the author and his *New Yorker* editor. When the author especially pleads for inclusion of a passage to which Mr. Shawn unwaveringly objects, what happens is that Mr. Shawn calls the author up and patiently explains why he is opposed to the inclusion of that passage. This author always relented. I would do anything for Mr. Shawn save join the Communist Party, and I am happy that it is unlikely he will ever ask me to do so.

All of this is by way of background, given that some critics a) concluded that I expanded by force-feeding into a book (about 75,000 words long) what I had written for the *New Yorker* (the *New Yorker's* version ran about 45,000 words); while others b) pretended to flirt with the idea that Mr. Shawn had coaxed me into writing a self-parody, that he had acted as an editorial agent provocateur — a reading of Mr. Shawn wildly ignorant of the kind of person he is; leaving also c) a few critics who, though reviewing my book, obviously had not read it, having clearly read only the excerpts published in the *New Yorker*. One critic especially comes to mind, who warned, "Readers seeking the tart side of Mr. Buckley will be disappointed." The tart side of Mr. Buckley is well-represented in the book, less so in the *New Yorker* excerpts because Mr. Shawn explained to me over the telephone, after I had pitched for the inclusion of one very tart episode, that the *New Yorker* does not have a letters column in which editorial targets can fire back, and that therefore he feels it morally important to avoid anything that might be thought as hit-and-run.

In due course (January, February 1983), the *New Yorker* excerpts were published, and the reaction to them was, well, out of the ordinary. The *Washington Post's* Curt Suplee reported joyously in his column, "That incessant scrunching noise you keep hearing to the north is Wm. F. Buckley Jr. attempting to squeeze his ego between the covers of the *New Yorker*. The behemoth first half of his two-part personal journal makes Proust looks positively laconic. Buckley maunders along like Macaulay on Quaaludes about his house, limo, kids and friends, gloating and quoting his snappiest ripostes . . . *And yet you can't put the damn thing down!* Odd anecdotes bob up in the verbal spew (e.g., the time a typo in his column made it seem as if Pat Boone and his wife were wild about porno movies). The rhythm becomes hypnotic and . . . is there such a thing as smug-o-lepsy?"

I think I can only describe the reaction of *Newsweek* as hysterical. Before the *New Yorker's* ink was dry, Mr. Gene Lyons published an excoriation in high tushery of indignation ("So who is this preposterous snob?"). Not satisfied with this, *Newsweek* then published letters from readers for whom the mere mention of my name is obviously emetic. And not content with *that*, *Newsweek* then published a piece speculating on who might be the successor to William Shawn when he retires as editor of the *New Yorker*, including reference to unnamed critics' concern over Mr. Shawn's wilting powers, as witness that he had published the "self-indulgent" journals of Mr. Buckley. (The three assaults prompted me to write to *Newsweek* to observe that I hoped their obsessive concern over my self-indulgent journals had not got in the way of their enjoyment of the two million dollar party *Newsweek* had given itself in New York to celebrate its fiftieth anniversary. The letter was published, but in bowdlerized form.)

Now, leading up to publication of the book and fired by the *New Yorker*, came the parody-makers. There was one by Jon Carroll of the *San Francisco Chronicle* which was quite funny, burlesquing among other things my occasional use of Latin phrases. He had me referring to "Nihil Obstat, our Cuban-American cook," summoning my "Honduran-American driver, Pari Passu," sailing my "71-foot sloop, Malum In Sea," and using the services of my "ever efficient secretary, Gloria Mundi." There was another treatment by Richard Cohen of the *Washington Post*, good-natured and clever. Another in the *New York Review of Books*, some of it very funny, and still another in the *New Republic*.

I have elected to publish here in full the parody I thought funniest. It was written for the University of Chicago daily, the *Chicago Maroon*, by an undergraduate, David Brooks, the week before I went there as a visiting fellow. I put it all here in part because it is exuberantly readable but also because it communicates the nature of the irritation felt by some of the readers of the *New Yorker* articles. He touches, in the manner of the parodist, on themes that would be sustained by many of the critics when the book came out in August.

THE GREATEST STORY EVER TOLD

William Freemarket Buckley was born on December 25, 1935 in a little town called Bethlehem. He was baptized an Episcopalian on December 28 and admitted to Yale University on the 30th.

Buckley spent most of his infancy working on his memoirs. By the time he had learned how to talk he had finished three volumes: *The World Before Buckley*, which traced the history of the world prior to his conception; *The Seeds of Utopia*, which outlined his affect on world events during the nine months of his gestation; and *The Glorious Dawn*, which described the profound ramifications of his birth on the social order.

Buckley attended nursery school at the School of Soft Knocks, majoring in Art History. His thesis, "A Comparison of Michelangelo's David and My Own Mirror" won the Arthur C. Clarke award for Precocious Criticism and brought him to the attention of world luminaries.

His next bit of schooling was done at Exeter, where he majored in Pre-Yale.

Buckley's education was interrupted by World War II, during which he became the only six year old to fight in Guadalcanal and to land on the beaches of Normandy. Combat occupied much of his time during the period, but in between battles he was able to help out on the Manhattan Project, offer advice at Yalta, and design the Marshall Plan. His account of the war, *Buckley Versus Germany*, perched atop the *New York Times* Best Seller List for three years.

Upon his return to Exeter, Buckley found that schoolwork no longer challenged him. He transferred his energies to track, crew, polo, golf, tennis, mountain climbing, debate, stock brokerage, learning the world's languages, playing his harpsichord and, of course, writing his memoirs. By this time he had finished his ninth volume, *The Politics of Puberty*, which analyzed angst in the international arena and gave advice on how to pick up women. A friend at the time, Percy Rockefeller-Vanderbilt III remembered, "Everybody liked Bill at Exeter. His ability to change water into wine added to his popularity."

The years at Exeter were followed by the climax of his life, the Yale years. While at Yale he majored in everything and wrote the bestseller, *God and Me at Yale*, which was followed by *God and Me at Home*, and finally, *God and Me at the Movies*.

His extracurricular activities at Yale included editing the *Yale Daily News*, serving as President of the University, and chairing the committee to have Yale moved from New Haven to Mount Olympus. He also proved the existence of God by uttering the cartesian formula, "I think, therefore I am."

While a senior, Buckley founded the publications which would become his life's work: one was a journal of politics entitled *The National Buckley*, and the other was a literary magazine called *The Buckley Review*. Later, he would merge the two publications into what is now known as *The Buckley Buckley*.

On the day of graduation, Buckley married Miss Honoria Haight-Ashbury and fathered a son and a daughter (Honoria helped) both of whom would be named Yale.

As any of you who read the *New Yorker* know, life for Mr. Buckley since then has been anything but dull. On any given morning he will consult with a handful of national leaders and the Pope, write another novel in the adventure series, "Bill Buckley, Private Eye," chat with a bevy of Academy Award winners, write a few syndicated columns, and tape an edition of his TV show,

"Firing Pin." He also tames a wild horse, chops down trees to reduce US oil imports, and descrambles some top secret Soviet spy transmissions.

In the afternoons he is in the habit of going into crowded rooms and making everybody else feel inferior. The evenings are reserved for extended bouts of name-dropping.

Last year, needing a break from his hectic fast lane life, Buckley sailed across the Atlantic in his yacht, the HMS Armsrace, and wrote a book entitled *Atlantic High*. In one particularly riveting scene, the Armsrace runs out of gas in the middle of the ocean and Buckley is forced to walk the rest of the way.

Buckley has received numerous honorary degrees, including an MBA, an Ll.D, a PhD, an MD and an LHD, all of them from Yale, of course.

During his two days at this University, Mr. Buckley will meet with students, attend classes, deliver a lecture and write four books.

So that as the countdown approached for the publication of *Overdrive*, one had the feeling that pens were being taken to the smithies to be sharpened. My son Christopher has a sensitive ear for these matters and advised me to batten down the hatches: I had seriously provoked, he warned me, substantial members of the critical community. And sure enough, his Farmer's Almanac proved reliable because the flak from the most conspicuous critical quarters (the *New York Times*, the *Washington Post*, the *New York Review of Books*, the *New Republic*, the *Nation*, *Atlantic*, and *Harper's*) was instantaneous, and heavy. These critics were uniformly . . . upset, might be the generic word to describe their emotions. They expressed themselves differently, and at different lengths, ranging from the four-thousand-word review by John Gregory

Dunne in the *New York Review of Books*, to the two-sentence review in the *Atlantic Monthly*. They found the book variously boring, boorish, presumptuous, vain, arrogant, illiterate, solipsistic, and other things.

The Virginia Kirkus Service, which is a prepublication bulletin designed for bookstores and libraries, summarized that "most readers will probably find this [book] tedious at best, sleekly loathsome at worst." The writing is "sloppy." An example of the kind of thing one finds in it is that at one point I ask myself why I labor, and answer, " 'the call of *recta ratio*,' and 'the fear of boredom.' He then goes on, patronizingly, to explain what *recta ratio* means." I think this means either that everybody already knows what *recta ratio* means, or that if not everybody knows what it means, an author should not explain the meaning, as to do so is patronizing. Writing for the *New York Times*, novelist Nora Ephron was oh so scornful. "He has written a book about money," was her principal finding. She imputed anti-Semitism (ever so deftly, but more readers would catch that, than the meaning of *recta ratio*) and insensitivity to the suffering of my friends all in a single sentence: (". . . it's appalling that Mr. Buckley should mention Shylock when discussing *National Review's* landlord or discourse so blithely on the physical infirmities of his friends"). And closed by suggesting that my affectations might best be understood by using a little ethnic imagination ("The English used to say, give an Irishman a horse and he'll vote Tory, but never mind").

So certain was Miss Ephron that much would be made of the fact that I get about in a chauffeur-driven limousine that she led off with it, quoting from my book at some length, to wit:

> I cannot imagine that anyone who reviews this book will fail to mention the part about the limousine, so I

may as well begin with it. Only a few pages into *Over-drive*, WFB gets into his limousine . . . and the occasion inspires him to reveal the circumstances under which he had the car custom built. "What happened," he writes, "was that three years ago when it came time to turn in my previous car, which had done over 150,000 miles, the Cadillac people had come up with an austerity-model limousine, fit for two short people, preferably to ride to a funeral in. The dividing glass between the driver and driven was not automatic, there was no separate control for heat or air conditioning in the back, and the jump seats admitted only two. . . . This simply would not do: I use the car constantly, require the room, privacy, and my own temperature gauge. . . . There was, as usual, a market solution. You go out (this was in 1978) and buy a plain old Cadillac. You deliver it to a gentleman in Texarkana [I should have said Ft. Smith, Arkansas]. He chops it in two, and installs whatever you want. Cost? Interesting: within one thousand dollars of the regular limousine, and I actually don't remember which side."

Don't you see, Miss Ephron asks, "the story of the limousine is *emblematic*"? (My italics.)

My colleague Joe Sobran, on seeing Miss Ephron's review, sent me a memorandum: "Dear Bill, The critical reaction is interesting: Nora Ephron calls it 'a book about money,' when it's her *review* that's about money. I can't imagine you dwelling on the subject as she does; for that matter, I can't imagine you writing about your worst enemy as she writes about her ex-husband. Wonderful to hear such a woman lecture on poor taste, vulgarity, the nouveau riche. . . . My impression was that you can only be nouveau riche for the short-term; she seems to want to make you out as *second-generation* nouveau riche. She sees bigotry in a Shakespearean tag, then proceeds to make a crack about the Irish which the *Times* wouldn't tolerate about just *any* ethnic group."

Grace Lichtenstein, writing for the *Washington Post*, leaned heavily on the tease that William Shawn was pulling a fast one. "When parts of this book first appeared in the *New Yorker*, I thought it was a joke, a Buckley parody of how some leftist might view Buckley's preoccupation with material possessions and his aristocratic lifestyle. Alas, it is not an intentional parody, although there are, swimming in this sea of trivia, some amusing anecdotes. . . ." Again, the business about my obsession with wealth, the slouchiness of my writing style; and then, to preserve her credentials as an even-minded critic, "Now let me tell you the most awful part of *Overdrive*. After plowing through a third of it I realized . . . I was also (deep breath here) [her deep breath] quite envious. I mean, who wouldn't want a stretch limo in which to dictate one's letters? [etc., extending to a cook and a chauffeur] — plebian clod that I am," said Miss Lichtenstein, teasing us, because we are all supposed to know she is not *really* a plebeian clod.

Harper's took pretty much the same line, done by Rhoda Koenig, and the *Atlantic Monthly* saved space with a two-line review. "Mr. Buckley has assumed that a move by move record of one week in his bustling life, together with such recollections, reflections, and droppable names as occur to him en route, will be of benefit to the public. Ah, well, to err is human, and Mr. Buckley is not divine." There is a heavy burden, one can see, placed here on the word "benefit," as in "benefit to the public." Is Mr. Shawn, the revered longtime tutor of the editor of the *Atlantic*, engaged in "benefiting" mankind when he publishes the *New Yorker*? And if so, how do we measure these benefits (given that we are not divine)?

The *San Francisco Chronicle* also elected a short dismissal, by Patricia Holt, "Buckley has produced an overdone, overwritten, overblown 'personal documentary' whose preview in the *New Yorker* earlier this year provoked a brilliant sendup by Jon Carroll in these pages. Better to read that column than waste your time with this book." The revelation to the citizens of San Francisco that an editor of the *San Francisco Chronicle* was actually concerned about wasting their time was apparently met with such exuberant skepticism that *Overdrive* became, in that city, a modest best-seller.

The attack in the *New York Review of Books* was hefty and unexpected, this because its author, John Gregory Dunne, an acquaintance of long standing, had written to me after the *New Yorker* articles had been published to say in a pleasant context that he had "inhaled" the *New Yorker* pieces and looked forward to the book treatment. Usually, if you hear that something you created had been "inhaled," you are likely to conclude something other than that your friend had been bowled over by a mephitic encounter. In any event, when Mr. Dunne's attack was published, the editor, Robert Silvers, punctiliously offered me space to reply. The gravamen of Mr. Dunne's objections was, really, my technicolored view of life. Unhappily, the descriptions he gave of episodes touched on in the book justified his criticisms of them. If I were to write that Hamlet was a man who never could make up his mind and therefore manages to bore us to death I am, as a reviewer, fully protected — except against anybody who proceeds to read *Hamlet*. In my reply to the *New York Review of Books* I was concrete in the matter, excerpting exactly Dunne's description of one episode in the book (my quarrel with the *Boston Globe*) and then describing the episode itself. Mr. Dunne's version will live as a locus classicus of distortion (Locus Classicus, I should say for the benefit of Jon Carroll, is my Shangri-la).

A week after seeing Dunne's review I received a letter:

"If they ever listen [to what you wrote] (which must be a question) you will teach them not to take the sacred elixir of life and splash it all over the roadside, as they are too prone to do." That was the comment on *Overdrive* by Louis Auchincloss, whose profound advice is not heeded, even by writers some of whom can no longer blame their afflictions on youth. Lance Morrow (I anticipate my narrative) wrote, "I was just thinking about your book again, and about several exceptionally stupid reviews of it that I read. It seems to me that there was some massive point-missing going on there, but I can't quite account for it. Well, maybe I can at that."

Not easy. *People* magazine said of it, "Less self-confident men would be embarrassed to flaunt themselves so openly, but Buckley is obviously never shy." By contrast, Mr. Dunne was complaining: "[Buckley] is really not very giving of himself." *People* magazine would shrink to four pages if the editors suddenly found it "embarrassing" to express a curiosity about People ten times more inquisitive than any I would consent to satisfy. But Dunne was relentless in at once protesting the lack of profundity, while trivializing or ignoring what is there. Thus (in pursuit of the general vision of my hedonism), "[Buckley] spends every February and March skiing in Switzerland." That was on the order of my reporting, "Mr. Dunne spends every morning brushing his teeth." (My skiing occupies as much of my day in Switzerland as Mr. Dunne's stair-climbing does his days in Los Angeles.)

But oh how he worries about me! — as you would see if you read his entire review. I closed my letter to the *New York Review of Books* by quoting Dunne's final strictures, and my reaction to them:

"The show has been on the road too long," Dunne pronounced. "Mr. Buckley has spread himself so thin that he has begun to repeat himself, repeatedly. *Overdrive* is *Cruis-*

ing Speed redux as last year's *Atlantic High* is *Airborne* redux. As might be expected, Mr. Buckley is unrepentant." I answered, "As well complain that I edit a 28-year-old magazine which will celebrate the fourth of July again on the fourth of July. I have written a dozen non-fiction books, six novels, and a few books that are not routinely classified, though they are, by some, glibly dismissed. In 1985, I shall write a book called *Pacific High*, patterned after the first two. The literary technique explored in *Cruising Speed* — I think of it, occasionally, as on the order of the invention of that stage — is so majestically successful I intend to repeat it ten years hence, and ten years after that. At which point I shall be happy to review John Gregory Dunne's *True Confessions IV*, inasmuch as I am certain there will be great wit in it, as there was in its progenitor; as also in *True Confessions Redux*, published last year. [My reference was to *Dutch Shea Jr.*] I promise in my next book to scratch up a friend about whom I can say something truly unpleasant if Greg Dunne promises in *his* next book to come up with a murdered woman who doesn't have a votive candle protruding from her vagina."

But I shouldn't delay much longer in reporting that others viewed *Overdrive* very differently. Take, for instance, the question of snobbery. A number of critics came gleefully to the conclusion that *Overdrive* was the work of a snob. Mr. Charlie Slack of the *Chattanooga Times* said it quaintly: "To call William F. Buckley Jr. a snob is to call the U.S.S. Nimitz a boat, the Sahara Desert a sandbox." The charge, widely if less picturesquely framed, struck the sensitive ear of *Time* essayist Lance Morrow. Now Morrow was himself disturbed by what he apparently deemed an unnecessary elongation in this book of hedonistic passages

— at least that is what I think he is saying here: "Buckley luxuriates in his amenities a bit too much, and one hears [I wish he had written: "one hears, if one strains to do so"] in his prose the happy sigh of a man sinking into a hot bath." But he scotches conclusively, in a striking passage, the correlations so widely drawn about people who luxuriate in soapsuds. "So his enemies [note the mot juste] try to dismiss him as Marie Antoinette in a pimpmobile. They portray him as, among other things, a terrible, terminal snob. To make the accusation is to misunderstand both William F. Buckley Jr. and the nature of snobbery. Buckley is an expansive character who is almost indiscriminately democratic in the range of his friends and interests. He glows with intimidating self-assurance. The true snob sometimes has an air of pugnacious, overbearing self-satisfaction, but it is usually mere front. The snob is frequently a grand porch with no mansion attached, a Potemkin affair. The essence of snobbery is not real self-assurance but its opposite, a deep apprehension that the jungles of vulgarity are too close, that they will creep up and reclaim the soul and drag it back down into its native squalor, back to the Velveeta and the doubleknits."

Closely related to the charge of snobbishness was that of arrogance (egotism, vanity, what you will). The reporter for *Palm Beach Life*, who should be familiar with the phenomenon, wrote, "His book is outrageous in its egotism" (he concluded, "but amusing withal. Treat yourself to it"). Phillip Seib, writing in the *Dallas Morning News*, took arrogance for granted but ventured an explanation: "A certain arrogance is essential if one is to publish what Buckley calls 'a personal documentary.'" The trouble with that extenuation, as far as an author is concerned, is that it gives such comfort as you would get from reading, "Mr. Joseph Blackburn, who traverses Niagara Falls on a tightrope, is said to be a damned fool. But who else but a damned fool would be expected to traverse Niagara Falls on a tightrope?"

Thomas Fox of the *Memphis Commercial Appeal* evidently thought he caught it all when he pronounced *Overdrive* "nothing more than the product of a smug exhibitionist who likes to wave his ego in public," while Peter Richmond, writing for the *Miami Herald*, gritted his teeth: *Overdrive* "may be the most egregious example of the abuse of literary license since Jack Kerouac, well into fame, actually published 250 pages of his dreams." The publisher of the *New Republic*, James Glassman, wrote in *USA Today* that *Overdrive* was "an act of sheer gall" but he quickly gave an individuated explanation for it. "My theory is that Buckley wrote *Overdrive* as proof of his own security in social and literary matters. He must have known that the literati would make fun of the book, but he wrote it anyway, just to flout them." That is an interesting insight, but it fails to explain why I should go out of my way to slight so many critics in this special way, since I tend to do so routinely in so many other ways. And it is incorrect to say that I expected anything like the reaction *Overdrive* got, about which more in due course.

Pamela Marsh of the *Christian Science Monitor* said that, really, it was worse than sheer arrogance. "Add to that his obvious relish in what seems an overwhelming arrogance — he is in fact proud of his pride." That tends to ask for more thought that one is routinely prepared to give to such facile statements, unless they come in from philosophers. (Let's see: John is proud to be an American. John is proud of his pride in being an American. How about: John is proud of his pride in his pride in being an American. I wonder if Miss Marsh ever thought of that? Ever *worried* about that?)

Doug Fellman, a student writing for the *Hopkins News-*

letter, tried to be reasonable about the whole thing: "Naturally, some persons will complain that Buckley, in recording his life in such a journal, is committing an act of great egotism and conceit. Yet the autobiography is a common and accepted form of biography, and Buckley simply chooses to record his life in the present and as an excerpt." But untuned objections were everywhere. The *Chicago Booklist* said comprehensively that, for some readers, *Overdrive* would prove "a cross section of everything that is wrong with America, from elitism to Reaganomics." The *Cleveland Plain Dealer* found "the private Buckley who appears in this book . . . laced with pride, unflinchingly materialistic and self-centered — all in all, a popinjay."

I (happen to) prefer temperamental reactions to the lorgnetted sort of thing *Overdrive* drew from what one might call The Social Justice Set. I especially preferred Miss (Ms. would here be safer, I suppose) Carolyn See of the *Los Angeles Times*, who saw the author of *Overdrive* as "an American institution . . . lounging elegantly in his talk-show chair, driving Norman Mailer into a conniption fit, teasing and torturing Gore Vidal until he just can't take any more, driving at least 49 percent of the viewing audience into a state of mind that can't really be described in words, but it involves lurching up out of your chair, burying your hands in your hair and shrieking 'Yuuggh! Turn it off! Make him go away!' " There's no quiche in Ms. See's diet, 100 percent All Bran.*

The refrain on the matter of wealth was widespread, the popular corollary of which was to reason on to insouciance, with respect to poverty, as (Ann Morrissett Davidson, *Philadelphia Inquirer*) for instance: "But there is some-

---

* Sometimes such wholesome antagonists go on to blush. Ms. See concluded her colorful review, "Buckley shows us a brittle, acerbic, dutybound, 'silly,' 'conservative' semi-fudd, with a heart as vast and varicolored and wonderful to watch as a 1930s jukebox."

thing rather beguiling and even enviable about this over-driven patrician and his way of life. Perhaps it is his apparently blithe blindness to most of the world's miseries." The patronizing explanation is both sweet and deadly. Jack the Ripper just didn't know it was wrong to strangle ladies, don't you see?

Two weighty voices, however distinct, came in from the Big Leagues.*

One of them Eliot Fremont-Smith of the *Village Voice*, the other Norman Podhoretz, the editor of *Commentary*. Fremont-Smith, in voicing qualified approval of the book and its author, is a prominent liberal who found himself teeming with with things to say.†

He began with the novel point that those who harp on the theme of the privileged life of the author of *Overdrive* tend to neglect a not insignificant point. "I think of *his* dilemma. No public figure I know of has been so chided by people he likes or is willing to admire or takes it with such aplomb." He insisted that *Overdrive* (a point made by several other reviewers) was ultimately a book about friendship. "Friends are more important, indeed all important. *Overdrive* is a record and celebration of connection, of how association (memories, locales, daily working intercourse, surprise, pleasure) improves the soul and perhaps the cause of civilization and bestows grace on all and sundry, by no means least of all" on the author. Fremont-

---

* I am grateful to a score of critics whose reviews, appearing in newspapers and magazines that seldom penetrate the Eastern Seaboard Establishment's switchboard, were understanding in every case, in some cases even encouraging, in a few even affectionate.

† His task was concededly complicated by a personal friendship, recently formed.

Smith, unlike the automatons who approached the book with floodlights in search of Social Justice and a hemorrhaging psyche, had eyes for *detail* (of which, in many reviews, there was a total absence). "He . . . discourses on Bach and Scarlatti with the likes of . . . Fernando Valenti and Rosalyn Tureck, and also mediates between them (the sections on music and the ego requirements of great performers are among the funniest, most scrupulous, and moving in the book)."

F-S becomes concrete, and it is interesting to reflect here on observations by one critic, alongside observations by two others.

On what I wrote in *Overdrive* about homosexuality, Fremont-Smith: "His riff on homosexuality, for notorious example [of my occasional waywardness], seems deliberately blind to all sorts of subtleties he should, at his age, with his antennae, be less innocent of."

On my treatment of homosexuality, Franz Oppenheimer in the *American Spectator*: "Another pernicious myth touched upon in *Overdrive* is the supposed biological and hereditary nature of homosexuality. . . . My father, who practiced psychiatry, first in Germany and, after his emigration in San Francisco, collected substantial evidence in support of Buckley's impression that homosexuality is a disease that can be cured. During my father's entire professional life he endeavored to find a true 'biological,' i.e., an incurable homosexual. He never did."

And then at a personal, more evaluative level, referring to a eulogy and a testimonial I gave in my book, Fremont-Smith:

"[In *Overdrive*,] love is couched in courtly encomiums that are heartfelt but nevertheless embarrass."

Norman Podhoretz: "He is so good at delivering tributes that one would choose him above all others (well, perhaps not above Daniel P. Moynihan) to deliver the eulogy at one's own funeral, or better still, the speech in one's honor on some appropriate occasion. There are samples of both kinds of speeches in *Overdrive* and they are, without exception, masterpieces of the extremely difficult art of praise." Some say tomayto; which of course is to be preferred.

Fremont-Smith, finally, declines to accept my implied proposition that the literary form I adopted (one week in the life of X) is generally viable. He rejects the notion that the form is widely useful. Rather, he insists that it must be taken as a singular phenomenon. "Two questions [in fact] arise: a) How is all this activity possible? b) Can we stand it? Particularly, can we stand Buckley's glorying in it? . . . basically *Overdrive* is a log — not a how-to-do-it but how-has-it-been-done in a particular frame of time by one particular energy."

I come now to Norman Podhoretz, who in November led the Book Review section of *Commentary* with an answer to the critics of *Overdrive*, interrupting a long silence as an active book reviewer. I am moved by the self-pride abundantly so designated in quotes already cited — but above all by feelings of gratitude most readers in my position would, I think, understand — to quote from this review. Podhoretz began, no less:

"The first thing to say about *Overdrive* is that it is a dazzling book." And then, of course: "The second thing to say is that it has generally been greeted with extreme hostility."

Podhoretz went on to examine the causes of such hostility, discarding routine ideological antagonism as a satisfactory answer. "I do not believe that the injustice done to

Overdrive can be explained in strictly political terms. Something deeper and more interesting is at work here." What that is is not easily distilled, though I will have a few thoughts on the subject at the end of this essay.

To those who declaimed first against the insubstantiality of *Overdrive* and then against the craftsmanship in *Overdrive*, like the lady who thought it should have been subtitled "Dictated but not read," Podhoretz replied: "The material is fascinating in itself and all Buckley's virtues as a writer are called forth in the recording of it. The prose flows smoothly and elegantly, its formality tempered with colloquial touches that somehow never jar, its mischievous wit coexisting in surprisingly comfortable congruence with its high rhetorical solemnities, its narrative pace sure-footed enough to accommodate detours and flashbacks without losing the necessary forward momentum." (Compare Grace Lichtenstein in the *Washington Post*: "What Buckley needed was a snappy rewrite by an experienced *People* hand. . . .") Podhoretz, who does not like to give ground, dealt defiantly with the matter of Money: "I for one do not doubt that the delight Buckley takes in his privileges is an exemplary spiritual virtue. If I do have a doubt, it concerns the extent of this delight. I mean, is he always so cheerful? Does he never suffer from anxiety?" (Eliot Fremont-Smith was more direct on this point: "In the book, Buckley has exquisite sandwiches but never takes a pee." (I wrote to Mr. F-S that I had trained myself never to pee, but he has not answered this letter, nor publicly celebrated my achievement.) (". . . What I was most struck by were the parts in which you tell us what you have to be sober about," my colleague Richard Brookhiser wrote me.)

To Mr. Podhoretz, I take the opportunity to say that I thought the shadows were there, in *Overdrive*, and that if they were not discernible to him, I do not know what is the appropriate reaction. Angst, in this volume, would not work.

Well, then. I have before me page after page of excerpts from reviews that make interesting observations. But economy requires that I put aside these notes and conclude. I do so by probing two questions, one concrete, and in its own way heuristic, the second general and critical.

The first is the matter of the limousine and the prominence it was given.

There was remarkably less fuss about my limousine when it figured in *Cruising Speed*. What, then, was the provocative difference between my *1970* limousine and my *1981* limousine? Hard scrutiny of the reviews suggests that the second *having been custom-made* caused it to be marginally insufferable. This is very interesting, especially so since the offended reviewers did not (many of them) hesitate to quote my narrative, in which, as Miss Ephron has reminded us, I revealed that, in 1978, buying a limousine with roughly the same features as the traditional, i.e., pre-austerity, limousine, cost approximately the same as the regular commercial limousine now being offered by the Cadillac company.

What then was it about the customizing that so inflamed? — that caused the *New York Times Book Review* critic to begin her review by concluding that *everyone* would focus on the limousine, whereafter she proceeded to devote almost one-third of her review to it?

Is it — I explore the question again — simply, the economic point? That a limousine is expensive? If so, isn't it odd to weigh in so heavily on this, given that a limousine costs only about twice what a Ford sedan costs? It does not require that one belittle the figure to ask: Why is it, when other finery of affluence is there to choose from, that a limousine is so conspicuous? I explain, in *Overdrive*, how I spend my days; and it quickly becomes obvious that it would no more be feasible to spend my days as they are spent in the absence of a car and driver than it would be to run a taxi service without taxis. Without going over a time sheet, in the week I recorded I would guess that eight hours of work resulted from being driven rather than driving. What is it that especially affects so many about this particular auxiliary to one's commercial life? The cost of it?

But that is hardly rational. Well then, is it the point that one ought not to expect rationality in a review of how one American (this American) leads his life if his *modus vivendi* is judged obnoxious? I say it is irrational because hardly anyone bothered, in reviewing *Overdrive*, to dilate on his objections to extravagances even when clearly unrelated to productivity. E.g., owning and maintaining a 36-foot sailing auxiliary which (by the way) costs three times what a limousine costs (ask any of the hundred thousand Americans who have one). I own a grand piano worth more than my limo; used less, and mutilated more. Or consider articles of unquestioned and unmitigated professional uselessness, like a 33-year accumulation of one's wife's jewelry. . . . What *is* it about a limousine?

Sometime after the first dozen reviews appeared, I lunched with Sam Vaughan of Doubleday and told him I was astonished by the intensity of the concentration on the matter of my limousine, which at this point I was tempted to paint khaki. Sam observed that typical luxuries go largely unobserved, but that a chauffeur-driven car is the single most provocative possession of the modern urban American. "Everyone," he expanded, "no matter who, has in New York been caught on a street-corner in the rain, waiting for a bus, or trying to hail a taxi. And inevitably they will see a limousine slide by, with the lumpen-bourgeois

(Drawing by Ed Arno; © 1984 by The New Yorker Magazine, Inc.)

figure in the back seat, maybe smoking a cigar; maybe even reading the *Wall Street Journal*. That is the generically offensive act in the big cities." A good point, if the idea is to explain the spastic hostility toward limousine-owners. Not, I think, a sufficient point to understand the peculiar emphasis put on the limo in some of the reviews of *Overdrive*.

I think that of the several points raised in opposing the book, this concrete point puzzled me the most. I dwell on it because American culture has tended to be guided — not finally, but substantially — by utilitarian criteria. Does John Appleseed produce more using a tractor than a horse-drawn plow? Does Tom Wicker perform more efficiently using a typewriter, and, going on to a word processor, than with a pencil? Why isn't the utilitarian coefficient dispositive in the matter of a limousine? Is it because the critic cannot distinguish between the limousine qua limousine, i.e., a luxury vehicle associated with inaugurations, weddings, and funerals, and the limousine as mobile office? If so, there are two problems, the first the failure of the critical intelligence. The second, whether the envious view, transformed to resentment on that rainy day, on the sidewalks of New York, of the man comfortable in his limousine isn't, to use Miss Ephron's freighted word, "emblematic" of a public, rather than a private, disorder?

The second point touches on the corrosive use of the word "gleeful" to describe a reaction to one's material situation. I have especially in mind, because it was so frequently adduced by reviewers, my reference to a swimming pool. What I said about it parenthetically — words (if I may say so, gleefully reproduced) — was that it is "the most beautiful indoor swimming pool this side of Pompeii."

Now I found it odd that several reviewers of obvious intelligence bridled at this. (They might, at one level, have passed it by, as "I saw the best movie last night since 'Birth of a Nation'" would presumably have been passed by.) In doing so it seems to me, on hard reflection, that they must have understood me to be saying something different from what I intended to say, so that the fault is either mine or theirs, and it is worth inquiring: Whose?

My indoor swimming pool is of modest dimensions (I give them, in *Overdrive*). In the book, as a matter of course, I acknowledge the architect who designed the pool, and the artist I engaged to give me a mosaic pattern to decorate it. My delight, therefore, was clearly not with my own doing, but with theirs. I cannot imagine resenting any expression of pleasure uttered by the man who, having, say, commissioned the Parthenon, goes on to describe it in his diary (presciently) as "the most beautiful pre-Christian temple ever constructed." What would he have been saying that a rational, self-respecting critic could object to?

Mine was the voice of acclamation: a celebration of the architect, and of the artist: hardly of the author who accumulated the money with which to pay them.

But how odd, so widespread a reaction at an expression of delight at others' competence and artistry (many made as much of my reference to an "exquisite" sandwich made by our cook). Isn't it the job of the critic to distinguish between a compliment slyly paid ostensibly to someone else, actually to oneself, and a genuine compliment? Or are the critics reading self-congratulations by the man who had the wit to commission the pool, and the taste to appreciate the singularly well-made sandwich? That surely is reaching, isn't it? Would a reviewer single out a diarist's encomium on the performance of a visiting artist as an effort to draw attention to the author's piano? Or to his leverage on the artist?

I focus, finally, on what appears to have been a highly provocative literary proposition, namely my contention that a scrupulous journal of a week in an individual's life is at least a literary form worth thinking about, at best a literary idea worth celebrating. Many years ago the editor of the humor quarterly *Monocle* (it was Victor Navasky, now editor of the *Nation*) asked me to do a review of the work of the columnist Murray Kempton. I replied that he was asking me for the equivalent of a review of the work of Walter Lippmann, never mind that it would be more fun. Was I supposed to go back and read, or rather re-read, fifteen years of Murray Kempton in order to write three thousand words?

I came up with a formula that satisfied Navasky, satisfied me, and planted, I think, the idea that blossomed, if that word is not too tendentious, in *Cruising Speed* and, now, *Overdrive*. Why not take a week of columns by Murray Kempton — next week's columns, say — and talk your way through them? He was writing five times a week back then, so that the chances were on your side that you would catch Murray Kempton reacting to a satisfactory range of challenges, phenomena, provocations, scandals, whatever. Enough to acquaint the reader with the moods (penetrating), style (incomparable), and thought (unreliable) of Murray Kempton.

It worked, in my judgment.

And so does it work, again in my judgment, on a larger scale in *Overdrive*.

To ask and quickly answer the most sensitive question, let me simply blurt it out:

Not everyone can write such a book. Or, if it goes down more smoothly to put it so, not everyone would read such a book if written by anyone.

William Murchison, the columnist from Dallas, Texas, wrote, "Few indeed are the authors who could bring off such an enterprise as this. A week, literally speaking, with Ralph Nader; or Walter Mondale; or Phil Donahue; or General Westmoreland! To think of it is to weep."

Now Mr. Murchison has a point here, but not of the kind that should cause the egalitarian furies to howl.

We seem to concede, without any problem, that only people who are technically qualified can satisfactorily perform on the piano before an audience. So we concede, again without any apparent problem, that unless one deftly uses paint and canvas, one ought not to expect to be able to merchandise one's art. I do not see why there should be so much difficulty in applying the same implicit criteria in order to distinguish what one might call the "performing writer." Perhaps the problem exists at all only because very few people without the technique to bring it off would undertake to play the "Flight of the Bumblebee" on the piano. Not many weekend painters would expect to sell their canvases even to the very little galleries.

By contrast, everybody — writes. And, in writing, there

is progressive fluency that approaches artistry. No one can say exactly where the line is, but it is to comply with the requirements of the full disclosure laws to admit: it would probably separate those who, using this standard, could, and could not, publish their journals, only the former being "performing writers." Okay. So why should it be difficult to accept the proposition that, from a writer, one expects work of a distinctive quality, even as one would from a painter or musician or plumber? If one managed that problem, one would cope with the preliminary objection: to a journal based on a single week in a person's life. The person needs to be a writer.

But if the writer *is* qualified, what besides that does the reader, in order to be satisfied, require?

The reader would want an interesting sensibility. What is in process, in such an undertaking, is a literary self-portrait. I say "literary" only because the author's reactions are sometimes limned with operative emphasis on *the way* in which the reactions are expressed: and what then happens is that you collect, one by one, the little colored dots which, when they are, however chaotically, assembled, leave you with a mosaic, at best a pointillist portrait of — one human being.

Why should you care to have a self-portrait, as done, for instance, by William F. Buckley, Jr. — or by Groucho Marx? Or by Kay Graham?

Because, I think, self-portraits of many people can be interesting. If they work, they amuse. Enlighten. Explain. They provoke. And — I cling to the point — although the formal autobiography lets the actor stage his life and thought with more regard for conventional architectural prominences, the week's journal has complementary advantages. If I were offered today the alternative of reading an autobiography of Walter Lippmann, tracking his career, with which I am routinely familiar, or another comprehending his activity and his thought hour by hour during a single week, I *think* — I'm not sure — I might not lose by choosing the former. Remember that the supplementary alternative isn't necessarily excluded.

A book like *Overdrive* written by Ralph Nader? Well — who knows? He has not, true, achieved a reputation as a writer. Indeed one might go further and say that the authors' oligopoly is one he has not cracked. On the other hand, if he had the training to carry it off, would I be interested in reading a journal of a week in Ralph Nader's life? My own answer is, Yes: I would. So would I — I mean it — a week in the life of Phil Donahue. In fact, I would sleep outside the bookstore, waiting to put my hands on such a book; if it were such a book. It would take only one or two other explorers to set the form in concrete. Murray Kempton comes to mind as ideal. Or Patrick Moynihan. Or how about Jesse Jackson? If he would speak Honest Injun, as I do.

I regret many things about the reception of *Overdrive*, though I am obliged to record here two qualifiers. The first is that the book has been a solid, if not spectacular, entrepreneurial success. The second is that the book has generated an extraordinary amount of mail from strangers, strangers who, after reading it, thought to write to me, their motives varied. The volume of that mail I was unprepared for — the reach of the *New Yorker* always astonishes me but — I think no book I have written (with one exception) has got such a response, overwhelmingly grateful — for what I take to be the sense communicated of a common and joyful search for serenity, in which the readers appear to have been helped. (One wrote, "Rambling, idiosyncratic, amused, cranky, occasionally flamboyant — your observations and recollections were most enjoyable testaments to a vital life. You actually believe *something*: Something old, something blue, with flecks of tweed, patches on the elbows, old Nantucket and Martha's Vineyard before everyone else came, in short: the right way of doing things." Another: "In a confusing world, I must express my gratitude. . . .") For that reason, among others already given, I regret the facile dismissal of the literary form by some reviewers (there were exceptions: *Time*'s Roger Rosenblatt wrote me, "I think you've invented a genre. Pepys on speed, but better") who, in their haste to disparage, did not give sufficient thought to the potential uses of such a form by people whose thought and careers they would read about with less resistance. I hope, before I die, to see others using this form. In my reply to Greg Dunne of the *New York Review of Books* I said airily that in ten years I intended to write a sequel to *Cruising Speed* and *Overdrive*, and ten years after *that*, a fourth journal. The prospect of this will cause a disturbing number of people to wish me . . . retired sooner, rather than later. But I caution them against strategic optimism in these matters. My limousine has miles to go before I sleep.

One

MONDAY

Gloria brought in my lunch on a tray—two pieces of whole wheat toast each with tuna fish covered with some cheese-something my wife Pat had read about somewhere, a salad, a half bottle of Côte Rôtie (I remember the wine's name only because it's the one I have in half bottles) and coffee. I leaned back in the big desk chair that reaches to my withers, tucked the napkin under my chin in case bits of tuna oozed out, and looked out at the lawn as I ate. I was looking through two huge windowed doors that had served as garage doors before we bought the house in 1952, converting the number four garage into my own office, and the number three into an office for a secretary. Pat had been prowling about the area for seven or eight weeks, and one day telephoned to the office of the *American Mercury*, where I was working, to tell me she had found just what she was looking for, I must hurry out with her to see it, but I was to ignore the furnishings when I did see it, as they might distract me.

We met at the Stamford railroad station, and the real estate agents, a couple in their late sixties, drove us to the little headland, through the private gateway, turn right, second driveway on the left. They explained to us chattily the circumstances of the house's availability.

It had been constructed in 1907 by a doctor, who with his wife brought up their children and, pursuing his passion for horticulture, lived in the house and tended its lawns and gardens until the early forties when both the doctor and his wife died. The house had then been picked up by a wealthy Stamford industrialist. He had a mistress; in due course he decided to replace her with tenderer flesh, but being a man of stout conscience he resolved to give the retiree a substantial farewell gift, and so bought this house for her. Here she, with her rather distracted husband, lived for a few years, but their economic fortunes had waned. So, in order to save on that winter's heating bills, they had

moved out of the main dwelling into the top floor of the garage in one of whose converted cubicles I now sat.

We were shown the house by the proprietress. In the living room alone I counted twenty-two chairs—the room would have made an excellent workshop for those social critics who remark every now and then America's obsession with chairs. The walls were papered in a purple print, out of which every here and there plastic flowers protruded. The other rooms were decorated congruently.

The following Sunday, Pat and I traveled back to the house to take a more exact inventory of the rooms, and one of us (memory chivalrously forgets which) forgot the key the owner had given us (she and her husband would be out of town, but we must make the house our own—we had agreed to buy it). So I broke a windowpane in the kitchen door to gain entry, wrote out an explanatory note for eventual perusal by the returning owner, and we wandered about.

That was the very first conscious experience I had with the reality that books don't necessarily figure in everyone's life. There wasn't a single volume in any of the eleven rooms, though in the garage apartment there were four neatly standing editions of Reader's Digest Condensed Books. (Do these count? I asked the question seriously of Mortimer Smith, whom I came to know slightly, soon after he had published *And Madly Teach* and *The Diminished Mind* and founded the Council for Basic Education, devoting his life to the reclamation of phonics as the basis for learning how to read. "Marginally," he answered.)

I remembered taking Whittaker Chambers to my office here one day in 1955, with lighthearted trepidation. Not because of the mess (he wouldn't mind messy offices—he'd mind people who minded messy offices), but because I had had fixed windows installed in the top half of the garage doors, giving me a copious view of the lawn and garden, though not the eastern view, into Long Island Sound. (That had been the mandate to the real estate people. We desired a house a) close enough to New York to permit commuting, but b) by the sea, because I wanted to live by the sea and didn't see any particular reason why, if the whole southern tier of Connecticut squats down on the sea, I shouldn't be among those who squatted down in that part of Connecticut however sadly remote from the beautiful but isolated northwest corner of the state where I grew up, and where most of my siblings dwell.) Whittaker had once told me, on taking me down to his own cellar office in Pipe Creek Farm, which had no windows at all, that an engaging view was distracting to a writer; but his discipline was always self-directed—I never knew a less censorious man about others' ways. And he did not say anything about the seductive view to the left of my desk. Chambers had told me that a scenic view from one's desk is the great enemy of productivity.

I shook myself free of reminiscence, and observed for the thousandth time the great cock pheasant that makes this point his own preserve. He was picking his way confidently across the semifrozen yellow-green grass. I reflected on the curiosity that the pheasant, full-grown, had apparently always been full-grown. For thirty years now I had seen what I call "him," though it must have been "they," since it is my impression that pheasants do not live for thirty years, let alone forever. It occurred to me that thirty years hence "the" pheasant might well be strolling by, viewed by different eyes. And perhaps halfway between now and then I will still be seeing him. From a wheelchair? I hope not; though it is so for most people who grow old, my father among them, and the geriatric imperative suggests it will be so even more in the years ahead. The thought is glum, but not so much as its complement, that fifteen years hence I should magically find myself fifteen years younger. The only quality of youth I covet is their health, not their age; life is wonderful, but the thought of reliving it is altogether repelling; spiritually, and even biologically, exhausting. When the character in Catch 22 said he intended to live forever or die trying, I sensed an exalted fatalism, nicely captured by the easy superficiality of the biological paradox.

In any case, no matter how long I live, certainly I'd never willingly live elsewhere. My wife and I know what it is to learn to love a piece of property wholly; defiantly; truculently, even. I have lived in (two) beautiful homes (my father's specialty) and been blasphemously happy in them. This by all objective standards is by far the least of the three, although it is not (I do not pretend any such

thing) Tobacco Road. For a while my private nightmare
was that the eight houses along the point here would one
day be taken over by the city of Stamford to provide more
public beaches and swimming space, but presently a huge
swimming area just a little way north was developed by
the city (which already disposed of a huge beach area
southeast), and neither of the two outdoor areas is heavily
patronized. It seems unlikely, then, that the twenty-four
acres on this point will be violated. We'll always be here,
then, in the warm summers when the leaves make invisible
the houses of our neighbors to the south and north; in the
spiky fall season, days like today with the little chill that
makes one feel freshly laundered; and in the truly cold
cold of the cold days, although we haven't spent a February or a March here since 1959, when we took to going to
Switzerland.

I looked over at the telephones. There are two. One is
an extension of my son's line—his official home is above
where I sit, the garage apartment upstairs. He occupied it
the whole of this last year, completing his first book,
Steaming to Bamboola. He then returned to *Esquire* magazine, and on that Monday his boss gave him a welcome-
back party. On Wednesday he was asked by a man he had
never seen or heard of before (nor had I, when told the
name) to go down to Washington to discuss some urgent
business in the Vice-President's office. There and then he
was offered (based on his past writings for *Esquire*) the
job of speechwriter. On Thursday he told me he had
accepted the offer but was mortified by the thought of
having to tell his *Esquire* boss, who had been so cordial in
welcoming him back after a year's leave of absence. I suggested he broach the subject by saying that on Friday
he was available, in the event *Esquire* wanted to give him a
goodbye party. Christopher's laugh is wonderful.

Well, Christo is in Washington now, and so I pick up

his telephone when it rings. Half the time I serve as his social secretary ("No, Christopher isn't here, he is in Washington; would you like his telephone number?"). The rest
of the time I find myself responding to commercial calls,
because Christopher's number is listed, mine isn't. Those
conversations go, typically:

"Mr. Buckley?"

"Yes."

"Mr. Buckley, we have a special offer of *Time* magazine, for thirteen weeks, for only seven dollars and twenty-
five cents."

Calls such as these are difficult because the process of
self-extrication is complicated. I can't now say, "I'm not
Mr. Buckley." And to say, "I am Mr. Buckley's father" invites informality. Unlike Waugh, who wrote that he understands formality and understands intimacy, but can't
stand informality, I like informality; but not when it is
conducive to conversation I wish to avoid. I can't say I *already* have two subscriptions to *Time* magazine, which is
the truth, because that invites the questioner to ask how is
it that her records show me delinquent? So I say something about having a subscription that goes to the office,
thanks very much, and hang up. They are trained not to
be too persevering. I know, because Jim McFadden,
keeper of all the secrets at *National Review*, once told me
he uses the system; for all I know, the same girls.

The second telephone has three lines. One of them I
think of as my wife's telephone. The light is regularly lit,
as her friends have in common not only their kindness, but
their loquacity. A second line we call "Eudosia's phone"
after our Cuban cook, retired after twenty-five years with
us. The third is a tie line to my office in New York, and
when that indicator is depressed, the telephone operator at
my office answers, and puts me through to whomever.

The desk itself is decrepit in appearance, but superbly

shaped. Back in 1951 everything in Mexico was cheap, and I had this huge, indulgent desk constructed for a few hundred dollars. It resembles in shape a bow, and I sit where the arrow would cock, with plenty of room to my right, and to my left, enough room for as many as three people to occupy it simultaneously. When I went to Mexico, it was for the CIA. The rules are that if you resign your post in less than one year, you must reimburse the government the cost of having shipped your household goods abroad. If you stay one year, you need not reimburse the outbound shipping costs, but you must pay the cost of returning your goods to the United States. If you stay two years or more, you can claim the cost of shipping your household goods both ways.

I stayed less than one year, as it happened; but I made an elementary deduction, namely that the customs charge on the furniture I acquired in Mexico was legally subtractable from the total sum due. Why? Because while in Mexico I was (however secretly) working for the government of the United States, and household goods purchased in connection with government duty performed abroad are not taxed on returning home. But as a deep-cover agent I could not reveal to the customs official that I was properly immune from customs duties. So I paid customs. I then took the figure—it was approximately five hundred dollars—and subtracted it from the total owed to the CIA, making out (as instructed to do) a personal check to an anonymous person residing at some address or other in Washington. I thought this not only just, but resourceful.

A few weeks later, my secretary told me that downstairs to see me was a gentleman who identified himself as an old friend from Yale, Robert Lounsbury. And indeed it was he.

Lounsbury, a tall, talented student at the law school while I was an undergraduate, had, for reasons I've forgot-

ten, learned fluent Spanish as a child, as had I. So acute had
been the shortage of Spanish teachers in the fall of 1946,
and so inflated the student demand for instruction in the
language, that Yale had had to take three students—one
law student (Lounsbury), and two undergraduates (me
and an American raised in Argentina)—and admit them to
the faculty. So that Bob Lounsbury, who lived with his
wife and child in a little house near the law school, and I
met daily in adjacent classrooms and became close friends.
(I never knew a man who took more voluptuous pleasure
from opera recordings.) Lounsbury, I also remembered,
had caused a slight ruffle in official Yale during my junior
year, because one of his students was Levi Jackson, the
amiable and formidable black captain of the football team.
Ten days or so before the Yale-Princeton game, Lounsbury grabbed me as we were both leaving our classrooms
and gestured me to the end of the room, where he triumphantly produced from his briefcase two letters. The first,
addressed to him, was written by the Director of Athletics,
and said (I quote from memory): "Dear Mr. Lounsbury: I
note that Mr. Levi Jackson is having difficulty with
Spanish. The rules of the College automatically place on
probation, forbidding extracurricular activity to, any student who fails a subject in the midterm exam. The midterm comes one week before the Yale-Princeton Game. I
trust Mr. Jackson will have no problem in this regard.
Yours, (etc.)." A huge smile on his face, Lounsbury then
gave me his freshly typed answer, which he was about to
drop in the post office: "To the Director of Athletics, Yale
University. Dear Mr. Kiphuth: I am sorry to say that the
probability is *very* high that indeed Mr. Levi Jackson will
have a considerable academic problem before the Yale-
Princeton game. Sincerely, Robert H. Lounsbury, Princeton 1943." He howled as he licked the envelope. But Bob
was good-natured; Levi played in the game. And Yale lost.

After a few minutes Bob revealed he was here on official business—that he was an agent of the CIA, and had been instructed to arbitrate the financial differences between me and the United States Government. I was genuinely astonished that Bob was a spook (Lounsbury, I had felt sure, was headed right to a senior law firm), but even a short period in the CIA prepares you not ever to be astonished for long. I appealed to Lounsbury, honors graduate of the Yale Law School: Had not the identical government that had taken five hundred dollars from me in customs duties also immunized from customs duties all government employees stationed abroad? Hadn't I therefore forfeited that five hundred dollars only because I had kept silent, as a government agency had pledged me to do, my reason for being in Mexico? Bob agreed that the judicial poetry was all on my side, but said that the books simply made no provision for what I had done. He smiled: Would I agree to pay two hundred dollars? I agreed: provided it was put down as a gift from me to Uncle Sam, so that I could reserve the satisfaction of having won the juridical point. Again he smiled, said nothing, and I gave him a check made out to cash for two hundred dollars.

I never, I recently explained to someone, revealed the secret of my former employment until I was blown—by William Sloane Coffin, Jr. It was Watergate-time and for some reason he and I found ourselves at opposite ends of a telephone line. At the end of the business he was calling me about he told me that while he had served as chaplain at Williams College no doubt I would be pleased to learn that he had taught ethics to Jeb Magruder, one of the White House people freshly sentenced for conspiracy to obstruct justice and defraud the United States. It was public knowledge that Coffin had himself been a member of the CIA before going to Yale, so I blurted out, "And *you* will no doubt be pleased to learn that my superior in the CIA was Howard Hunt." We cackled—but he indiscreetly (on the other hand, does it really matter, at this remove?) used the information at a public meeting, and my (and the government's) twenty-year-old secret was out. Poor Bob Lounsbury, who had become moderately prominent in Democratic-intellectual affairs in New York, committed suicide about ten years ago. I don't know why, but happily assume his tragedy was unrelated to any contrition felt for what he had done, or almost done, to Levi Jackson, and to the Director of Yale Athletics.

In the drawers of this desk is an accumulation, twenty-five years of assorted matter, but I know where the paper clips are and, indeed, the loaded pistol. (I loaded it after my friend the Columbia University philosophy professor Charles Frankel and his wife were shot at night, in their country home, a few years back.) The office has two armchairs, one of them folding out into a cot of sorts, good for a catnap. The walls are packed with books, research materials, and photographs. Most of the surface of the table is piled high with papers and the usual paraphernalia—dictating machines, reference books, a large Royal standard typewriter, purchased at Yale when I was a freshman and in perfect operating condition. I am content here, and productive.

The car, coming down the drive, has passed my window: Jerry has come for me. I looked at my watch. No problem; I will be in New York easily by three. My column has been phoned in, and I had written that morning the promised piece for *TV Guide* on "memorable guests of 'Firing Line.'" ("The most effective guests on 'Firing Line' are those who talk, listen, and who plead seductively, masters of their argument, serene in their convictions. The most effective guests are not, however, always the most memorable.") I wrote of guests who had appeared ten years earlier, in 1971. Of Huey Newton (as in "Free Huey") who had flummoxed me by an absolutely perfected double-talk, *absolutely* inscrutable as to meaning. Of Bernadette Devlin, the young Ulster militant whom *I* had flummoxed by instinctively lighting her cigarette halfway through the show, causing her inadvertently to say "Oh, thanks very much"—thus shattering her carefully cultivated bellicose front. (Afterward she told me heatedly that lighting her cigarette was a typical act of male chauvinism.) Of Harold Macmillan who, having reached the sixteenth century in the course of making a historical *tour d'horizon*, suddenly said, "Oh, isn't this program over yet?" And of Jimmy Hoffa, who told me how necessary it was to be tough in this world if one wanted to survive; soon after, disappearing below some cement somewhere.

Jerry was back at the garage within ten minutes, with Rebeca and Olga, respectively a solicitous and fussy Guatemalan and an otherworldly and gay-spirited Ecuadorian, who have been with us for a number of years. Neither speaks English, both are infinitely good-natured. And of course my beautiful old pooch Rowley, who had already made one round trip in his beloved car, Jerry having driven Pat to the city earlier, while I stayed behind to write and attend to correspondence. Jerry Garvey is a huge man who, while a firefighter, ran a driver service when off duty, his reserves of energy being inexhaustible, even as his competence is complete in all but mechanical matters: He shares my difficulty in distinguishing between pliers and tweezers.

When Jerry was on duty in the Fire Department Tom, also a fireman, would substitute for him, it having been contrived that Tom and Jerry would never simultaneously be on duty at that fire station. Jerry elected to retire from the service after twenty years, and now drives full time for me. In fifteen years I have never heard him complain, not even about his brain-damaged but apparently contented daughter, whom he permits to sit with him in the front seat, but only on weekends, and when the car is empty, or when I alone occupy it.

It is a large car. I remember having no exact figure in mind when the manager of the garage in Texarkana asked me how long I wanted it, so I simply extended my legs from the desk chair I was sitting in and suggested it be two feet longer than the current standard model. What happened was that three years ago, when it came time to turn in my previous car, which had done over 150,000 miles, the Cadillac people had come up with an austerity-model limousine, fit for two short people, preferably to ride to a funeral in. The dividing glass between driver and driven was not automatic, there was no separate control for heat or air conditioning in the back, and the jump seats admitted only two, because now the axle was raised a good six inches, making it impossible to furnish uninterrupted seat space stretching across the middle (all these features were Cadillac's accommodation to the fuel economies specified by Congress). This simply would not do: I use the car constantly, require the room, privacy, and my own temperature gauge, else I'd have to live off Jerry's, and how could that air, cold or hot, find its way aft with the partition closed, which is how I usually keep it, so that Jerry can listen to the radio, while I do my telephoning or dictation?

There was, as usual, a market solution. You go out (this was in 1978) and buy a plain old Cadillac. You deliver it to a gentleman in Texarkana. He chops it in two, and installs whatever you want. Cost? Interesting: within one thousand dollars of the regular limousine, and I actually don't remember which side. The only problem is that people who come into the car will, unless warned, wheel about and sit down allowing for the conventional interval.

They land on the floor, because the back seat is—two feet behind where it normally is.

Olga is up with Jerry. Rebeca sits with me. Rowley is sleeping, over the heat ducts, but we are used to this. The briefcases and other paraphernalia have been carried out of my office. I asked Jerry if he had turned on the burglar alarm in the house (Gloria had taken the train, to meet an early appointment), and he said yes, he had. For fifteen years we didn't even have a key to the house, having lost the one the owners left us. But then there was a burglary, and they took all the silver. I say "they" because notwithstanding that there were servants sleeping on the third floor, the burglars took their time, and evidently were, or became, hungry: the next morning, when the police came, the remains of two table settings, rather formal under the circumstances, I thought, were still there on the kitchen table with the apple cores, bread crumbs, and so on. The diners had plenty of silver for their modest needs.

So now we have one of those alarms which ring first at the switchboard of the company's headquarters in New Jersey. From there, someone reacts by dialing your number. If there is no answer, or if the person who answers does not recite the code word, then the switchboard immediately notifies the police and a neighbor (you have given the switchboard two neighborly neighbors' numbers). The plot is that everyone then convenes at your house, and your neighbor, who has a passkey, opens the door, the police arrest the burglar, and you feel your money was well spent. Several times the police have arrived at our place to find an empty house. The false alarms are embarrassing, but it is also true that there have been no further burglaries.

I turned on my Dictaphone, and checked to see that the battery was alive. It was. It always is. Dictaphone has managed to construct a portable recording machine which is

about the only thing around to remind us that we actually won the war against Japan. You turn on the unit, and start to look through your pile of papers. But the difference between this machine and others is that unless you actually depress the microphone button and talk into the machine, it does not expend battery energy. This is a datum of huge importance. For the sake of experiment, last spring I took a measurement. During five hours of uninterrupted work flying to San Francisco, I accumulated only eighteen minutes of dictation. Five hours—three hundred minutes—divided by eighteen. That adds up to one minute of dictation for every sixteen minutes of standby. I then calculate: the Japanese machines, which burn up energy once you've turned them on, whether you're talking or not, use up batteries sixteen times as fast as my beautiful Dictaphone which, I suppose it is fair to add, costs about six times as much.

I'd have written to Dictaphone to volunteer a testimonial, save for my experience with Smith-Corona. That was seven or eight years ago when we reached Switzerland, as usual, at the end of January. I lugged out a Smith-Corona I keep there, having bought it ten years earlier—a $170 portable electric. I turned on the power switch, and as ever it performed perfectly. I was seized by the moment, stuck in a sheet of yellow paper and wrote to the president of Smith-Corona, "Dear Sir" (not knowing his name): "I wish to advise you that your portable electric model so and so is the most wonderful electric typewriter I have ever experienced, having given me no trouble whatever during ten years. You may use this tribute in any way you desire, so long as you make clear that I was not paid for it." The letter was never acknowledged. Five years later, an advertising agency most decorously approached my secretary to ask whether Mr. Buckley ever gave testimonials to a commercial product? His client, Smith-Corona, was interested. (Mr. Buckley does not.)

On the seat between me and Rebeca is a briefcase, and I take a plunge. The Public Agenda Foundation desires me to serve as a member of its Policy Review Board. Ugh. But careful—it is my old friend Frank Stanton, longtime president of CBS, who suggested my election; mustn't hurt his feelings. I read about the duties of the Policy Review Board I am asked to join. It "serves a critical function in this work. The Board, consisting of leading citizens with many different backgrounds, philosophies, and experiences, functions to guarantee the objectivity of the Public Agenda's work. Board members review Public Agenda projects, publications, and other materials to insure that they are free of ideological bias, that they are balanced and thoughtful, and that they represent the highest level of analysis and research." Prose like that gags, doesn't it? I mean, if leading citizens with different backgrounds, philosophies, and experiences guarantee objectivity, then why isn't the United Nations objective? And are we so sure we *want* to be free of ideological bias? Isn't a hierarchy of values valuable? And if so, do we then not inherit a working bias of sorts, susceptible of rearrangement—e.g., when we elect to go to war?

And just when is a bias "ideological"? Is ours for democracy ideological? And in order to be balanced, does this mean that every time we make the case for human freedom, we need to present the *other* case? I do not tire of quoting Randall Jarrell in *Pictures From An Institution* who spoke of the professional toleration of Flo, the wife of the professor of sociology . . . "If she had been told that Benton [College], *and* [her husband] Jerrold, *and* [her son] John, *and* [her daughter] Fern, *and* the furniture had been burned to ashes by the head of the American Federation of Labor, who had then sown salt over the ashes, she would have sobbed and sobbed, and said at last—she could do no other—'I think that we ought to hear *his* side of the case before we make up our minds.' "

But these are well-meaning and gifted people, and the organization no doubt does good, whatever exactly it does; but would it do better for my efforts? I write that my schedule is hectic and my availability for meetings therefore uncertain, but that of course I will happily discuss the question with Frank Stanton when he calls, which he never did, and I take the matter to be closed.

John LeBoutillier is a young and very energetic congressman. Having experienced him, I can understand how he contrived to get an interview with the most reclusive man in America, Alexander Solzhenitsyn. I don't know just *how* he managed, but his tenacity evidently paid off: and now he wishes *National Review* to publish his interview, which we'll almost certainly do. John wrote *Harvard Hates America*, an exposé of his alma mater; and perhaps at this remove (the book was written three years ago) I can confess my opinion of it, namely that the title is the very best thing about it. But John will go far, and no doubt, in encountering him, Solzhenitsyn detected one or two familiar Bolshevik traits. The interview says nothing entirely new, but Solzhenitsyn speaks with continued force, and I marvel at his capacity to sustain the high level of his rage. "In December 1973," he tells LeBoutillier, "when I was still in the Soviet Union, I have published (*sic*) the *Gulag Archipelago* in the West, and the Voice of America—one speaker, one announcer—has immediately read an excerpt from this book, and immediately Radio Moscow was up in arms. There was an uproar, and they said that the Voice of America has no right to interfere in internal affairs of the Soviet Union. And what did the Voice of America do? Together with the State Department, and with the consent of the State Department, the Voice of America prohibited the reading of the *Gulag Archipelago* over the radio. Not only that, they went even further. They prohibited even any mention of Solzhenitsyn so as not to antagonize the Soviet leaders, meaning that my book was written for the Russians—in the West, millions of people have read it. And in my country nobody can read it. . . . Your radio broadcasting does not provide the needed spiritual help for people."

More. The *Firing Line Newsletter*, describing the program that would air that Sunday, rates it three stars each (out of a possible four) for Public Interest, Performance, and Entertainment. The newsletter goes out to all television critics and program managers in the cities that air "Firing Line," approximately two hundred and fifty. I am pleased with the idea, which I generated fifteen years ago when "Firing Line" was in its infancy. When a show goes on week after week, television critics (and program managers) should have some idea what's in it, and how it came off. The trick is to get someone of independent turn of mind who, notwithstanding that his/her editorial stipend comes in from "Firing Line," will make ruthlessly objective judgments. Such a woman exists—in Columbia, South Carolina, the administrative home of "Firing Line." I have never met her, know nothing about her, but her judgment is excellent, her critical style sprightly. The format begins with a comment: "Mr. [Mark] Green wields a wicked needle, attempting to stick Mr. Buckley with Budget Director Stockman's views on supply-side economics, and also with the envisioned sumptuary laws of the Moral Majority. Mrs. [Harriet] Pilpel zeroes in on the subject of abortion and announces, with the authority of Moses, what the law is. Sometimes the questions are too long, including a rebuttal to Mr. Buckley's supposed reply before he can answer. Some arguments reach an impasse. . . ." That critique is followed by the text of my introduction to the program, which is useful in supplying background material on the guest(s). And, finally, the newsletter contains a page of excerpts from the program's transcript.

"Firing Line" celebrated its fifteenth birthday earlier this year, its guest invitation list comprising everyone alive who had ever been on the program. Shortly after the party began I was yanked from the receiving line by the maitre d' of the New York Yacht Club who informed me that within one minute, the President of the United States would be on the line; that when he spoke, I was to hold the telephone up against the microphone so that the crowd could hear the exchange. Silence was secured with the weighty announcement that the (freshly inaugurated) President was on the line, and of course it was a technological fiasco. President Reagan began by greeting me and the program. I replied that at hand were Howard Hunt and Gordon Liddy, and did the President have any instructions? But the result of the neat little scheme of push-

ing the telephone up against the mike was that the President couldn't hear my replies and the audience couldn't hear his voice, so the colloquy dissolved in a blur of congratulations and reciprocal compliments.

"Firing Line" is now one of the twelve oldest consecutively run television programs. I am constantly astonished by the *variety* of people who look at it. A fairly recent poll reckoned that 980,000 households tune in every week, and that figure is not of course impressive as television goes. Contrast 100 million viewers of the Super Bowl. On the other hand, contrast one million households viewing "The Dick Cavett Show," which runs only a half hour. A careful reading of additional data encourages certain tentative conclusions. It transpires that the average viewer will stay tuned to the Cavett show for eight minutes, to "Firing Line" for thirty-eight minutes. The reason why is readily discernible. The Cavett show is on nightly, and the listener can tell in a few minutes whether the guest interests him. "Firing Line" is known to be comparatively exhaustive. It would follow that the prospective viewer would first establish the identity of the guest before reaching a decision whether to tune in. If interested in the subject (or the guest), he will tune in. And, already aware of the tempo of the program, he is not made restless by its pace. Television talk programs in recent years have quite intentionally paced up their talk segments, so that typically they run five or six minutes. Five or six minutes is long enough to declare war, recite the Gettysburg Address, or seduce Fanny Hill, but isn't generally enough for a satisfying, measured analytical exchange.

Ken Galbraith and I worked "The Today Show" in Miami in 1972 (he was backing McGovern, I Nixon), back when the time limit of a segment was fifteen or twenty minutes, and the exchange was lively, useful, and, the record suggests, popular. Four years later in Kansas City we were asked back, but were limited to the new time allowance. We were both dissatisfied with the outcome, even as (we take it) the network was. "Anything that requires us merely to exchange wisecracks doesn't work," was Galbraith's postmortem, and I agree with him. Later in the season I was asked by "Good Morning, America," Would I debate on Election Day with Norman Mailer on the subject, Carter or Ford?

"How long?" I asked the producer.

"Six minutes."

"No."

"What!"

"No."

"Why?"

"Because in six minutes you can't count on getting anything said."

There was a most awful consternation at the other end of the telephone, and after a summit conference, no doubt attended by major stockholders, it was decided to give us eleven minutes. Two years later I caught the same program, on which Alfred Kahn, President Carter's inflation czar, or rather anti-inflation czar, was given six minutes to explain the reasons for the then-current sixteen percent inflation rate. At the end of six minutes he was cut off, so that we might, with a guest plumber, view the causes of, and requisite ministrations to, a leaky faucet.

I summarized the lesson learned from watching that self-help segment in a column that same day: "Turn off the water valve. Tape the nut at the top of the faucet's base, to protect the chrome. With a wrench, loosen the nut by turning counter-clockwise until the unit lifts up. Unscrew the handle, and behold a leaky washer. Loosen the screw (with a Phillips screwdriver). Remove the offending washer, and replace it with a new one. Screw back, handle back, base back, tighten wrench, remove tape, turn on water valve, open the faucet, let there be no leak!" It leaves one a little breathless, and poor Mr. Kahn, one of the most articulate economists in the business, couldn't really explain Mr. Carter's policies, let alone check inflation, in the six minutes given him, but I did suggest: "Take a President. Turn him clockwise, till he vetoes 15 percent of the money voted by Congress. Take Congress. Pass four laws: 1) savings are no longer taxed; 2) dividends are no longer taxed; 3) depreciation schedules are cut in half; 4) sunset legislation on the regulatory legislation goes into effect. Then, beaming, open the valve: Presto! No more inflation!"

Norman Mailer, I would learn on the program, was greatly impressed by candidate Carter—which, given the record of those who have politically impressed him, makes his judgment consistent. We breakfasted after the program at my apartment, after which, while I was standing with him at the street corner to flag him a taxi, we were almost run down by Daniel Patrick Moynihan being driven in a station wagon. That very day, Mr. Moynihan would unseat the sainted junior senator from New York, my brother Jim. Now he leaned out the window of the car, wearing his usual tweedy Irish walking hat, and said, "Damn, I could have gotten you both with one swipe!" I replied that Norman had already been killed once that morning.

More correspondence. Clif White writes to thank me for writing an introduction to his book, which is an account of his labors over a lifetime on behalf of political candidates (he managed Goldwater's presidential primary race, and my brother's successful 1970 race). . . . Robert Makla, Esq., solicits my approval (as co-executor of Harry Elmlark's estate) to reimburse Harry's son-in-law for expenses in connection with the schooling of Harry's grandson Kevin. I wonder, is it the executor's responsibility, in such situations, to act as he thinks the benefactor would have acted? I am afraid to ask myself that question too rigorously, because Harry could be very tough in money matters. The boy's mother (Harry's only child) is dead, the father remarried. Or should the executor use his own judgment? Probably the soundest course of action is to decline to act as executor in the first place, if your temperament is like my own. But with Harry, I like to think I never refused to do anything he asked, which was very little. The last time I saw him, at the hospital a year ago, I told him I was leaving the following morning for the Caribbean. Lying on his back he asked, expressionless, in a faint voice reduced to hoarseness, When would I return? He had no measure of time anymore, so I said, "In a few days." His thin arm clutched mine, and he said nothing.

In the event his grandson isn't living at age twenty-one,

Harry specified that his money should go to my son, Christopher.

I spoke about Harry, that enterprising newspaper syndicator, at the memorial ceremony three weeks later:

In Harry's will, in the draft he wrote in 1975, he specified that there should be no religious element to these services, and that I should serve as the eulogist. He revised that will in 1977, specifying that a rabbi should be asked to say a few words, and, again, that I should serve as the eulogist. I conclude that between 1975 and 1977 Harry discovered that I was not capable, all by myself, of doing the Lord's work. However, as a eulogist he had me under contract, and, as was Harry's wont, the termination date of contracts he wrote tended to be vague. Unless you noticed, Harry was unlikely to notice that at a specified moment in history you were, in fact, free. That part of the Constitution did not make up Harry's bedtime reading. And so I exercised what little authority I have, in common with Mr. Ira Cohen [the co-executor], to invite others to whom he was personally or professionally close, who gave him such pleasure, to share the burden, which burden is a great joy, because knowing Harry was a great joy. A vexatious joy, to be sure; but such are, finally, the most enduring joys. If Harry had not been, in his own way, difficult, he would certainly not have been Harry; and he would not have passed through our lives with so singular an impact on each one of us—each relationship somehow different. No two people knew exactly the same Harry, and although I know how fully he satisfied, in different ways, different people, I would not exchange the combination of qualities I experienced for any other mix. One day, two or three months ago, he told me three times, within a twenty-four-hour period, a witticism he had uttered to Helen [a friend]. Finally exasperated, I told him that he had already three times told me his *bon mot*, to which he replied that three times was insufficient to do justice to it, so deep were its reserves of wit and eloquence. I told him to call Mary McGrory and tell it to her, and he replied that he already had, but come to think of it, he would call her again, and say it again. Harry.

I wrote once (it was in my book, *Cruising Speed*) about our first conversation. It was over the telephone, and this proved prophetic, because our relationship was primarily telephonic, and even as such—perhaps because it was such—proved profoundly satisfying. I had physically to go to him when he first learned that his wife, Lillian, would die; had to go to him when he learned that she had died; I had to see him in the hospital bed, during those final days, when we exchanged platitudes, because we knew what we were feeling, and knew that a platitude is a great and noble convention for sparing pain. But, for the most part, it was the telephone; and I suppose if I said we spoke two thousand times, I'd be underestimating the number. In this matter he was, however, remarkably disciplined. He would speak as long as you wished; but if you said you had to cut off, he would stop instantly: the man of affairs, recognizing other priorities, other obligations. When he called and you were occupied, he would not call again. "I always know you'll call me back," he said to me once; and it is a sadness very nearly disabling to know that I cannot call him back again.

That thought crowded my mind yesterday afternoon, when with Christopher, and Pat, and Marvin Liebman, I poured his ashes into the sea, in front of my house on Long Island Sound. The wind was northwesterly and bitingly cold, and the tide was falling, so that his remains fell and drifted out into the currents, whence, I do not doubt—like the leaves that rustled in each other's company from the tall boughs of the two great trees into which the god transformed Philemon and Baucis—I do not doubt that the remains of Harry, and of Lillian, who also elected to be put to sea, will come upon each other; and that a union consecrated by God, so tragically interrupted in 1973, will resume.

Christopher and I, who believe in life after death, sought diligently not to take sectarian advantage of our role yesterday; but one cannot travel far with the psalmists without coming upon that hope which sustains the Old and New Testaments alike. So that I found myself reading, as Harry's ashes rested, those final seconds, in the urn, above the sea, "Behold, He that keepeth Israel shall neither slumber nor sleep. The Lord is thy keeper; the Lord is thy shade upon thy right hand. The sun shall not smite thee by day, nor the moon by

night. The Lord shall preserve thee from all evil: He shall preserve thy soul. The Lord shall preserve thy going out and thy coming in from this time forth, and even for evermore." And Christopher, as I let fall the ashes into the water, summoned the words spoken over the ages when men are buried at sea. "Unto almighty God we commend the soul of our brother departed, and we commit his body to the deep in sure and certain hope of the resurrection unto eternal life through our Lord. The Lord bless thee and keep thee. The Lord make His face to shine upon thee. The Lord lift up the light of His countenance upon thee and give thee peace."

We bid goodbye to Harry. We promise not to miss our deadlines. We are confident he has not missed his final deadline.

It is because of Harry, I reflected, that this morning (and Wednesday morning, and Friday morning) I opine for syndication my views on this-or-that. It was nineteen years ago that Harry induced me to write a regular column.

Ralph Davidson, board chairman of Time Inc., sounded confused when I told him at one of those charity affairs last week that I was sorry I couldn't go to his affair on February 10, as I'd be in Switzerland. He was obviously confused, and it was foolish of me to forget how incessant is the use of useful names in the business of organizing charity dinners. He writes, "Actually I am devastated that you can't come on February tenth! When you threw the date at me last night I must confess that I did draw a blank. For God's sake, anybody who spends eight weeks in the Swiss Alps ought to be able to find more than an hour and a half a day in which to ski. I'm going to send Killy over to whip up your enthusiasm." That was the pleasantest encounter with *Time* magazine I had all week.

I had made a note that a formal protest must be made to Doubleday. "Sweet Betty [Prashker]: Would you be so kind as to direct the enclosed to the offending party? Love, Bill." Important to make it clear to Betty that you know *she* is not to blame. "Dear Sir/Madam: I was appalled to see [in the final, uncorrectable galleys] that the dedication in *Marco Polo, If You Can* was jumped over onto the copyright page. For sheer tastelessness this one is hard to beat. The casual reader will believe the book is designed to be stowed in the Hugh Kenner [to whom the book was dedicated] Wing of the Library of Congress. Except in mass paperbacks, and then only very seldom, the publisher does not begrudge an entire page to the person to whom the book is dedicated. And, of course, it should happen to perhaps the supreme arbiter of literary taste living today. Yours . . ." With a blind copy to Hugh Kenner.

There were several matters pending at the office, at which Jerry dropped me along with my clerical baggage, taking Olga and Rebeca uptown to the apartment. I walk up the two flights, turn right, open the door, passing by Rick Brookhiser's little office (once it was my secretary's, before that Whittaker Chambers', before that it was shared by my two sisters Maureen and Priscilla). We have occupied these offices since the second year of our existence, and I am reminded that that, now, was quite a while ago. Indeed, a young journalist recently observed that since no national magazine in 1955 was being edited by the same person who edits it today, save here, at *National Review*, that makes me the senior editor in the United States, if you count only longevity. Meaning? Oh, that your wife, the counterpart of the wife of the Guatemalan ambassador, gets to sit to the right of the Secretary of State if he has a dinner for editors, or that you're the one who says, "Thank you, Mr. President," calling an end to a press conference. The opportunity was perfect for me to answer in the style of George Bernard Shaw when asked did he know that in the English language only two words containing the letters "su" required that those letters be pronounced, "shoo," namely, *sumac,* and *sugar?* To which Shaw observed, "Sure, I know." To the journalist's observation I was able to comment, "Sure. And William Shawn?" The editor of *The New Yorker* has been in the saddle since 1952. Nice try, though.

I remembered that when I put out the offering circular, seeking to raise the capital to begin *National Review,* I committed myself to ten years' service to the enterprise. My father frowned on this, deeming the obligation excessive. He was a strict constructionist respecting any commitment, personal or professional. *National Review* continues to be the center of my professional life, and I once calculated that it takes up about forty percent of my time, even though I am reliably in the office only three days every fortnight, during which we take an issue to press. The balance of the work for *National Review* is done elsewhere, in automobiles, or over the telephone, or aboard airplanes, or at home. The magazine was conceived as a vehicle for responsible, informed, and inspired conservative thought, and it has been exactly that, playing a not insignificant role, I am quick to inform its patrons if caught with their zeal flagging, in its influence on charter-subscriber Ronald Reagan. So, through the corridor opening the door to my own office, greeting Dorothy McCartney, the young and resourceful head of research, who has the office on the left, and Susan Stark, equally young and pretty, who helps with research and correspondence, in the office on the right. The incomparable Frances Bronson's office is adjacent to mine, and the door is now open, so I greeted her (probably we have spoken ten times already today over the telephone). She told me that Bill Rusher was waiting for me.

Bill Rusher keeps a little appointment book, and no computer is programmed with greater exactitude. When our appointment is for three o'clock, I used to amuse myself by telling whoever was in the room that if he was curious as to when it would be 3:01, he had only to wait until the intercom rang. At 3:01 Bill advises me that it's after three. In the twenty-five years of our association Bill Rusher has made no effort to change these little habits, and there are three explanations for this. The first and least interesting is that in his case it would be like trying to forget he was right-handed—that, simply, is the way he is (he once told me that if he opens the door to the bathroom and finds the light accidentally already on, momentum will cause him to turn the light *off*, before ratiocination sets in, to advise him that if the objective is illumination, and the light is already on, then you shouldn't touch the switch at all). The second explanation is that having associated so long with persons of informal habits (I am probably the worst of the sinners, though one or two of *National Review*'s editors are not far behind), he feels the need to compensate for us by watching the clock, and living according to its beat. The third explanation is that, having come to be accepted as something of an eccentric, he rather cultivates the idiosyncrasies, which are annoying for the first ten years or so, but finally grow endearing.

In any event, I walked back through the corridor, past the elevator to the opposite end of the building, where Bill's suite has been for lo these many years. In front of him, neatly labeled and stacked, are his files. They are where they are FOR A REASON, and you must not on any account pull this-here file over to that-there end of the table. I sat down, and we moved instantly into the problem of our lease.

Our landlord, an elderly and attractive attorney named

Fred Scholem, told Bill a week ago that he would be requiring an increase for a lease renewal in December. Both Bill and I knew that dread moment would come, and braced for it, but the news would have caused Shylock to raise his eyebrows: Mr. Scholem wanted a *three hundred* percent increase over the price we were paying under our current lease.

National Review, like all journals of opinion, survives on charity. When we first got the news about the rent, we made inquiries—and learned that the square-foot rate Scholem was asking was in fact competitive for the area. Next I went to several brownstones and offices that had rentable space of ten thousand square feet, our requirement. The rental offices were asking about the same as Fred Scholem was asking, and the brownstones ranged in price from $750,000 to $1.2 million. Having established that the cheapest of these had enough space, I asked Rose Flynn, our accountant, bookkeeper, factotum, and Dutch uncle, to get the property vetted by a real estate inspector, and now Bill handed me the check sheet, which included such items as:

TERMITES: Evidence of
☐ Not observable
☐ [checked] Suspicion of
☐ See "Remarks"

I asked Bill to tell me simply whether the building passed muster, and the answer is Yes, but that to put it right for our company would cost about $100,000, or four fifths of a year's rent under Scholem. The next question is how to finance a hypothetical purchase. The only money we have access to is the Employees' Retirement Fund, which is under the supervision of three members of the board of directors, and a preliminary inquiry tells us that anything it invests in should yield a minimum dividend of fifteen percent. So the mathematics were quickly done, and we wound in and out of that one, calling in Rose for a half hour or so. Meanwhile, a telephone call from Bill establishes that Fred the Non-Red, as I now call him, will permit us the time to think the matter over: i.e., he will lease us our eighteen suites in the building on a monthly basis beginning when the rise goes into effect.

I mused with Bill that we were poorly situated to get mad at a capitalist who asks of us what the going price is of equivalent quarters, to which Bill quite properly responded that our rabbit warrens, adapted over twenty-five years to our particular requirements (what *other* tenant would need a dumbwaiter from the corner of my room, next to my desk, descending to Priscilla, into a cavity she can plumb from her desk chair, or Kevin Lynch from his?), are not all that easily rented to other parties, and that Fred rather likes getting a single check from one tenant, instead of (conceivably) eighteen separate ones; and that one other tenant just finished moving out rather than pay the increase.

I pondered the extraordinary hold on you that a property, and an area, can develop. We would move to Queens, or to New Jersey. . . . But this would also impose a burden on most of the (fifty) employees, who over the years have made their own arrangements with some reference to the fixity of their employer's. There is that, and also the psychic need of a journal of opinion for accessibility—to writers, visitors, foreign editors. "It isn't far, no further than downtown New York—and really, from the other end of George Washington Bridge you're practically there," a friend trying to coax me to lunch in his office in New Jersey once told me. It may be true—that you can reach some parts of New Jersey in about the same time it takes you to get downtown. But it *is* different, isn't it? That would appear to be the verdict of the marketplace, as witness the prices people are willing to pay to be housed in central New York. We decided to pursue the investigation of the brownstone, and to go once more to Fred Scholem, suggesting a compromise. . . .

Bill then went through his stack, and by 4:15 I was back in my office, and Frances gave me the day's telephone messages. WNET wants me to act as host for the television series, *Brideshead Revisited*, whose huge success in England I have read about. They need to know, said Frances, whether I am even remotely interested—enough so to sit through the thirteen hours of videocassettes. I told Frances I'll let them know within a day or two, and please to try to find Alistair Cooke's November telephone number (he has about twelve) since preeminently he would be in

a position to advise me on what is involved in hosting a series. I am taken by the idea, since *Brideshead* is a haunting and controversial book. . . .

The New York *Times* called to ask who had taken the photograph of me and Pat on the Orient Express that they will use in the Travel section, as they will want to send him a check (for $75). I told Frances that the picture in question was taken with my own camera by the waiter, and it would not be feasible to locate him. The spread will not be out until next Sunday and I haven't seen it, but the galleys, corrected over the weekend, amused me because I had privately gambled that one sentence I used would never see the light of day. On learning that the *Times* had a strict limit of $500 for any travel piece, a sum that

hardly returned me my costs, I had written: "Aboard the Orient Express, the consumption of [drinks from the bar] is encouraged, by the way, and they are cash-and-carry, and there is no nonsense about special rates. A gin and tonic is $4, a liqueur $6. These prices, weighed on the scales of the Old Testament, are not prohibitive, unless you are trying to make a living writing for the Travel section of the New York *Times*."

I won—the third sentence did not survive. It's a funny thing about the *Times:* I don't know anybody who works for it who *doesn't* have a sense of humor (big exception: John Oakes. But then he retired as editorial page director several years ago, and is understandably melancholy about having to live in a world whose shape is substantially of his own making). Abe Rosenthal, the working head of the newspaper, is one of the funniest men living. Punch Sulzberger is wonderfully amusing, and easily amused. And so on. But there is some corporate something that keeps the *Times* from smiling at itself; don't quite know what.

Frances tells me that a reporter for the *Harvard Crimson* has called three times, that he is working on a deadline, and that he wishes from me a) a comment on the resolution to be argued against John Kenneth Galbraith in a televised debate at Harvard in January, and b) my ideas as to what I "hope to accomplish." The resolution is: "Resolved, That this House approves the economic initiatives of the Reagan Administration." I told Frances to call the reporter back and say that my view of the resolution is that "it is satisfactory," and that my "hope" is that "my knowledge of economics should have trickled down to Professor Galbraith and his colleagues."

I occasionally like to tease James Jackson Kilpatrick by calling him "Jim," because on "Meet the Press," candidate Ronald Reagan once referred to him as "Jim" (he is "Jack," or "Kilpo"). I mentioned this, in January of election year, to Reagan's then campaign manager, John Sears. Sears smiled. "That's nothing," he said, making reference to New York's principal Republican, "he calls Perry Duryea *'Dan'!*" Kilpo had called to say he wasn't sure he could make connections with us in Switzerland in January, we having postponed our departure by three days. . . .

Other calls I can't delay, but not that of Bob Bauman. I hadn't spoken to Bob since the scandal over a year ago, in the fall of 1980, when it was revealed that, while drinking, he had solicited sex from a young male. The news came as a considerable blow, needless to say, to the Bauman family, but also to the conservative community, not least because in Congress Bob over the years had acquired a considerable reputation as a parliamentarian at the service of the right, but also as a heckler of others' moral weaknesses. The government dropped the charge, on the condition that Bauman promise to take part in a rehabilitation program.

Bob (whom I'd known, as also his wife Carol, since he helped to found the Young Americans for Freedom) had made an announcement of some dignity at a press conference, in which he made no attempt at self-justification, contenting himself to say that since the time of the offense, he had succeeded in curing himself entirely of alcoholism, and that any tendency to homosexuality had gone with the alcohol—and that under the circumstances, he would *not* retire from the race for re-election to Congress. I was in Seattle, lecturing, when I got the news, and I don't remember a column I ever wrestled with more than the one I wrote that night, calling on Bauman to resign from the race. Although he never wrote to me, he is said greatly to have resented my declaration; and now he was calling.

I greeted him. He answered amiably and told me that he had just come from a press conference at which he had announced that he was reentering politics and would be a candidate in 1982 for his old seat. "Someone asked me,

'What does Buckley think of this?' and I said 'I don't know, I'll call him and ask.' So this is that call." I told Bob that if he thought himself cured, by all means he should do what he wanted to do, and if it meant anything, I was with him all the way.

The phenomenon of the sometime homosexual, wholly cured, is not one with which most of us are familiar. I am not talking about men who had an experience as school-boys, or even at college, of the kind intimated with such taste in *Brideshead*.

I remember being stunned when in 1976 I read that Professor Allen Weinstein, who was then preparing the definitive book on the Hiss case (*Perjury*, A. Knopf, 1978), had got hold of a handwritten letter to the FBI volunteered by Whittaker Chambers disclosing preemptively (lest Hiss's lawyers came up with it at the trial, which they never did) that Chambers had been an active homosexual during five years in the thirties. But that, since leaving the Party (he wrote), he had been cured, being a faithful husband, and father. My astonishment was at learning that the man I had known so well had ever been a homosexual. I have probably known ten people who knew Chambers extremely well, dating back many years before the year I met him (1954), and none of them had any intimation of this chapter in Chambers' history. It is fashionable nowadays to say that a person's sexual "preference" is not a datum of any consequence. That question is best saved for another exploration. My point here is the discrete one, that the assumption that homosexuality is an enduring condition (like alcoholism) is simply mistaken, by the evidence of anyone who knew Chambers; and, as of now, presumably by anyone who knows Bob Bauman.

Frances brought me the issue of *Time* magazine, just out. What they had done was as bad as could be.

Several years ago the Securities and Exchange Commis-

sion launched an investigation of the Catawba Corporation, founded by my father in the late forties, and owned
by his ten children. The idea of Catawba was simple
enough, namely to set up a service organization which by
commanding top administrative, geological, financial, and
legal talent could offer the best service to small explor-
atory companies which, dependent on their own resources,
would not have been able to come up with quality service.
For thirty years, Catawba in effect managed six explor-
atory oil companies founded by my father. What was
wrong, though neither illegal nor immoral in the circumstances, was that the same people who decided, in their capacity as officers of Catawba, what Catawba should charge
its client companies also approved, in their capacity as
officials of the serviced companies, Catawba's charges.
What made the relationship substantively defensible was
the reasonable fees and royalties charged, the performance
of Catawba over the years, and the disclosures regularly
made in public documents of Catawba's role.

Still, as anyone who has dealt with the SEC or become
involved with it (as I protractedly was during 1977–79)
knows, ethical criteria for conducting publicly owned
companies are an evolving moral art, and that which was altogether okay in 1950 would not necessarily get by in 1980.

When it files its complaints under Rule 10b-5, its most
infamous weapon, the SEC Enforcement Division can elect
to allege a violation of clause 1, or 2, or 3—or all of said
regulations that fall under Rule 10b-5. But only the first
and third clauses speak of "fraud." Now "fraud," as used
by intelligent and cosmopolitan men and women, has a
pretty nasty connotation. The SEC in recent years has
tended to use the word with abandon, cunningly calculating that although a *securities* "fraud" is very different
from garden variety fraud, the use of the word has considerable intimidating power if the people against whom it is

used are prominent other than in the securities business, as of course was the case with Catawba.

Steve Umin, the learned family attorney in Washington, was greatly gratified that the SEC, when finally it framed its complaint against Catawba, did *not* use the first or third clauses. In not doing so, it acted conspicuously—i.e., it said in effect: Although certain practices followed by Catawba we allege to be in violation of the Securities and Exchange Act and the regulations promulgated under its authority, we specifically do not include, as among those violations, any intent to defraud.

When the complaint was issued, together with the consent decree signed by my brother John (the only Buckley directly concerned with the litigation), what one might call the professional business press, most conspicuously *The Wall Street Journal*, gave it a routine story (the *Journal* ran it on page 17). But because my brother Jim and I are public figures and are stockholders of Catawba, notwithstanding that Jim has been essentially unaffiliated with Catawba since he was elected to the Senate in 1970, and that I hadn't had anything to do with Catawba since a brief spell in 1954, the New York *Times* gave the consent decree front-page treatment. It was hard, reading the story, to understand why it rated such prominent attention. (A headline accurately communicating its news might have said: "COMPANY OF WHICH JAMES AND WILLIAM BUCKLEY ARE STOCKHOLDERS/SIGNS THROUGH BROTHER WHO ONCE WAS COMPANY'S PRESIDENT/CONSENT DECREE WITH SEC AGREEING TO KEEP SEVERED/CATAWBA TIES WHICH WERE SEVERED IN 1978.")

But a young reporter for *Time* mag, hoping for much much more, had devoted a great deal of effort to the whole complicated business, and when the SEC declined to move in a more stentorian mode, he undertook to do so himself, and persuaded his superiors to go along. Accordingly, two

weeks ago *Time* had devoted an entire page—not even in
the business section, but under National News—to Catawba.
The story said:

> . . . the Securities and Exchange Commission, after a
> 3½-year investigation of Buckley-controlled oil and
> gas companies, last week portrayed the family's own
> business practices as unethical and even unlawful. In
> effect, it accused the companies of having defrauded
> stockholders to feather the family's nest.

Now that story had an extraordinary effect on the new
director of the Enforcement Division of the SEC. John M.
Fedders had been for a number of years a securities lawyer, and had clients who had suffered from the arbi-
trariness of Fedders' predecessor, Stanley Sporkin—gone
now, after Reagan's election, to the CIA, as chief counsel,
where, one hopes, he will be instrumental in doing as much
damage to the Soviet enterprise as he did to American enterprise. John Fedders, shown by Umin the article in *Time*
magazine, joined in Umin's indignation and undertook to do
something absolutely unprecedented in the history of the
SEC. He wrote a letter and addressed it "To the members
of the Buckley family." (It is perhaps prudent to add here
that Mr. Fedders, unknown to me, is also unknown to my
brothers and sisters—i.e., his spontaneous action was not
motivated by particular attachments.) Fedders' letter read:
"Your counsel have expressed to me their displeasure with
the article in the November 16 issue of *Time* magazine. I
am concerned with the impression left by the article that
the Commission's complaint alleges that the Buckley family
'defrauded stockholders to feather the family's nest.'

"Although the Commission's complaint alleges violations
of Rule 10b-5 (2) under the 1934 Act and Section 17 (a)
(2) of the 1933 Act, it does not allege that the described
transactions were 'fraudulent.'

"It is important that the results of the Commission's work not be misunderstood."

What then happened is in part reconstruction, in part narrative contributed by participants. *Time* magazine, confronted with this challenge, told the young reporter to justify what he had done, by God, or —— . . . John Fedders was thereupon approached by the reporter.

Informants do not reveal whether the reporter wept at that meeting. But either Fedders authorized the researcher to report back to New York that Fedders had changed his mind; or, more likely, the researcher improvised a retraction by Fedders. At any rate, the issue this morning, its unpleasantness for my brother John aside, makes an absolute fool of poor Fedders. Here we all had, over his signature, the flat statement that the SEC did *not* allege fraud. And now *Time* prints, "Mr. Fedders told *Time* his letter was not intended to address the question of whether *Time*'s interpretation of the transactions was accurate." What then *was* it intended to address? Why had Fedders written that he was "concerned" with the "impression" left by the article that the SEC's complaint "alleges" fraud?

I was angered by what *Time* had done, the more so on learning from Steve Umin over the telephone that three times the reporter, having first *asked* for the opportunity to hear the case against concluding "fraud," had not availed himself of that opportunity, presumably to guard against seeing evidence that might cripple his beloved story, which was no story at all in the absence of fraud, the story's vertebral column. I wrote a violent letter to the managing editor of *Time* (whom I have never met, and about whom I hear only pleasant things; and in the interval that has gone by I concede that, after all, one should understand . . . If the director of the Enforcement Division of the SEC can be made to look contortionate by the writhings of a reporter, why not also *Time*'s managing editor? Editors necessarily *rely* on staff).

Dear Sirs [I wrote to *Time*]:
    Having surveyed not a few of the nests provided by the stockholders of Time Inc. to executives of *Time*, my comment is that that which my father created, *ex nihilo*, he was modestly compensated for. You hide behind the term "in effect"; your use of the word "defraud" was explicitly declined by the SEC, whose standards are severe. *In effect*, you have demeaned your responsibility to weigh the evidence and speak the truth with verbal precision. That calling is higher than any dumb loyalty to subordinates whose demonstrated misjudgment you are evidently too insecure to disavow.

A mutual friend subsequently wrote me:

I dissuaded [the managing editor of *Time*] from sending a rather scathing two-page reply to your very trenchant note. [His] draft said in part, and I quote for your amusement and with his permission: "I cannot comment on the living standards of *Time* executives or the Buckley family. This *Time* executive lives in a 2½-room Manhattan apartment which you have not had an opportunity to survey because I fear the appointments would strike you as distasteful and the company boring."

I cannot say what would be my reaction to the former, but I doubt the latter. I replied to my friend:

I have a book-length manuscript describing the outrages attendant on my own brush with the SEC three years ago. I haven't published the book because my friends tell me it is too goddamn boring, and that part of me which is an editor agrees. But I don't really understand why [*Time*'s managing editor] should want to send me a scathing reply. After all, the SEC did not allege fraud, [*Time*'s] writer did; the SEC dissociated itself from [*Time*'s] interpretation, and then [*Time*'s] writer, having told the SEC his job was on the line, reported verbally that the SEC had contradicted itself, and *Time* —again without consulting the Buckley lawyer, or the language used by the SEC—went on to reaffirm a charge. You and I and, I expect [the managing editor], know that civil fraud [as the term is used by the SEC] . . . needn't be all that grave. That is the[ir] technical use of the word, but the layman's use is different, and it is the burden of my unpublished book that a) no one appears to care; but b) people should care. And when *Time* suggests my brother committed fraud, I care enough to risk receiving a scathing letter from the managing editor to set the record straight. So there we are, my friend. . . . There was a day, and I genuinely regret its passing, when people genuinely guilty of fraud were ostracized. The dissipation of the social sanction has its convenience but I doubt that it is altogether healthy.

In New York, we live uptown, on Seventy-third Street, and Jerry got me there only minutes before our six guests convened for a drink and sandwiches (we would dine later). We piled into the car to go hear Rosalyn Tureck perform the second of her three scheduled fall concerts at Carnegie Hall. I have managed over the years to hear her perform publicly a dozen times (she presumes to perform even when I am out of town). For one whole season she stayed abroad, doing her scholarly editions; another season, for a month or so, she was ill. Two years ago she played five concerts, repeating works she had performed forty years back when, as a young woman, she began her New York career. I met her nearly twelve years ago, when I asked her to do a program with me for "Firing Line" at which we would explore the question, "Why are they afraid of Bach?"

I tease her sometimes, because it's fun to do so when two people absolutely agree on the same proposition, in this case that she is the best piano interpreter of J. S. Bach at large. She likes to hear a compliment, but is never quite surprised by it. I suppose in this respect she is like many artists. I remember returning from our honeymoon in 1950 and finding that my father's graduation present, a Challis clavichord, was—I feared fatally—constipated by the moisture in northwest Connecticut where I had left it. In desperation I took it to the house of the legendary harpsichordist Wanda Landowska, off neighboring Lakeville Lake. I had never met her, but assumed she would share my distress and give me counsel. She palmed off the instrument on Denise Restout, her musician-assistant, and proceeded to chat with me, her very first question being, Had I heard her new recording of *The Well-Tempered Clavier?* I was able truthfully to reply, Yes. She closed her eyes, and said: "Magnificent, no?" I agreed.

Rosalyn combines self-esteem with great artistic maturity. I think it safe to say that if she were *not* good, she wouldn't think she *was*. Along the line, sometime in the late thirties, she resolved to abandon her vast repertory and play only the work of Johann Sebastian Bach. I read somewhere that the great Chilean pianist Claudio Arrau once calculated that he held in memory enough music to play forty two-hour concerts. That would be eighty hours. It is only a guess, but it is reasonable to assume that it would take about forty hours to play all the works of Bach written for keyboard, but some of these works are of absolutely terrifying complexity. It is one thing to commit to memory

Grieg's Concerto, another to remember a couple of Bach's English Suites. Or, for that matter, the first six preludes and fugues in the second volume of the forty-eight preludes and fugues. The problem is that the story line is totally polyphonic, with two, three, and four melodies pursued in counterpoint. To play romantic music can be horrifyingly difficult (one thinks of the Transcendental Etudes of Liszt), but I think that memorizing them would be easier than memorizing much of Bach.

In any event, it isn't a secret that there is a certain amount of professional resentment of Tureck because of her single-minded focus on one composer. Her reputation as an artist in other literatures was well established, and I have heard cassettes of her doing remarkable things with Paganini, Chopin, Liszt. But her devotion to a single composer, while certainly idiosyncratic, can hardly be judged as narrow, for the reason that we are dealing with Bach. No more would an actor be judged narrow who determined to act only in the plays of Shakespeare. We might regret the decision, even as I regret that Rosalyn doesn't play the other composers—unless I thought that were she to do so, she would dilute her talent, playing Bach less magnificently than she does.

Her second offense against the professional world of music is that she elected, somewhere along the line, to perform not only on the piano, but also on the harpsichord. Moreover, she plays the harpsichord with stunning effect, though in that instrument she has competitors. "They" don't like it when you perform on more than one instrument. Rosalyn rubbed it in by deciding a few years ago to do something probably never before done, namely to play the Goldberg Variations on the harpsichord before dinner, and on the piano after dinner. When she does the Goldberg she takes all the repeats, and it clocks in at about one hour and twenty minutes of the most exacting keyboard work imaginable, evoking every mood, every technical problem, including the musical problem of cohesion. And it takes the concentration required to play without any interruption for twenty-five minutes longer than it takes to perform Beethoven's Ninth Symphony.

She invited Pat and me to her apartment three days before the double Goldberg and played the thing through for us on her harpsichord, a marvelous experience. And then a year later Pat told me that Rosalyn had a present for my birthday. She was scheduled to play at Carnegie Hall the following Tuesday. On Saturday she would give the same concert at our home in Stamford. We invited about twenty guests, and she came down from upstairs with consummate presence (she doesn't like to be introduced to people individually *before* she plays). I presented her at the piano by recalling an old story I heard at college, about the boy who, weary of the school band, says to the girl, "Let's go to my car and listen to Guy Lombardo and his Royal Canadians." She says, "I didn't know you had a radio in your car!" He says, "I don't. I have Guy Lombardo and his Royal Canadians." "I feel," I said proudly, "as though I have here Guy Lombardo and his Royal Canadians!"

Guy Lombardo [this rhetorical device, I once learned— I'll talk about that—is called "antonomasia"] sat for a breathtaking hour and a half at the Bösendorfer. I recorded it, and gave a copy to David Oppenheim, dean of the School of the Arts at New York University, and he told me he thought the last half, in particular, one of the finest piano recitals he had ever heard.

And then, when I was out of town, a friend taped her on CBS, playing in London at Temple Church. One half hour, videotaped from a concert during the first half of which she had played the harpsichord, the second half the *organ!* I have shown that videocassette to terribly cosmopolitan types who have been uniformly swept off their feet

by what she accomplishes on an organ with the *Chromatic Fantasy*: one walks away convinced that Bach must have meant it for the organ, but forgot so to designate it. Until one hears it again on the harpsichord. Or on the piano. "Bach wrote tonalities," she once said to me, stressing the success with which Bach himself took identical themes and expressed them on the keyboard, the violin, or cello.

Tonight at Carnegie Hall she would play four preludes and fugues, the Partita in E minor, the Chromatic Fantasy and Fugue, and the Italian Concerto. That, for the baroque crowd, is the rough equivalent of going to a Shakespeare recital and hearing, oh, the soliloquies of Hamlet, Lady Macbeth, King Lear, and then Romeo. The four preludes began (only a showman-artist could do this) with the triumphantly simple C major, which Gounod practically ruined by coming up with his Ave Maria all over it, much as kindergarten music teachers forever ruin Schubert's symphony by teaching the children to remember it with the melodic mnemonic, *"This is* the-sympho-*nee*/That poor old Schubert never *fi*-nished."* Rosalyn's rendition was so enthralling one had the sensation of hearing that minute-long masterpiece for the very first time.

And so it went, through the balance of the preludes, including the marvelous G major she also played at Stamford (and at Temple Church), a rendition breath-catching in its lyrical speed. Rosalyn loves and reveres the Sixth Partita, and the combination is perfect. After the intermission, the Chromatic Fantasy, with the deceptive slowness of the fugue, and her remarkable capacity to increase the tension. She looked small from the dress circle where our seats were, and the sound she produced was all the more imposing, the dominion of a mid-sized, handsome woman with dark hair, ample bosom, dead serious in her devotion to the agent of our delight; a memorable experience. The Italian Concerto, with which she concluded (she gave three encores), has—the marvelous slow movement apart—never done for me what it does for others, and it intrigues me that true connoisseurs gravitate to it, giving it such serious attention ("Nobody plays the Italian Concerto like Alicia de Larrocha," Fernando Valenti once solemnly told me). When judgment by very particular people is passed on something, which judgment isn't in accord with one's own, one must pay such judgment presumptive respect. I understand what I have just said as an intellectual proposition. And yet I am required to reflect that there are serious people who think the Rolling Stones make captivating sound. I cannot agree. I would go so far as to say only that the Rolling Stones captivate their audiences, not that their sound is captivating; but perhaps I resent it when I reflect that there were a few empty seats in Carnegie Hall tonight, but none a few days earlier when the Stones played at Madison Square Garden; though perhaps I am being foolish. As if a reading of the sonnets of

Shakespeare could be expected to bring in as large an audience as would flock to hear Billy Graham.

I wired Rosalyn the next morning, before catching the plane. "YOU BROUGHT GREAT JOY LAST NIGHT. WAS THERE A LITTLE TOO MUCH PEDAL IN FIRST FUGUE? I COULDN'T HAVE DONE BETTER MYSELF. YOU CAN BE MY SECOND THIRD AND FOURTH LOVE." On the first point she later expressed some concern, but we ended by agreeing that where I was sitting, off at the right, and high, there must have been a little distortion.

The last is an inside joke. On a "Firing Line" program, years ago, that touched on the question of love and marriage, someone was making some point or other about artists and marriage and I blurted out that what-the-hell, Rosalyn Tureck had been married three times, and that this datum hardly advanced whatever point my guest was seeking to make. A few weeks later Rosalyn accosted me at the premier of Jerome Robbins' Goldberg Variations ballet, and asked me whether what she had heard I had said was true. To answer her truthfully (I had quite simply forgotten making that reference to her) I needed to consult the transcript, which I subsequently did. I *had* said it; and I was wrong. Rosalyn has been married twice, one of her husbands having died, so to speak, *in situ*. In my apology I told her that I could only think to do the right thing by offering my hand as her third husband, so that *retroactively* it could be said that she'd had three.

Ah yes, antonomasia. A dreadful episode, though I acknowledge that my more disreputable friends found it awfully funny. It was several years ago and I was on the Merv Griffin program to announce the publication of my most recent book, which I attempt routinely to turn into a national holiday. The other guests certainly completed the spectrum. They were Mr. and Mrs. Arthur Murray—after

Terpsichore, the principal sponsors of modern dance; a young woman—a movie producer; and—well, here is how I wrote it in my column: ". . . a rock-ballad singer, envelopingly warm, talented Pat Boone-type who sings songs about father-son relationships."

My office, confused by the balance of my text and unable to reach me as I had flown off to the Fiji Islands, cut out the word "type" so as to leave it as, merely, "Pat Boone." This was consistent with the balance of the column, in which, secure in the knowledge that such a literary convention existed, I had referred only to "Pat Boone," even as one might write, say, "The Californians that year elected a Robin Hood-type as governor. The moment Robin Hood reached Sacramento, he came out for a wild program of redistribution. . . ." I didn't know that that device was called "antonomasia."

Not that knowing would have kept me out of trouble.

I had gone on to describe what "Pat Boone" had said on Merv Griffin's program about the activity in which the woman producer was engaged. What was *her* line?

Well, [I wrote] she produces and directs porno flicks. The hard stuff. She looks rather like Kay Kendall. How old are you, dear? Twenty-three. What religion were you brought up in? Catholic. Still practice your religion? Well—tee hee—no, not really, don't go to church much. Did you go to college? Yes, Michigan State. Graduate? Yes. Major? Phys. Ed. What made you go into . . . porn movies? Wanted to get into the business, and worked for a while as a cashier at a movie house that featured X-rated movies, so got interested in the business, asked around, and went to Hollywood. Do you make . . . all . . . kinds of . . . films? No, we don't go into, well, bestiality, sado-masochism, that sort of thing. Just, you know, the regular stuff, only, in a way, you know, we try to experiment, new positions, that sort of thing.

After that paragraph I had written:

> Pat Boone came in and said he thought it was all a pretty good idea. He and his wife had an X-rated film which they showed on their home videocassette system, and he thought it was very healthy, after all we're all part animal, and we have animal instincts, and what's wrong with recognizing anything that obvious?

I had, on Merv's show, contributed at that point something to the effect that it was also an animal instinct to eat other animals, but we don't make movies about people eating other people.

> And Merv said to the author [me]: Have you ever seen a pornographic film? "Sure, the author said, I've done a lot of reprehensible things." The audience, I noted, hadn't liked that very much—
> That did it. What was so reprehensible about it: I mean, here's a sweet young thing, 23, Phys. Ed. from Michigan State, making the kind of movies that Pat Boone and his wife show in the privacy of their living room, so what's so bad about that?

I was calmly scuba diving in the Fijis when that column hit the fan. Someone close to Griffin read it when it arrived in mimeographed form at the Los Angeles *Times* and telephoned my office in New York to ask how was it that I had mistaken the singer John Davidson for Pat Boone? Frances Bronson called Harry Elmlark, who sent telegrams to three hundred newspapers. Half the clients made the correction in time, but the others did not. The first call awaiting me on my return to New York was from Pat Boone's lawyer.

After it was all settled I had a letter from Pat Boone which is surely one of the most lugubrious ever composed. "I appreciate your letter of November 20, and your expression of concern. I don't think you can have any idea of how this article has wreaked havoc in my life. I'm getting letters from all over the country from irate and terribly grieved people, most of them in the evangelical Christian community, who feel that I am a hypocrite, a traitor, and worse. . . . We've only got a partial tally so far, but it appears the column ran in almost every place I've ever called a 'home town,' including my birthplace of Jacksonville, Florida, and folks by the thousands, at least, must now be quite convinced that I have pornographic films at home, and that Shirley and I sit around drooling at them in the evenings. The terrible irony of this is that I was the *only entertainer* who came out in favor of Proposition 18, the anti-pornography measure on our ballot in 1974, and earned the disfavor of the whole entertainment community. . . ."

I was terribly grieved at the hurt I had done him. His lawyer said it would not have made a substantial difference if the column had retained the qualifier "type" after the first mention of "Pat Boone." (Ignorant of antonomasia? That will be a fine of five thousand dollars!) Five thou was how much money I had to send to compensate the lawyer. I confess that when I wrote out the check, I permitted myself, just that one time, to reflect, with a wink ever so discreet, on one of the clippings I had been sent. It was in the White Plains daily, featured a large picture of Pat in a most pious posture, head slightly downturned on the stage. The caption? *"At night he watches the pornies."* Oh dear. As Hugh Kenner tells me, and I do not tire of repeating, "Newspapers are low-definitional instruments. Never rely for the exact meaning of what you wish to say on the correct placement of a comma."

Two
TUESDAY

I tried to rise without waking Pat, didn't succeed in doing so, and she kissed me bon voyage with that combination of listlessness, habit, and implicit affection that somehow works, or must, because without it the day begins incompletely. She muttered that I must not be late for the ballet, and I promised. Jerry as usual was a few minutes early, and we got to Kennedy at 7:30, in plenty of time. In the aircraft I checked my speech folder, wrote out an appropriate new introduction, and turned to the mail.

A couple of weeks ago I did a column devoted to examining a public letter sent out by the television producer Norman Lear ("All in the Family," etc.) which letter he had announced as "probably the most important" he would ever write. Its contents were a denunciation of the Moral Majority and a hair-raising description of the threat it poses to the American way of life. My reaction was that that sort of thing (The Moral Majority Is the Greatest Threat to America) has become altogether too easy and fashionable, rather like denouncing Joe McCarthy a generation ago, then looking up expectantly as though your physical and moral courage had clearly earned you a standing ovation. I was careful to point out that Norman Lear is a man of enormous talent, and incidentally that no single simplification urged by the Moral Majority, e.g., in the area of creationist theology, could hold a candle up against the hilarious flights of reductionism at the expense of religion, patriotism, and the free market system regularly urged by Mr. Lear's most famous creation, Archie Bunker.

I myself became addicted to "All in the Family" back during the years when it played at eight on Saturday, when I am generally home. I remember greatly resenting it one Saturday a few years ago (before the age of videocassettes) when Pat reminded me we were scheduled that Saturday night as guests of the Nelson Rockefellers, who were giving a big party at Pocantico in honor of Henry and Nancy Kissinger. This meant I would miss "All in the Family." But life is full of such pitfalls—and at 8:30 on that fabulous terrace, we sat down in our designated seats; and lo, the man seated next to Pat and me was none other than Carroll O'Connor—Archie Bunker: who proved a charming dinner companion.

He had just returned from Rome, he told me, having traveled there with an old friend, a Jewish Hollywood producer who was the *original* anti-fascist. "I mean, when he was a kid, no baseball for Al, he was out there selling flags for money to contribute to Bundles for Britain, distributing leaflets at public gatherings about Hitler and Mussolini, the whole thing. Well," O'Connor's face lit up, "so we travel together to Rome, and a couple of nights ago— Al's crazy, I mean *crazy* about jazz piano especially, and we wander into one of those late-night clubs and there's a piano player, and Al orders drinks and he says, 'That guy's *good!*' So he signals to the headwaiter to come over, and he says to the headwaiter, 'What's the piano player's name?' And the waiter says, 'Mussolini.' And Al says, '*What did you say?!*' And the waiter says, 'Mussolini. Romano Mussolini.' Al turns white, and says, 'Any . . . relation?' And the waiter says, 'Yes. Son,' and off he goes. And so Al looks at me as if he was seeing a ghost, and orders another drink. Well, two or three drinks later, there's just the two of us, and old Romano playing away, all the songs requested by Al. And by now we're seated right up against the piano. Al orders a last drink. And suddenly he turns to the piano player and says, 'Romano, you know something? That was a *hell* of a thing they did to your father!'" Archie was never funnier.

Norman Lear says a lot of things, and encloses some material, but concretely tells me I was wrong in saying that he, Lear, had produced a great extravaganza on behalf of Jerry Brown during the 1980 primary campaigns. His efforts had been in behalf of John Anderson. I answer: "Dear Mr. Lear. That was a silly mistake I made, and I apologize for it. I remembered the large spectacular in favor of Jerry Brown and it was only after receiving your letter that I researched my memory to find it was Mr. Coppola who put it together, not you. Thanks for the enclosures. I will let you know when I feel threatened. Cordially."

My classmate McKinney Russell—we had come to know each other better in Moscow in 1971—writes to me pleasantly from Rio. He had to give cover in the embassy to Henry Kissinger for three hours, until a hostile crowd dispersed. In the course of the affair he met my son Christopher, who is traveling with Vice-President Bush as speechwriter. In Moscow, you are not allowed to designate anyone on your staff as the "Cultural" Affairs officer (sometime, somebody in the Kremlin decided that any such designation implied that there was less than sufficient culture already in the Soviet Union), so McKinney was called something else, though that was the job he executed. His special genius is in language. A few years ago he returned from a three-week vacation in Sweden speaking the language fluently. In Rio, he is probably moonlighting by teaching Portuguese.

A correspondent reacts to the column in which I registered dismay that the documentary on the North American operations of the KGB is not being aired. What happened was that two young Canadian producers became interested in the KGB and were astonished to learn that no treatment of the KGB's operations had *ever* been aired, so they set out to do one, using Canadian capital together with money put up by ABC for an option to air it in America. But after the three-hour documentary was completed, ABC backed down—not giving a reason. The Canadian people asked me, through Bill Rusher, if I'd have a look;

and so, mounting the cassette, one night I did so: and saw some of the meatiest spy stuff I'd ever seen on a screen, including reminiscences from one or two people who had worked with Alger Hiss within the Communist Party—pretty sensational fare. Also, a great deal about activities of the KGB in Hollywood.

On impulse, I made a copy and a few days later when Ronald Reagan (Jr.) and his wife were staying with us, whence they were heading for Camp David, I pressed the cassette in his hand and said his father ought to see it. A few days later, El Presidente called to say how much he had been impressed by what he had seen. In the course of discussing it, it transpired that he had seen only the first hour, missing entirely the section on Hollywood, among others. I couldn't understand why the tape had been defective, but discovered the following weekend, on looking at it again, that the delay between the first and succeeding segments is about two minutes, giving the viewer the impression he has seen it all.

I don't know whether Mr. Reagan ever got to see the balance, but it seemed plain that the balance is never going to be seen by the American public, because although there was a fuss of sorts after the column was published, and although ABC said they would have another look at it, it hasn't been shown (it was broadcast locally in New York City the following spring). There is a preternatural fear among many Americans that to show what in fact the KGB does—i.e., to depict its workaday techniques of intelligence gathering, dissimulation, and disinformation—is to run the risk of being accused of McCarthyism. As a matter of fact, those Americans are correct. That is exactly the risk they run. . . .

I gave the name and address of the Canadian producer to my correspondent.

A note from Howard Hunt. He lodged a libel suit

several years ago against *The Spotlight*, a publication of the Liberty Lobby, of which a principal figure is Willis Carto. *The Spotlight*'s distinctive feature is racial and religious bigotry. Howard writes, "So far Carto has avoided deposition by staying on the West Coast, allegedly; this delays my libel suit's progress." He says he has heard from Carto's lawyer that "Willis Carto . . . is by coincidence a target of yours." More exactly, it is the other way around, Carto having attacked me and *National Review* for years, presumably upon learning that we thought the Protocols of the Learned Elders of Zion a forgery. We were finally ourselves forced to sue Carto (or, more exactly, counter-sue), and the stuff (depositions, motions) is in the hands of the judge—the slowest judge in history. (A few weeks later, Howard called me in high exultation to say that the jury had awarded him a judgment of six hundred and fifty thousand dollars. *The Spotlight* had alleged about Hunt, among other jocularities, that he would probably be im-plicated in the assassination of John Kennedy.)

Howard was my boss during the nine months I spent in Mexico working for the CIA. He was always cheerful, opinionated (our biases were in sync), and bright, and we became good friends. Indeed, when his wife Dorothy, who was killed in the United Airlines accident a few months after Watergate, decided she would revert to Catholicism and bring her two daughters and her son with her, I was asked to become their godfather. We had, in Mexico, many amusing experiences together, but I remember most viv-idly the extraordinary speed with which Howard Hunt would write his spy thrillers. Every three or four months he would go uninterrupted from desk (at the office) to desk (at home), where he would begin typing. In seven to ten days his book would be finished. By company rules, the books could not be published until after they had been screened for security at CIA Headquarters; but after about

Book 25, Howard received a note from the office of Allen Dulles, Director of the CIA, whom he had known from service in Germany, something on the order of: Howard, you write books faster than our staff can review them, so let's put you on your honor. From now on, *provided you don't use your real name*, we'll let you, until further notice, publish your books unreviewed by us, *trusting* you not to reveal any information that might hurt the United States.

I was present at the conference at which Howard and Dorothy reflected on noms de plume, where finally it was settled that he would write under the name "Gordon Davis." Four months later, Howard proudly showed me a copy (which had just arrived that morning from New York) of his latest paperback: "*Appointment with Death. By Gordon Davis.*" I congratulated him and leafed through it. When I came to the last page, I read, "*You have just finished another exciting spy mystery by Howart Hunt.*" It was funny. But I groaned for Howard. If only that groan had resonated forward twenty-one years, warning against snafus, to that epochal night in June 1972. Or is that an immoral thought? I don't think so, really. I'd rather the burglary, however reprehensible, had succeeded, than that Watergate and the collapse of a foreign policy should have happened. Put it this way: If the Scotch tape at Watergate had stuck, maybe there wouldn't have been any boat people.

The business about who in the CIA, past or present, can write what, came up as a First Amendment case when 1) Frank Snepp, formerly with the CIA, wrote a book about his last days in Vietnam; 2) he didn't show the book to Stansfield Turner, director of the CIA; 3) Turner asked the Justice Department to sue, adducing Snepp's pledge not to reveal any information developed while at the agency without first clearing it; 4) the court found in favor of the CIA, penalizing Snepp the whole of his income from royalties; upon which he appealed, and 5) ultimately the Supreme Court refused to overturn.

Snepp accosted me at a social function a few months ago, asking how it was that I could write novels that contained knowledge gotten while I was at the CIA, and he couldn't. The differences struck me, then and now, as obvious: i.e., my CIA stories are imagined, save only an account of the training I received in 1951, which was accurately transcribed in *Saving the Queen;* while Frank's disclose events, during the months in 1975 preceding the great exodus, which enmesh dozens of people and, arguably, reveal CIA habits. Abstractly, however, he has a point.

I told him so, and gave him a useful episode for his complaint inventory, even while acknowledging that clearly the context was humorous. I was lecturing to the CIA at Langley (I have done this only once), and was introduced, with some wit and jocularity, by Snepp's nemesis, the director, Admiral Turner, part of a small group with whom I had in 1972 traveled to the South Pole, so that it happened we were friends. I replied to his spirited introduction by revealing to the audience that our most recent exchange of communications had taken place only a month or two before. I was in Hawaii, and wrote to Turner, "Dear Stan: I seldom join committees, but this one, in which I was offered membership yesterday, I simply couldn't resist. I'm writing to ask whether you yourself shouldn't join it? It is called 'The Pearl Harbor Committee to Keep One's Eyes on the Russian Fleet.'" Admiral Turner replied that ex officio he was a member of that committee. "But I am also a member of another committee, which you presumably have never heard of. It is called 'The Committee to Keep One's Eyes on Former CIA Agents Who Write Spy Novels Without Having Them Checked for Security.'"

Malum prohibitum, non malum in se—a distinction I cherish. Is it really wrong to go through a red light when there
isn't a soul within miles of the intersection? I favor the rule
that says you must stop anyway, because the habit of self-
discipline can save your life, and more importantly, others'
lives; but if I were a judge I'd hand down a lesser sentence
than I'd have done to a man who went through the red
light when there were children running about.

Last spring, from Switzerland, I was moved to repay the
debt I have felt to peanut butter. "I have never composed
poetry [I wrote in my syndicated column], but if I did,
my very first couplet would be:
  "'I know that I shall never see/A poem lovely as
Skippy's Peanut Butter.'"
My addiction is lifelong, and total. I reminisced. "I was
hardened very young to the skeptics. When I was twelve,
I was packed off to a British boarding school by my father, who dispatched every fortnight a survival package
comprising a case of grapefruit and a large jar of peanut
butter. I offered to share my tuck with the boys who
shared my table. They grabbed instinctively for the grapefruit—but one after another actually spit out the peanut
butter, which they had never before seen and which only
that very year (1938) had become available for sale in
London, at a store that specialized in exotic foods. No
wonder they needed American help to win the war."
   The volume of mail attracted by this column was extraordinary, most of it from p/b addicts, come out of the
closet, and most of them with declarations as to which
brand they were enslaved by. One letter interested me in
particular, because it was accompanied by a case of peanut
butter labeled "Red Wing." I tasted it skeptically—and
forthwith put all competitors aside.

It is quite simply incomparable. Charlton Heston, who had sent me a jar of *his* favorite stuff, just plain surrendered when I introduced him to Red Wing. But Pat told me her problem, and so I wrote to my benefactor, at 196 Newton Street, Fredonia, New York, "Dear Mr. Marcy: The manager of Grade A Market, a huge concern at which my wife does the shopping for our place in Stamford, Connecticut, (a) never heard of Red Wing, and would like to know (b) where he might order your product. Could you give me information on this subject?" He could, and he writes now to inform me that it sells under various names in various places—nearly always with the house label of the store selling it. But you can tell if it's the real thing, because the screw-on cover is yellow plastic.

My "detail sheet," as they call it in the lecture trade, disclosed that no one would be at the airport at Tampa to meet me, that I was to hail a cab and direct it to take me to the Don CeSar Beach Hotel in St. Petersburg.

There are advantages and disadvantages in being met for lecture engagements, of which this would be my forty-fourth (out of forty-eight) this year. If you are met, then there is no possibility of confusion. Moreover, during the car ride you will learn something about the social or political auspices of the speech, and such stuff is not only interesting but useful, particularly in angling the opening remarks of the talk. On the other hand, being met imposes social burdens which can be tiring. Not unusually, the forty-five minutes between arrival and deposit in the hotel are devoted to answering questions to which in any event you propose to devote yourself during the talk, and this lets a little air out of the speaker, who may very well need all the air he has.

The airport at Tampa is proud of its automated trains

that run you from the skirt around which the airplanes gather, one thousand feet into the terminal. Thus you avoid the long walks characteristic of so many airports. Florida is sunny and bright, this November 17, and, brief-cases in hand, I located a taxi. At the Don CeSar Beach Hotel there will be only one hundred people, invited to pay two hundred dollars apiece to attend a day-long program sponsored by Jack Eckerd, the retail drugstore entrepreneur who ran a losing race for governor of Florida in 1978. He has begun an educational institute which, in cooperation with Hillsdale College, is sponsoring today's event. There are several speakers, including Robert Bleiberg, editorial director of *Barron's* and a trenchant libertarian analyst; George Roche, president of Hillsdale College in Michigan and a keeper of the libertarian tablets; and Frank Shake-speare, formerly head of the USIA, with whom I was associated as a member of the U.S. Advisory Commission on Information, an ardent anti-Communist now serving as president of RKO General.

Old friends these, and today I'd be speaking to men and women of kindred economic inclination, and they include Perry I. Prentice, former publisher of *Time* mag, who has written to tell me he hopes I will devote my talk to an ex-amination of the principles of Henry George, as he knows me to be an admirer of George's single-tax theories. (H. George, 1839–1897, believed in taxing the rental value of land to protect society against land-grabbing specula-tors.)

In his letter, Perry had been quite specific. "In these clippings [Prentice enclosed several] I think you might find it most interesting to note that Governor Graham [of Florida] and all but one of his cabinet members are big land owners who owe their personal fortunes to the way nearly 95% of all the land in Florida is almost tax exempt! And in the story headlined '70% of Pinellas' Property

Taxes Are Borne by Residential Owners' I think you may find it worth your while to note that we 'rewarded' the Bank of Clearwater for giving us our finest buildings by piling a $335,000 land assessment increase on top of the $3,659,150 assessment on the new structure and we 'rewarded' the developers of Clearwater's finest shopping center by multiplying their land assessment from $960 an acre to $55,000 an acre, thereby piling a $2,720,000 land assessment on top of the $12,244,500 assessment for the new store buildings! . . . The President does not seem to realize that by far the biggest element in our overall inflation is the way land prices have soared far faster than any others to a total estimated at the census bureau at well over two trillion dollars, imposing twice as big a burden on our economy as the Federal debt." I agree, I agree. But I have discovered no way of interesting the general public in the subject.

Most speeches, at least in my case, are prewritten. One can't write forty-eight different speeches in a year—and if one did, they wouldn't be very good. I learned in conversation with my son of the harrowing schedule maintained by the Vice-President. George Bush has accepted as many as eight or ten speaking engagements in a week, and half of these may call for major speeches—e.g., before the American Bar Association, or the American Enterprise Institute. Christopher has to set out, day after day, and come up with a fresh speech. A pity. It isn't as if the Vice-President's speeches were reported in the daily press in such detail as to preclude his giving them more than once. A not entirely explicable imperative is at work here, in sharp distinction from the well-known, and universally accepted, tradition of campaign speeches that are sometimes given, unchanged, eight times per day by the candidates; seven days per week; thirty days per month.

My own feeling is that a prepared speech should be

polished, to which end I tend to write mine out. For that reason the question period is useful, to demonstrate to the audience that you can also think extemporaneously. A useful combination—not applicable, obviously, to special occasions, of which there would be one the day after tomorrow, when what is said has to be prepared *ad hoc*.

St. Petersburg is a substantial drive from the airport, and I was greeted by several old friends, but having arrived a little late I had missed the bloody mary and so, seated at lunch, I petition the waitress for a glass of wine, which she told me was only available at the bar, a statement the residual meaning of which was that she is too busy to go to the bar, but obviously the guest wasn't. At any rate, the wine was fetched up by a kindly volunteer, and I listened to George Roche speak with some excitement about the progress of his beloved Hillsdale, and the January launching of the institute at Shavano in Colorado. George's new director of development is John K. Andrews, Jr., whose name flickered briefly in the news in 1973 when he resigned his job as a presidential speechwriter with an unprovocative statement in which he nevertheless hinted at his discontent with regnant moral practices. John is highly literate, deeply religious, and a profoundly convinced conservative. He contracted to send me material on the forthcoming conference in Shavano for *National Review*. I was led to a press conference before the speech, where most of the questions had to do with David Stockman and his exchanges with the assistant managing editor of the Washington *Post* for the *Atlantic Monthly*; that and the huge size of the projected federal deficit. The local paper handled it all as follows:

> *St. Petersburg Beach*—A vintage William F. Buckley Jr. wowed business, educational and political leaders with an hour of biting political anecdotes and hard-line conservative economic philosophy here Tuesday. . . .

The 55-year-old New Yorker tossed five-syllable invec-
tives [animadversions?] and rhetorical subtleties to the
pinstriped crowd, interspersing his anti-government
theme between appropriate rounds of laughter and ap-
plause.

Well, it does sound rather gooey, doesn't it? On the
other hand it *was*, really. In my life, on the average, perhaps fifteen percent of the public appearances I've made
have been before audiences that profoundly agreed with me
(mostly I have spoken at colleges). But such time isn't, I
think, wasted; not for the lecturer, certainly not for those
lectured to. The lecturer can detect, by the inflections of
the audience's behavior, what it is that works, what doesn't
particularly work; what is readily communicable, what
isn't. And the audience can hear arguments, analyses, and
adornments by someone who believes pretty much as they
do and is presumably worth listening to. What isn't so easy
to forgive is the adapting of one's views to the inclinations
of the audience. I spoke early in the year at a Friends of Israel fund-raising banquet in Toronto, having been asked to
address general themes of foreign policy, which I did. The
first questioner asked how was it he had paid one thousand
dollars to listen to a speaker who only spent a few minutes
on Israel? I answered that I hadn't contracted to speak
only on Israel, that if I had been asked to, I'd have
declined, inasmuch as being myself a friend of Israel, I
didn't think myself equipped publicly to devote an entire
hour to the subject without first giving the subject more
time in preparation than I had; I wouldn't want to damage
Israel by making less than the best case out for it. So it
goes.

Today the questions were pretty much as expected,
with, as noted, special emphasis on the huge looming
deficit. One tries to make clear that in economics all mat-

ters are not necessarily weighed on the same scale. That is to say, although one dislikes large deficits, one doesn't therefore necessarily reason to the desirability of higher taxes. Better, I said, a rise in productivity and a relative decline in the public sector, though the symbol of the high deficit would hang heavy on Mr. Reagan's neck.

Mr. Eckerd asked that I be permitted to leave without social interruption, as I had to drive to Tampa in time to catch the flight to New York; which I did, uneventfully.

Tonight Pat and I (and others) were guests of Joe and Estée Lauder at a benefit for the New York City Ballet at the New York State Theater.

My feelings about ballet have been ambivalent over the years. On the one hand I find dance beautiful as vision, discipline, and exercise. On the other hand, my mind doesn't readily integrate the dance and the music, so that I find I am primarily viewing the dance—or listening to the music —when of course the idea is to do both. I have the same kind of problem with popular music, having for inexplicable reasons no idea at all what are the lyrics being sung, until someone, someday—maybe—sticks them in written form in front of me, without music to distract me. This is why I experience less than the satisfaction I should from the dance, though I am swept up by the beauty of what I see (Balanchine's Apollo, Robbins' Piano Pieces, Peter Martins' Symphony No. 1), and awed by the natural and developed talents required to make it all possible.

Arlene Croce, who reviews ballet for *The New Yorker*, worked for *National Review* for a number of years, and we experienced with this awesomely sensitive human being a clerical difficulty, the kind of thing *National Review* seldom encounters, in part because we are permissive, in part because in response to that permissiveness the staff is extra conscientious. But Arlene's problem was late-rising; and this was substantially owing to a hunger for the ballet that was fanatical in its hold on her. No religious order ever held more tenacious sway over a postulant than the ballet did over Arlene who, pressed on the subject, once revealed that that particular year she had attended 260 ballets. The excitement of seeing it, I assumed at the time, kept her up into the morning, which made it difficult for her to get to work at noon, let alone at nine in the morning. That kind of hunger for the ballet I confess not to share; and indeed, a ballet in prospect, I find myself fugitively thinking about the exclusively musical event I might have gone to instead; so it is.

As we sat down, I felt the end of a newspaper tickling my ear, looked back and it was Arthur Gelb, deputy managing editor of the New York *Times*. I greeted him warmly (we are old friends) and he handed me the Travel section of next Sunday's edition of the New York *Times*, which featured our trip on the Orient Express. I thanked Arthur, waved at his author-wife Barbara, and took a peek, showing it to Pat. I was dismayed that the picture on the cover page, of Pat and me dining in the railroad car, dressed in black tie, excluded Jack and Drue Heinz, our traveling companions, because I had told them that was the picture the *Times* was planning to use; and now I see they have been cropped.

Arthur had called me a month or so ago to say that the Travel section of the *Times* was being re-geared, and would I do a sailing piece for the first issue? I told him that *The New Yorker*, at just about that same time, would be publishing a 25,000-word piece by me on sailing across the Atlantic and I doubted *The New Yorker* would be pleased if another piece on sailing appeared simultaneously; but that I *had* promised to ride on the Orient Express with the Heinzes, two weeks hence, whereupon Arthur (who is very decisive) said fine, four issues after the grand opening the *Times* would still be promoting its revised Travel section, but please I must write it as soon as possible after taking the trip. I told him we would leave Turkey on Saturday, spend the night in England, and return to New York on Sunday. "You'll have it Monday," I promised.

The circumstances of that Sunday proved amusing. We had reservations on Pan Am business class, but as I reflected on my promise to Arthur, I thought I had better change that to first class, to permit me to retreat to the top section of the 747 to use my typewriter. Accordingly, at the airport, I asked the woman at the counter if there were two first-class seats available; she punched the computer and said, "No . . . *Wait a minute!* Yes! Somebody just canceled." While she made out the boarding pass, I was to go to the cashier, pay the differential, then come back to pick up the tickets. So I went to the cashier, who made the calculations and presented me with a bill for eight hundred and eighty odd dollars. I stared at her and said that surely she had made a mistake? She looked down and said no, first class is $440 more than business class. So I said, Thanks very much, but never mind. I put the original tickets back in the envelope, and walked back to the ticket counter.

I try to make it a point not to say or even think anything unpleasant about Pan Am that insinuates extortion on its part, since poor Pan Am has lately been losing an awful lot of money; on the other hand, it isn't my personal responsibility to redress their budget balance. So I returned to the patient lady and said, "I'm terribly sorry, I've changed my mind. Can I have my two business-class seats back, please?" Again she pushed the computer. Goodness! she said. They're gone! Business class is sold out. Under the circumstances you'll have to take the first-class seats. "At the same cost as business class, of course." I thought that most awfully sporting of her, and wondered at the providence of getting $880 worth of extra space at no cost. Was *this* supply-side economics?

But on arriving in first class and mounting the staircase, I discovered that the whole of an area once reserved for business and social use was now given over to regular first-class seats, for those who didn't particularly want to see the movie. All the seats were taken. So, descending to my own seat, I realized the article would not get written. It simply isn't socially possible to type while everyone around you is trying to see a movie, and I cannot compose in longhand.

So it was that I arrived at JFK with Arthur's article unwritten. We drove to the country, had some dinner, and then I went to the garage to write the piece. It was after midnight, or 5 A.M. London time, when I came to the final paragraph: "The reconstituted Orient Express may end up in Disney World, chugging its way around Orlando, but I hope not. It is good to travel to the ancient capital of the world aboard a train built two years after Lenin died (and 54 years after one wishes he had died) and one year before Lindbergh flew the ocean, and know that it still works. It is also good to know that traveling through Europe by rail, in circumstances almost stagily comfortable, can still be done—up to a point. At the Bosporus, Asia begins, and many things end, among them the journey." And thank God, I thought, this article.

I remember describing to Pat a complementary experience aboard another train, the longest journey I ever took. It was the early summer, 1945, pre-Hiroshima. I was a second lieutenant in the Infantry, stationed at Fort Gordon, Georgia, engaged in training recruits, when one of those Army dice-rolls spelled out my name, and I was handed orders to escort 160 enlisted men and noncommissioned officers, who had reenlisted in the regular Army, from Augusta, Georgia, to San Luis Obispo, California. I was nineteen years old and had been commissioned for about two and a half months. I was put in charge of veterans in their twenties and thirties who had seen combat in Europe, had returned home on furlough, and were now, as reenlistees, to be attached to a new outfit preparing for action in the Pacific.

My commanding officer, given to verbal economy, told me only 1) that I had the authority, as commanding officer, to conduct summary courts-martial if required to maintain discipline; 2) that I would need personally to sign for the eleven-car train, and was therefore technically responsible for anything missing when it arrived in San Luis Obispo, whether a fork or a sleeping car; 3) that the train had a low priority, so that the trip might last as many as six or seven days, depending on how many times it was shunted aside to give precedence to other trains carrying hotter cargo; and 4) that the conductor would confide to me the probable length of time the train would remain at a siding or station, but when asked by the troops "How long?" I was always to answer, "Just a few minutes"— because, explained my major, if the troops discovered that the delay would be for an hour or more, they would leave the train, get drunk, and contract a venereal disease. My success in administering this assignment, he told me, would be based substantially on the number of soldiers who, arrived at San Luis Obispo, didn't have to report to the infirmary.

It was endless. The soldiers rotated their sleeping arrangements. Lower berths were for two men who slept head to toe. The upper berth, one man. There was no air conditioning. The chow lines were boisterous. The clusters of poker players intense, indefatigable—some played around the clock. The beer and the booze seemed almost self-generating, as if a distiller were on board. One grizzled old soldier (probably he was twenty-five) had got uncontrollably rowdy near El Paso, and we had had to lock him into a bathroom where, sitting on the toilet, his hostility, along with the alcohol, gradually metabolized.

So to speak, the Upstairs and Downstairs of train travel, over against the Orient Express. One hedonistic, the other spartan. It is terribly vexing that it isn't obvious that the one was ultimately more pleasurable in memory than the other.

From the ballet we went to the home of Mica and Ahmet Ertegun. She is, simply stated, one of the most beautiful and interesting women in the world. Ahmet is many things, most conspicuously a rock music entrepreneur-tycoon. He either owns the Rolling Stones or else they own him, something of the sort; but the relationship is symbiotically profitable, and Ahmet is always going around the world in his Gulfstream jet to attend this or that rock recording enterprise, while Mica either accompanies him, or attends to her interior decorating business in New York. Ahmet has also been a trustee of St. John's College in Annapolis, with which Stringfellow Barr was associated for so many years, and which stresses the importance of the Great Books. Albert Jay Nock, the eccentric and dazzlingly erudite essayist, belletrist, and neoanarchist, incidentally a personal friend of my father's, spoke so highly of St. John's that my brothers and I all very nearly ended up being sent there. In any event, Ahmet talks to me about St. John's. He is still using a cane, having had a hip operation, concerning the post-surgical care of which he has received extensive lessons from Pat, who went through it two years earlier.

To everyone's dismay (people don't quite like it if operations end by being hedonistic experiences), Ahmet enjoyed every moment of it, declaiming about the fine care the doctors and nurses took of him, the pleasure he took in receiving visits and best wishes from his friends. It was all really quite irregular, so that it came as enormous relief to his wife and friends when, having been brought home for the post-hospital part of his recuperation, *Ahmet turned absolutely impossible*, expressing his displeasure with everybody and everything, though not I think the Rolling Stones. From this other extreme, he has emerged in recent weeks as a man of dignity and fortitude, but then what else would one expect of a former trustee of St. John's, Annapolis?

Back home, Pat and I chatted. Then I read, but my eyes soon wandered. For a moment I thought I might, as an exercise, apply Henry George economics to the problem of ballet deficits; but I decided to put it off and, come to think of it, I haven't yet undertaken that exercise.

Three
WEDNESDAY

Wednesday is one of the three days a week in which I write a newspaper column, and of course the day generally begins with that special kind of newspaper reading during which your subconscious, and indeed your conscious, minds are scanning the news in search of a nubile subject to write about—because it is either this or a column about something that has been nagging you. Or, finally, there is the drawerful of articles, clippings, book excerpts that cry out for comment. Gene Shalit, a marvelously amiable and perceptive—personality, I suppose one calls him—with lethal verbal powers, did an interview with me two or three years ago on radio, the subject being my then-current novel, and as he wandered about hill and dale with amiable discursiveness, I gradually lost my guard, so that when he asked me, "How do you decide what you're going to write a column about?" I answered that after you have written a column for many years, you could, if your back were up against the wall, close your eyes, and let your index finger descend on *any* story on the front page of the New York *Times*—and proceed to write a column on that subject. "Oh yes," Gene said. "I remember reading that one."

Fair enough, and a nice way to transform into braggadocio what wasn't meant as such. But one should not expect someone of Shalit's prehensile wit to let such an opening go.

George Will once told me how deeply he loves to write. "I wake in the morning," he explained to me, "and I ask myself: 'Is this one of the days I have to write a column?' And if the answer is 'Yes,' I rise a happy man." I, on the other hand, wake neither particularly happy nor unhappy, but to the extent that my mood is affected by the question whether I need to write a column that morning, the impact of Monday-Wednesday-Friday is definitely negative. Because I do not like to write, for the simple reason that writing is extremely hard work, and I do not "like" extremely hard work.

I work for other reasons, about which mostly dull people write, dully. (I have discerned that those who are given to the formulation, "I am one of those people who . . ." would generally be safest concluding the sentence, ". . . bore other people.") Is it some aspect of a sense of duty that I feel? Moral evangelism? A fear of uselessness? A fear that it is wrong to suppress useful, here defined extramorally as merchandisable, talent? I do resist introspection, though I cannot claim to have "guarded" against it, because even to say that would suppose that the temptation to do so was there, which it isn't. Indeed, these very words are prompted by an imperative handed to me by my friend and editor Sam Vaughan, the least imperious of men: but curiosity is, in such circumstances, his professional business. Why do I do so much? I expect that the promptings issue from a subtle dialectical counterpoint. Of what? Well, the call of *recta ratio*, and the fear of boredom. What is *recta ratio?* The appeal of generic Latin terms (*habeas corpus, nihil obstat, malum prohibitum*) derives in part because the language is indeed dead and therefore unmoved by idiomatic fashion. In part, however, it is owing to the complementary character of its tantalizing inscrutability. It is just faintly defenseless; so that one can, for instance, interpret a Latin term—use it metaphorically, even—without any decisive fear of plebiscitarian denial. We know that the term translates to "right (rightly) reason(ed)," and that the Scholastics used it to suggest the intellectual instrument by which men might reason progressively at least to the existence of God, at most to how, under His aegis, they should govern themselves in all major matters, avoiding the major vices, exercising discipline, seeking virtue. The search for virtue is probably best drowned out by *commotion*, and this my life is full

of. It is easier to stay up late working for hours than to
take one tenth the time to inquire into the question
whether the work is worth performing.

And then, as I say, that other, the fear of boredom.
Thoreau is known for his compulsion, day by day, to discover more and more things he could be without. But I
have enough of everything material, at least measured by
ordinary standards. But not the reliance to do without dis-
traction; so that I would not cross the street without a
magazine or paperback, lest the traffic should immobilize
me for more than ten seconds. The unexamined life may
not be worth living, in which case I will concede that mine
is not worth living. But excepting my own life, I do seek
to examine, and certainly I dilate upon, public questions I
deem insufficiently examined.

I was saying that I do not enjoy writing. I envy those
who do. John Chamberlain once told me that if he has not
written during the day he will not sleep, and it is only
when he wonders why he cannot fall asleep that he re-
members that he has not written during that day; and so he
rises, and writes. John Chamberlain is as incapable of affec-
tation as Muhammad Ali of self-effacement. It is simply
the case that some people like to sit down hour after hour
and write, and with some of them the disease is so aggra-
vated that it doesn't particularly matter whether what they
write will be published.

I elected to devote today's column to the fascination
politicians are showing over the lapse of David Stockman
in confiding to his friend Mr. Greider of the Washington
Post–Atlantic Monthly his misgivings about Mr. Reagan's
economic program. I set out to make the point that those
who ask Stockman to resign because his offense is hypocrisy have not considered the genocide that would result
from an impartial application of this rule. (How many
congressmen who express opposition to inflationary spend-

ing vote against inflationary spending?) A second observation is that Stockman, during 1981, found political obstacles to the execution of practically everything he sought, and that, after all, he never did attempt to call for a decisive reduction in the marginal rate of taxation—say, to twenty-five percent. Reduced to that level, in the estimate of Milton Friedman (as stated in a most measured article in *Newsweek*), you would organically affect the deployment of dollars away from tax shelters, thereby adding to the taxable base more than enough revenue to make up the relatively light (thirteen percent) loss in general revenues. (Friedman argues that reducing the top marginal rate of taxation to twenty-five percent would *increase* tax revenues.)

I had read the newspapers and breakfasted in the beautiful, cloistered, red-red library Pat so ingeniously decorated and then, in my dressing gown, I climbed up the stairs to my little study, which incidentally looks out, between 8 and 8:30, on the handsomest, gayest, most cheerful parade of children aged six to twelve, the youngest of them accompanied by nurses or governesses, all of them carrying sackfuls of books, bouncing off to the multifarious schools concentrated in the area. I dialed my private office number (the switchboard was not yet open) and Frances Bronson, who was as usual there early (she attends early to most of her problems, and all of mine) gave me late messages from yesterday and asked where I wished to meet my sister Priscilla (the managing editor of *National Review*) and Joe Sobran (one of the senior editors) for lunch before the scheduled performance of *Nicholas Nickleby*. I suggested Paone's (my favorite restaurant, which is also near the office), whence we'd drive to the theater, meeting Pat there (she has another lunch date). Doria Reagan is arriving independently, and Ron not until dinner, as he could not escape a rehearsal suddenly scheduled for that afternoon by his ballet troupe, Joffrey II. I informed Frances that as soon as I wrote my column I'd telephone it in to Susan at the office (who would record and transcribe it, after which Frances would copy-edit it). In due course this is done. And I turned, again, to my correspondence.

Harold O. J. Brown, a youngish scholar who did his divinity work at Harvard and in the past has written religious essays for *National Review*, sends me a copy of a reproachful letter he has sent to Bart Giamatti, president of Yale, on reading Giamatti's dressy excoriation of the Moral Majority. Giamatti's remarks were made in September, to the freshmen, and my own comment on it at the time had been that to be lectured on the perils of the Moral Majority upon entering Yale was on the order of being lectured on the dangers of bedbugs on entering a brothel.

Again I reflected on the ire provoked by the MM, and the fashion parade of those who have attacked it. Giamatti is a man of near-infinite sophistication and wit, who would normally spend no more time warning us about the Moral Majority than he would warning of the Flat Earth Society. He'd be much more at home warning of the dangers of gnosticism, or sciolism, or pridefulness. But the Moral Majority is the season's bug, and it has swept the country. The president of Georgetown University pitched in, with results similarly vulnerable. The first reaction to this kind of thing is the pleased roar of the programmed reactors—who was that singer who got so much attention, by merely stepping up to the podium during an entertainment at Nixon's White House, and declaiming on the Vietnam war? That kind of thing. But in the long run it's dangerous because the attack is clearly unbalanced and can damage your reputation for precise criticism, if you have a reputation for precise criticism.

The February 1982 *Commentary* would feature an article, alas at Giamatti's heavy expense, called "God & Man at Yale—Again," by Robert William Kagan, a recent graduate of Yale doing graduate work at Harvard. "The faction which Giamatti's speech served was that of the liberal intellectuals among whom he was raised and educated, and whose ideological dominance on the Yale campus has not abated for a moment since Buckley complained about it thirty years ago in *God and Man at Yale*. The fact is that the greatest threats to pluralism, to academic freedom, and to the values of a liberal education at Yale have always come from the Left, not from the Right or the New Right. The status quo which Giamatti has been trying to preserve against the destabilizing efforts of groups like the Moral Majority is quite secure within Yale's gates. Preserving it, however, may not necessarily be in the best interests of the University."

I wrote to Joe Brown thanking him for a copy of his letter, and expressing doubts that Mr. Giamatti would answer it. Here, though, I must sympathize, because it isn't possible to respond when the answer would require extensive analysis to mail that arrives in such volume as no doubt it does to the president of a major university. Sometimes I wonder whether no answer at all is preferable to a very brief, formulaic answer.

Brooklyn College wants a telegram sent to be read out when Stanley Goldstein is given the Alumnus of the Year award, which would happen tonight. Stan Goldstein is a high concentrate of ability and enthusiasm who launched an accountant's firm only seventeen years ago, and now it is huge. He is deeply conservative, and so to speak ex officio he became the accountant for *National Review*, the Conservative Book Club, and suchlike organizations, even as Monsignor Eugene Clark, and *only* Monsignor Clark, gives the benedictions at our functions. I wrote out the telegram and felt glad for Stanley, though I fear that he will attribute his winning the Alumnus of the Year award to his jogging every day. How hard he has tried to get me to take up that dismaying practice. But he always knows when it *simply won't work*. I told him I would endeavor to use an indoor bicycle every other day, and he is pacified; while I am troubled by my inconstancy. At my funeral, I know he will be saying, "I warned him, I warned him."

Hugh Kenner sends me a copy of a letter he has fired off to the gentlemen at the Heath Company, complaining of the incompleteness of the instructions that appear in the Personal Computing course distributed by Heath. The problem is that one is drowned with material after the reading of which one spends hours trying to find out *exactly what to do*. Hugh recites the difficulties he has had and, along about page three, writes with that terrifying clarity for which he is so famous:

"So let's outline something better. Suppose Manual ※595-2268-04, which comes with the machine, ended its nut-&-bolts section by saying, 'You now have the following: [outline of your hardware]. To make it do anything useful you need an Operating System such as HDOS or CP/M, both available from Heath.' Now let the HDOS manual commence, quite simply, 'An Operating System like HDOS configures the computer to receive data, execute programs, and communicate with outside devices such as disk drives and printers. In particular, it looks after the details of program and data storage on disks, directing traffic to and from these storage devices. It contains a number of Drivers (ATH.DVD, etc.) from which you will be selecting the proper ones to communicate with your particular disk and printer configuration. And it contains a relatively simple BASIC interpreter, so that you will have one high-level language at your disposal immediately.'"

One would want to kiss such prose, were it ever attached to an instruction booklet. But I must not go on to affect that all mechanical problems disappear on experiencing Hugh's prose. As I write, in Switzerland, I am simultaneously attempting to master not the internal mysteries of a word processor, but merely the technique of operating one; and I have here at my side identical counterparts of the machines Hugh Kenner has—the Z-89, the two disk drives, and the Diablo Printer. And, most valuable of all, sixteen pages of typewritten instructions conceived and executed by the great Hugh Kenner. Alas, after two days I gave up. I could not, from Switzerland, produce Kenner, who resides in Baltimore.

But providence arranged it that at the high moment of my distress two of my sisters arrived for a fortnight's skiing and brought with them nephew Jay Buckley—who is a computer expert. He pays me what he calls "office calls" after skiing, every couple of days, as I accumulate fresh desires I know not how to satisfy. Now, having been taught empirically by Jay, I can turn back to Hugh's instructions and read them like a road map. Some people write with total lucidity, but implicitly rely, for an understanding of what they say, on a level of spatial imagery some people just don't have. It is precisely this lack on my part that caused my essay on celestial navigation, first published in my book *Airborne*, to be such an unusual success: because it presupposes nothing at all. I am going to repay Hugh's courtesy, before I am through, by writing a fresh set of instructions on operating the computer, entitled: "Instructions for a Mechanical Simpleton. An Aprioristic Guide to the Use of the Word Processor." Practically the whole of it will be devoted to teaching the layman how to cause to be typed by the Diablo Printer, from the disk drive, as directed by the computer, the words that appear above between quotation marks.

I wrote to Mr. Clement at the Heath Company and told

him that if he should let H. Kenner slip through his
fingers, I'd sell my stock in Heath, if I had any stock in
Heath.

The fight over who will be the next director of the National Endowment for the Humanities rages. Two candidates are close to the wire, a third is held in reserve. The
last is Ronald Berman, who served as chairman with distinction under Nixon and Ford. The other two are William Bennett, of the National Humanities Center in North
Carolina, and Mel Bradford of the University of Dallas. It
is fair, but only roughly so, to say that the hard conservatives are backing Bradford, the neos, Bennett. I say it is
only roughly fair, because some enthusiasm for Bradford is
dissipated by speculation that he would fail confirmation
by the Senate, the consequence of certain animadversions
he has made in the past about Abraham Lincoln—none ob-
jectionable as historical speculation, but one or two the
kind of thing you can mount mountainous demagogic campaigns on.

One month ago, in San Francisco en route to the passenger ship Viking *Sky*, on which I was voyaging and lecturing, I had a call from an assistant to the President with
whom I have from time to time dealt, and she told me that
Bradford was "out" and asked, in my opinion, were Bennett's credentials as a conservative authentic? I said that
they were, and at the time thought the matter of the NEH
disposed of.

Why, why do they drag these things out so? In any
event, it is all very much alive, and now Irving Kristol
writes to denounce an editorial in *National Review* that
falsely, in his opinion, elaborates the qualifications of Bradford. "Last night I read my latest issue of *National Re-*

view, with its editorial on the NEH, and I must tell you that it depressed me enormously. I keep saying that the clear distinction that was once visible between 'neoconservatives' and 'old conservatives' is now so blurred as to be meaningless, but every now and then *National Review* will remind me that a gap still exists. The sad truth is that too many 'old conservatives' are so far distanced from the academic-intellectual world that they find themselves saying things, and doing things, that make the position of *all* conservatives in this world that much more difficult. Your editorial was a case in point."

Kristol proceeded to reject, at considerable length, the factual representations we had made; indeed, he did so so categorically that I simply assumed him to be correct, wrote him in that vein, and chose to disregard the general complaints, here quoted, about the difference between the new and old conservatives. I did, when I replied to Kristol, reflect on the fact that Jeffrey Hart, the single working academic professor on the staff of *NR*, who also writes editorials, happened to be the author of the editorial in question. *National Review* has never, in its twenty-five years, been in any significant sense "distant" from the academic scene: we have always roamed among professors and other intellectuals—it is simply amusing to denominate a journal whose principal editorial figure for twenty-three years was philosophy professor James Burnham as alienated from academic thought.

But Irving likes to make his points categorically, so I let it go. And now, having replied to him, I dropped a note to Jeff Hart, my learned colleague, full professor of English at Dartmouth, who is traveling on the West Coast so I couldn't now reach him on the phone. Did he, I asked, get the facts on Bradford wrong? Well, interestingly enough—having now seen both accounts—I would judge that Hart was much closer on than Irving; but, really, it turned out not to be important, or in any case that is my reading of it. The appointment was finally given to Bennett.

It is hard to devise a happier couple with whom to share lunch than Priscilla Buckley and Joe Sobran. Pitts (her nickname) is the single unmarried of the original ten Buckleys (two of my sisters died young, leaving between them fifteen children). I lured her from Paris where she was working for the United Press, bringing to the large office there the quiet pleasure she has given everyone ever since (alongside Nancy Davis Reagan) she graduated from Smith College. She combines extraordinary efficiency with the most obdurate affability, self-effacement, intelligence, and charm. Joe Sobran is one of the two or three wittiest men I have ever met, with a cultural intelligence as penetrating as that of anyone around twice his young age. He was doing graduate work in English at Eastern Michigan University, trying to support three children and a sick wife (from whom he is now divorced) when our paths crossed. He has now been four years with *National Review* as a senior editor, and his editorials, book reviews, and culture pieces are in every issue. He is also launched as a syndicated columnist, and (he will tell you) is writing two or three books.

The parentheses above are something of a joke, because Joe is terribly disorganized in the endearing sense that Samuel Johnson was disorganized, though I am not absolutely sure that Joe would have ended by actually producing that dictionary. Recently someone sent me, with the notation *"Can't wait to get it,"* a full page from *Publishers Weekly*, advertising a book: *"The Conservative Manifesto. The Philosophy, the Passion, the Promise.* By Joseph Sobran. Introduction by William F. Buckley, Jr." The final

sentence of the ad read, "Leading conservative spokesman
William F. Buckley, Jr. has written a cogent and entertaining introduction to this definitive work." And, embla-
zoned on the top of the page: *"Every disenchanted liberal
and every American who calls himself a conservative—or is
thinking of becoming one—must read this book.—*Wm. F.
Buckley, Jr."

On reading the ad I was faintly put off by my utterly
certain knowledge that the book did not exist; that I
couldn't, therefore, have written an introduction to it, let
alone a cogent and entertaining introduction (though when
it is written, it will of course be at least those two things);
and I didn't even remember composing a tribute to the
book that didn't exist, though on faith I'd venture to say,

sight unseen, at least as much about anything Joe Sobran undertook to write. So I sent along the *PW* page to Joe with a questioning note, and in his wonderful, reassuring, there-there way, he called and reminded me that *when* the publisher asked *whether* I would write an introduction for the book he was commissioning from Joe, I *had said* sure; but they *needed* something on the spot, so *I* had told *Joe* to say something *appropriate* to what he *proposed* to write, and his *memory* of it was that he did so, gave the text to Frances to check it out with me, and he simply *assumed* this had been done. Well, it is certainly safe to assume that something you give to Frances to do gets done.

So I asked my friend Joe, on November 18, as Priscilla and I silently raised our glasses to each other, how was the book coming along that would be *published* in April (books are usually published about nine months after the finished manuscript is submitted). And he smiled and said, "Now Bill, don't you worry. It will surprise you." It certainly will.

I apologized to Pitts, knowing she had heard the story before, and told Joe that speaking of book blurbs and surprises, I had had a jolly time a few years back with David Niven. I was given his book, *Bring On the Empty Horses*, to review. Thank God I was so favorably struck by it, because David has been for fifteen years one of Pat's and my closest friends. I found the book absolutely remarkable, said so in my review, and one line in my encomium was picked up by the publisher, and used universally, as follows:

"*Probably the best book ever written about Hollywood* —New York *Times*."

I have no doubt this is so, and other reviewers similarly acclaimed it. About a year later I received a telegram from my British publisher. Would I immediately secure from David Niven a blurb for my first novel, *Saving the Queen,*

which would be published in March? David was in Hollywood (filming *Murder by Death*), and I got him on the
telephone. He agreed to read the manuscript that very
weekend, and I got it to him. On Monday I had a telegram
from him that read: "DEAR BILL: HOW'S THIS: QUOTE
FASCINATING, EXCITING AND UNIQUELY DIFFERENT. WHAT
MORE CAN YOU ASK? UNQUOTE. IF YOU DON'T LIKE, FEEL
FREE TO CHANGE IN ANY WAY YOU WANT. DAVID."

The following winter, in Switzerland (as ever, during February and March), the evening before my departure for London where I would spend two days promoting *Queen*, I was in my study, the far end of which is equipped as an atelier centered about a Ping-Pong table. There, two or three times every week, I paint with David (he is expert) and whatever guests or friends are so inclined (we have a hundred guest-painted canvases lying about). David was concentrating most fearfully on his tulip or whatever, and I on mine, when I said, "David, remember the telegram, you know, the blurb for my book?"

"Umm," David said, rocking fore and aft on the balls of his feet, observing the petals of his daffodil.

"Well," I said, "I took you up on your offer, so I told the publishers that Mr. Niven had sent in a telegram: 'THIS IS PROBABLY THE BEST NOVEL EVER WRITTEN ABOUT FUCKING THE QUEEN.'" I swear it's true (though his friends and fellow professionals will never believe it) that for once in his life David Niven was caught off balance, for maybe half a second, which for him is a long time. His laughter was prolonged.

I am reminded that the next day, in London, during the press conference at which my novel was presented, the very first question was put to me by, no less, the young editor of *The Economist*, Andrew Knight.

It was something.

"Mr. Buckley, would you like to sleep with the queen?"

That was certainly an icebreaker, and I drew a deep breath. I explained to the journalists that anyone who had read my novel could not possibly confuse the existing queen with the fictional character I depicted. That being said, I thought it fair to respond with more spirit to the question of my friend Andrew, and added that, respecting the fictitious queen, my biological instincts were normal, but before undertaking any such irregularity as my character Blackford Oakes undertook, I would need to consult my lawyer, given the historical fate of some of the Englishmen who had dallied with royalty. Moreover, I pointed out, finally, it was important to remember that in my story the queen was the succubus, my American CIA agent most clearly not the incubus. The effort by Beautiful Andrew (they tease him with that—Andrew looks like a freshman, modeling) to transform my book into *lèse majésté* was unsuccessful, though here and there a reviewer tried to make a little—not, really, that much—of the royal seduction. Mostly the book was ignored there. But there was one character, an elderly Englishman residing during the winters in Gstaad—a Wodehousian gentleman alongside whom Colonel Blimp looks and sounds like a

dead-end kid—who assiduously telephoned ahead to all social hosts during The Season to ascertain whether I had
been invited, in order to be able to say, if it turned out that
I had been, that he would not be attending, as he did not
desire the company of anyone who would insult the
Queen. I confess that I greatly enjoyed it when, without
informing me, a year or so later my wife sent off anony-
mously to Lord Pomp the centerspread of the New York
Daily News, in which was a large picture of the *Britannia*'s
deck, featuring the Queen of England and her husband
greeting me and my wife at the reception she held to
commemorate the declaration of American independence
from Her Majesty's (I must reflect here, where Lord Pomp
would not need to) great . . . great . . . great . . . great-
grandfather.

Joe, Priscilla, and I ordered, and then there was a little editorial business to discuss, including the John Simon matter.
I reported on the lunch with our distinguished movie
reviewer and Chilton Williamson, the author and our
back-of-the-book editor. John had been most adamant
about continuing to require the extra space for his reviews
(they were running at about 1500 words), insisting that
shorter reviews would make him just that, a "reviewer"
rather than a "critic." A troublesome dilemma for an editor, on the one hand facing the possible loss of so fine a
writer and critic, on the other having to attend to basic editorial architecture.

I had mulled over the problem and now pulled out of
my pocket a copy of the letter I had already sent to John,
which Priscilla and Joe read and pronounced the only thing
to do under the circumstances:

"Dear John: I'm afraid that on the matter of extra space
the magazine cannot be flexible. The reasons why are not
new to you and so I shan't restate them. Nor do I need to

restate the pleasure I take from your work, or the admiration I feel for it. But there must be somebody, that semianonymous authority, who decrees that the pillars outside St. Patrick's can rise no higher, or that the dimensions of a canvas designed for a particular (finite) area cannot exceed the designated size. I know how deeply you feel in the matter, and therefore can only hope that you will undertake the adjustment. If not, I understand, and will go into mourning."

John never answered; but then he didn't quit either.

We arrived at the theater just as Pat did, as ever imposing, beautiful, elegant; followed, a few minutes after we were seated, by Doria Reagan, young, slight, especially pretty in the white dress she wore. The invitation to her and Ron came about as the result of an amusing effrontery. A few months earlier, Nancy Reagan had invited me and Pat and her son and daughter-in-law and Jerry Zipkin, an old friend, to go with her to the theater to see *Sophisticated Ladies*. Everything about going to the theater with a First Lady is somehow made enormously easy—no tickets to buy, or crowds to thread through; and so as we sat waiting for the lights to go out I flicked through the pages of that day's New York *Times* culture pages and came on the full-page ad for the great *Nicholas Nickleby*. The play would run for fourteen weeks beginning on October 4, eight and a half hours of theatergoing (four before dinner, four and one-half after dinner). I poked Nancy, pointing at the *Nickleby* ad, and said, "Let's take that one in too, while we're at it!" Nancy laughed and, getting into the spirit of it, I said, "I think when we go it would be nice if you also invited Ron and Doria." More laughter. And, at dinner later (it was a matinee), I told Ron that since his mother *obviously* hadn't taken my hint seriously, he and Doria would come as my guests; and here she was.

The play began at two and would run until six; then we

were to be back at seven. Pat had scouted about and been told that a handy restaurant where quick service was available was Broadway Joe's, a block and a half away. I had no idea then that it was owned by Sidney Zion, who greeted us at the door. I had first met him at an editorial lunch thrown by Victor Navasky, a founding editor of the short-lived humor magazine *Monocle*, now editor of *The Nation* (Vic peaked too early). Sidney is a gentle soul, a lawyer by training, and not *quite* responsible. He left the *Times* and co-founded *Scanlan's Monthly*, a radical mag, during the tail end of the wild period (1965–73). I remember his calling me in great indignation to tell me that *Scanlan's* printers had refused to publish the current issue because it had in it a diagram on how to make a home-grown hand grenade, or perhaps it was an atom bomb, I forget. I told Sid I could understand his abstract point, but that my natural sympathies were, really, with the printers. He never seemed to mind, no more did he mind it when I said to him, in some exasperation after a New York *Times* editorial lunch when he was arguing somebody's innocence, "Sid, the trouble with you is that you find *everybody* innocent." Well, Sidney proved not entirely innocent, that evening; he gave away our privacy, because sure enough, when we filed out, there was a newspaper photographer.

Ron arrived about five minutes late, dressed as if he had just left a ballet rehearsal, which is what he had just done.

. . . I remember when all *that* happened. It was Thanksgiving time, 1976, and Ron had matriculated at Yale as a freshman in September. It was arranged that the senior Reagans would come in from California, with Ron coming in from New Haven, to spend Thanksgiving with us. Thanksgiving Day (I had warned the Reagans) was traditionally reserved for my senior family, at Sharon. There the Reagans joined us, at about noon on Thanksgiving, where we would lunch with my aged mother, and brothers and sisters, at the family home. There was a wonderful scene in the patio with my senescent mother who, with her ineffable charm, was listening to a story from Nancy Reagan. The final, key words of the story Nancy was telling were, "You're not going to tell *that* to the *Reagans!*"

There was general laughter, including my mother's, at which point she turned her gentle, pretty face to Nancy, leaned toward her and whispered affectionately, "Tell me, darling, who *are* the Reagans?" Nancy's diplomacy was impeccable. I knew then she would go far.

After lunch we went to the area where traditionally we play touch football on Thanksgiving, and I asked Ron Sr. whether he would consent to referee. He looked at me most wistfully and said, "Can't I play?" I laughed and made him quarterback on my team, while my brother, the sainted junior senator from New York, acquired Ron Jr. The play was spirited, but I noticed with more than merely casual interest the extraordinary nimbleness of young Ron.

Because just before lunch, Nancy had drawn Pat aside, and Ron Sr. had taken me into another room: and each of us was told of their awful experience the night before. Their son had arrived in New York on Wednesday night to announce that *he had decided to leave Yale University and study ballet!* Such a decision is not easily received in any household. In their household, it was received with True Shock.

"Who am I to object?" the father said to me, pacing the floor of the music room. "I mean, *I* ought to know about show business, and the ballet is great stuff. But so few people make it. And pulling out of college . . . In the middle of a semester . . ." Reagan does not *act* excited, but one can sense when he *is* excited. He was thinking out loud.

He paused. And said that he was determined that his son should finish out the semester, because that way his record at Yale would be clean—"if he comes out of it. You know, if he doesn't make it."

It was perhaps my imagination but, an hour or two later, seeing his son jump six feet into the air to grab the football had me thinking of—a ballet dancer.

The multilateral conferences on the subject of Ron continued throughout the weekend, at our home in Stamford, to which we repaired after the football. Ron Jr. meanwhile told me that most ballet students begin at fourteen, and here he was at *eighteen*, so there wasn't a moment to lose, no, not even the months of December and January. And so his career began.

Now, at the restaurant, we reminisced happily about our day and night at sea a couple of months earlier. It had been August, and Ron was on vacation, and came first to us. I own a small sloop which sleeps four, and our date was boat-centered, so that in the late afternoon the Reagans and the Buckleys set out to cross Long Island Sound and spend the night at the little harbor in Eatons Neck. The journey was not quite typical because there were seven or eight gentlemen from the Secret Service superintending our departure and, to my great amusement, four of them squatted in an open Boston Whaler, trailing us by about three hundred yards. The wind was menacingly stiff that afternoon, and the combined knowledge of boating among the four of us was what I knew—period. So that when one of the boat's fenders (which I had, carelessly, failed to stow) slipped off the leeward deck, unwilling to lose it I announced I would come about: which I did, with my crew, or rather passengers, grabbing at lines I more or less pointed to, and more or less doing what I told them to do.

I made our way back a couple of hundred yards and brought the bow upwind, while Ron lay on the deck reaching out to scoop up the fender.

But he missed it; meaning that, in a 20-knot wind and building seas, we'd have to do the whole maneuver all over again. It was then that I thought to hail the thoroughly mobile Secret Service, who were unencumbered by sail; which I did, pointing to the fender, assuming that they would divine the message. But they did not acknowledge our signal. Ron then said brightly: "I know what'll bring 'em. *I'll* throw *myself* into the sea!" We laughed, and Doria looked just a little nervous. Finally the Secret Service zoomed up, and I communicated the message orally. They went back and fetched up the fender, while we resumed our southeasterly journey.

It was dark when we arrived, and I did not argue when the Secret Service vessel, with its weary, windswept, and probably seasick crew, volunteered to escort us in through a twisting channel I have known since 1952. It was a fine evening in the quiet little harbor, the anchor lights of a half-dozen other pleasure craft about us, the steak, wine, onions, salad, music, conversation, midnight swim. I teased Ron about that swim because seven or eight years earlier, spending a night with the Reagans at their beach house, I had announced I would swim before turning in, and Ron and his father accompanied me to the beach. But they thought me clearly mad to mingle at night with the sharks. I promised Ron that if there were sharks in the harbor to-night, I'd report them to the Secret Service, who lay a couple of boat lengths away as we slept, in that particular snugness that only a sailboat, anchored in the night, can radiate.

At dinner we did our best to brief Ron on the first half of *Nickleby*, and returned to the theater for what was surely the most captivating theatrical experience I've ever had. No one at first thought it could work. Of course it did, and the robust, ingenious kindliness of a sophisticated au-thor was made to flower in a performance so intricate in pacing and choreographical arrangement as to leave one in awe for those reasons alone. Going out, I asked one of the Secret Service agents, who had also been in Stamford that summer, what he thought of it, and his comment was that it would have been easier to spend the four and one-half hours sitting down. There had been no empty seats. We said good night, and plighted our troths to see *David Copperfield* together, if ever the Royal Shakespeare Com-pany does to David what it so wonderfully did to Nicho-las.

Four
THURSDAY

I had the whole morning clear, which is good, because there is a speech right after lunch at the Waldorf, which has to be thought through, as the occasion doesn't permit a regular lecture. I am to speak for only twenty minutes. I looked at the assignment and calculated the time it would take to prepare for it—say a half hour, leaning on familiar material. I have found that one can work with special concentration when hard up against that kind of a deadline. I had time left to attack the briefcase.

I had a very nice telegram from Walter Meade, the head of Avon Books, which has acquired the paperback rights to my novel *Marco Polo, If You Can.* I had been warned by Sam Vaughan of Doubleday that the market in paperback sales was way down, and that I mustn't be disappointed that the paperback auction fetched for *Marco Polo* less than it had for *Who's On First.* When Avon bought *Who's On First*, I persuaded Walter to purchase the preceding two novels (*Saving the Queen* and *Stained Glass*) from Warner Books, my prejudice being that the same publisher should have all the titles, to expedite multiple sales. Now I thanked Walter for his warm telegram, and encouraged the idea of a meeting with him, both because of the pleasure of it "and to discuss ways in which we can sell more of the softcover works. It seems to me that they have not done as well as they should have done, given the general [hardcover] reception to them. It may be that my name is unhappily associated with difficult material (long words, that sort of thing). We might consider how to undermine that rumor. In any event, it would be swell to see you."

Every time I bring out a novel, I feel compelled to play my little .45 rpm record which can be compressed into a single sentence: What is the *point* in personally advertising the availability of one of my novels, when all but a very few interviewers will dwell on *political* subjects?—which means that I will end up by alienating the majority of prospective book purchasers? Sam Vaughan smiles when I play my little record, and changes the subject; but it seems to me that my point is very strong. Take, for instance, the Donahue show, in which Phil (he is very good on this matter) will flash the book in front of the audience, but will resist (he is very good at this, too) conversation about the book—"because," he will tell you after the show is over, "after all, they don't know what's in it." One despairs of suggesting that that might be the very *point* in your appearing. But I have written about the general problems of book promotion for *Esquire* (my proposal: A compact among authors—fifty percent of TV and radio interviewing time has to be devoted to the book); but as often happens with my public proposals, no action has been taken.

Someone has sent me an account by Tony Castro, a columnist for the Los Angeles *Herald Examiner*, of an appearance in Los Angeles by Gore Vidal. Columnist Castro began the column by reproducing the well-publicized exchange between Vidal and me in 1968, which in due course resulted in a lawsuit. I decided, some time after writing what I considered a definitive piece on Mr. Vidal for *Esquire* (reproduced in one of my collections), not again (I am searching for a value-free word) . . . to write about him. Mr. Castro's column suggests the problem:

[Los Angeles *Herald Examiner*, Nov. 12, 1981, p. A3]
    Thirteen years later, novelist, playwright and potential U.S. senatorial candidate Gore Vidal has not forgiven William F. Buckley Jr. for his personal attack in the nationally televised emotional outburst whose venom matched the Chicago street violence at the Democratic convention.
    Vidal today remains in pain. He hurts so deeply still that the mere mention of Buckley's name rushes the

blood to his head and sends him into fits of hemophilic hatred, bleeding freely with vengeful anger and finally causing intellectual blackouts.

How else do you explain why Vidal can preach reason as a solution to America's problems, as he did yesterday in a lecture at Cal State–Los Angeles, and then lose touch with his own rationality in declaring Buckley a "criminal" and "a man who should be in prison."

It was no slip of the tongue. A writer of Vidal's rank doesn't trip over his words. But the only crook that came out of his performance yesterday appears to be Gore Vidal himself.

It is sad, especially when you have admired Vidal and even pulled for him in those tête-à-têtes with Buckley. But it's a bad worm that eats away at Vidal's insides. All you have to do to upset the man is mention the name Bill Buckley and you set him on a near-hypnotic state in which he destroys himself and his own credibility.

For what Gore Vidal proved yesterday was that he can be trusted no more than the "professional politicians" against whom he intellectually and cleverly ranted.

Vidal has a problem of taking as many liberties with the truth as he does with the facts in his historical novels. For certain, William F. Buckley Jr. triggers these fits, but who knows what else can get under the thin Vidal skin so as to rob him of so much reason that he can sink to Richard Nixon's understanding of American law and justice?

It was former President Nixon who, long before Watergate, committed the widely publicized major gaffe, especially for a lawyer, of publicly declaring Charles Manson "guilty," even though at the time Manson had yet to be tried on mass murder charges.

Vidal showed that he could plunge to that depth yesterday when a student asked him whether William F. Buckley Jr. was "a real person."

Vidal answered by telling a packed theater audience that an article in the latest issue of *Time* magazine indicated that the recent Buckley family business problems with the Securities and Exchange Commission are severe enough that "it appears a real prison door may be opening for the Buckleys."

"Whether William F. Buckley Jr. is a real person, I don't know," he said, "but Lewisburg Penitentiary is real."

The students, already in awe of Vidal, took his word as fact. They had no idea he was lying to them, or, in his vernacular, being an intellectual crook because this is not at all what the *Time* article either said or implied.

The third paragraph in the *Time* article even states that "the most illustrious Buckleys were not named in the 43-page (SEC) civil complaint."

Neither William F. Buckley Jr. nor his brother, former Sen. James Buckley, who Vidal also said is possibly prison-bound, were cited in the SEC action, which because it is *civil*—not criminal—would carry no prison penalty at all, even if the famous Buckley brothers had been included.

Later, pressed about the accuracy and ethics of labeling Buckley a "criminal" on the basis of a civil matter, a visibly frustrated Vidal countered:

"You don't have to be convicted by a court to be a criminal."

Somehow, you expected something better from Gore Vidal, something broader-minded, something a little less frightening than the way the crypto Nazis once carried out justice.

Pat Moynihan has written me. The whole thing skirted embarrassment. I was asked by the Millbrook School last spring to be the speaker at the fiftieth anniversary celebration of the school's founding. Ordinarily I'd have accepted the invitation, for the obvious reason (my three brothers and I attended Millbrook). But only a week before, Jack Heinz had written excitedly to say that he had confirmed our reservations on the Orient Express, that he had made the requisite hotel reservations in Zurich, and in Istanbul, that he had arranged with friends to take us about Istanbul, that a lunch and a dinner were being given. Whereupon I had called my old friend Alistair Horne in London to ask if it would be convenient if Pat and I stopped by and spent Saturday night with the Hornes in Wiltshire, en route back to New York. By all means, was the answer, and would the Heinzes (whom they had come to know) also spend the night? They'd be *most* welcome. Back to Heinz; they would be delighted; back to Horne, wonderful.

Now to scrub all of that would have been quite unthinkable. But I was too cowardly to say to the incumbent headmaster of the school, knowing that it would get back to the former headmaster of the school, the formidable Edward Pulling, that I could not accept the invitation because I had to frolic on the Orient Express; so I encouraged the vague notion that the future of Turkish participation in NATO tied in closely with my being in Turkey on the weekend in question. . . .

So Moynihan was asked to speak instead, and now writes me, "I was the fourth speaker at Millbrook's 50th and by the time I spoke, the temperature in the tent had dropped to well below 40 degrees. Accordingly, as a 50th anniversary present, much to the students' great relief, I announced that I would not deliver the enclosed speech, but would put it in the *Congressional Record*. Those present, I explained, could get the speech by writing to me.

The others who didn't write would be reported to 'The Boss' [Mr. Pulling]. Warm regards."

Moynihan had begun his address, "As many of us learned in the Sunday New York *Times Magazine*, William F. Buckley, Jr., graduated from Millbrook School, in Dutchess County, in the Class of 1943. That is the year I graduated from Benjamin Franklin High School in East Harlem. Although these places were apart in a number of senses, I was struck, on reading Mr. Buckley's sensitive and insightful [an awkward word for someone of such literary taste to use] memoir, by the similarity of our experiences."

After reading Patrick's speech, I wrote a column about it. Now I send it along, in case he had missed it. I had remarked Senator Moynihan's observation that the Reagan administration had brought "a time of meanness in American life when the very idea of education commences to be assaulted." "He did not make it clear who exactly in the Reagan administration is assaulting 'the very idea of education' [I wrote]. Whoever is doing this is showing that he is just mean enough to guard his anonymity." I analyzed a few other assertions of Moynihan's, and closed: "Ah well. Sen. Moynihan is lots of fun, and will be wise again soon after his reelection."

But, in addition to sending him the column, I thanked him for his courtesy in placing my own memories of Millbrook School, published in the New York *Times* the week before its celebration, in the *Congressional Record.*

The article, from which I now borrow as relevant, was a highly subjective reminiscence, primarily about the school, but substantially about my own childhood-at-school. . . .

My father did not go in for participatory democracy in the matter of children's schooling, and we did not know at exactly what moment in the thirties he resolved that his children should, having up until then mostly been tutored at home, be shipped out, gradually, to orthodox boarding schools, because one never questioned him on that, or any other grave matter. He had bought, and gradually expanded, a large house in northwestern Connecticut, in the town of Sharon, after being exiled from Mexico (he backed a revolution that sought to restore religious freedom—the churches in Mexico had been shut down for several years). His work in the oil business kept us in Europe during the late twenties and early thirties; but eventually we would settle in Sharon. My oldest brother John was fourteen, suffering from creeping unmanageability and an exuberant gregariousness which absolutely required that he be detached from the informal tutor system to which the younger of us were subjected, and go off to school. But go off where?

Just north of Sharon, five miles up, lay the Hotchkiss School, a venerable institution even then, with its ivied brick walls and private golf course. But there presided over Hotchkiss School a formidable gentleman named Van Santvoord, whose views on all subjects were highly pronounced, as were my father's. It would not have been easy, I dare say, for any stranger in the room to decide, on that spring day in 1934, who was interviewing whom. Nor is it exactly known why my father came away with a negative impression of Mr. Van Santvoord, a man of immense skills and cultivation. Probably it had to do with Mr. Van Santvoord's amazed reaction at learning from the father of four boys that the father wished to maintain residual control over his sons' schedules, for instance in the matter of where they would weekend, at school or at home, and that he assumed that Hotchkiss would be agreeable to such an arrangement. To have suggested such a thing to Mr. Van Santvoord would not have been different from my father's suggesting that he would take the liberty, now and then, of changing the school's architecture, as required.

In any event, the next we heard was that my father had traveled ten miles west, to interview the headmaster of another boys' school. Millbrook School was then all of three years old, and had thirty boys enrolled in it. My father's exchange with Mr. Edward Pulling was evidently satisfactory to both parties, because it gradually transpired within the household that in the fall my brother John would go to Millbrook. And, over the ensuing six years, my brother Jim, then I, then my younger brother Reid. Moreover, my father had worked out arrangements with Mr. Pulling as follows: The boys would be his until noon on Saturday, after which they would return home for one and a half days. This proved a singular, though not unique privilege. Probably now that Millbrook is fifty years old such latitudinarianism does not exist. But my father liked very much about Mr. Pulling that anything existed that Mr. Pulling elected to have exist. Including Millbrook School.

It is a quite splendid site. It was there the Hollywood people went, during the school's summer vacation, to shoot the early chapters of *The World According to Garp,* which readers will recall focused on the childhood of the protagonist and his energetic mother, who served the school as chief nurse. All that *Garp* evoked in a boys' school—tradition, civility, a great beauty of surrounding natural circumstances—is there. If you drive from Poughkeepsie past the town of Millbrook, where Timothy Leary ran a kind of anti-Millbrook School for drug users until the city elders finally ran him out (and he himself saw the light of day; do you remember the premonitory refrain in *Hair?*—"Now that I've dropped out/Why is life dreary, dreary/Answer my weary query/Timothy Leary, dearie"), toward Amenia, and you look out over the north, you can spot it there, in the dairy country, well over five hundred acres, with a dozen buildings, a church spire, a quadrangle, a few weathered buildings for the masters, the covered hockey rink. Only the old barn and the house across the way were there when the emphatic young man from England, married to Lucy Leffingwell, daughter of the senior partner of J. P. Morgan & Company, resolved that nothing would do but that he must start his own school.

Why? Edward Pulling is one of the most articulate men in the history of American education, but he cannot really give you an answer to that, short of the answer he would not give you, which is: manifest destiny. Some people were born to discover transistors, others strange lands; now and then there comes along someone whose personality is so overwhelming he cannot satisfy himself with anything less than an entire institution to absorb it. Edward Pulling had gone to schools in England and served as a young midshipman in the Royal Navy in World War I, then had attended Princeton, gone on to teach at Gilman School in Baltimore, and then to Groton under Endicott Peabody, who would influence him mightily, if it can be said of an Original Man that anyone influenced him. But here he was, in a huge country, in his early thirties, in the middle of the Depression, and he suddenly discovered that he must start his own school. At age eighty-three, at the school's fiftieth anniversary, he gathered there with six or seven hundred alumni and their families and celebrated one of the few institutions that can carry the imprint of a single personality on, often through, generations. They can say many things about Millbrook, never that it could have been the creature of any other man than Edward Pulling.

I had myself previously experienced only a single headmaster, and then only briefly. He was a Jesuit, at St. John's, the preparatory school for Beaumont College in Old Windsor, on Runnymede, a few miles from Eton, where my father had sent me (and my sisters to a nearby convent school) at the age of twelve—because, he mentioned to my mother after dinner in the presence of his spirited, amused, but cautious brood who never quite knew when my father's hyperboles would become the active agents of family policy—because, he said, as he reflected on it, at least five years had gone by since he had understood a *single word* uttered by any of his ten children. ("Oh, *Father!*" the groan went up. There he went again on one of his crotchets, about people who speak indistinctly.) But the next thing we knew, five of us were on shipboard to Great Britain, an educational experiment cut short by a world war. Father Sharkey had been a small man, of considerable temper, strict but affectionate, shrewd and understanding, with a highly developed sense of humor. When, eight months later, I left him, I had made a lifelong friend.

Then, for another year, we went back to the status quo ante, a house with tutors and visiting musicians and voice teachers. Half the year in Sharon, the winters in Camden, South Carolina, to which two tutors were shuttled. During that year my own thoughts were mostly on sailing, horseback riding, and the piano, my festering inability to master which probably compounded the natural unruliness of a fourteen-year-old. And so the word went out that the following fall I would enter Millbrook School. This meant that I would be interviewed by Edward Pulling, as my older brothers had been.

There cannot have been a more imposing figure in any educational institution. I am aware of the enormous literature describing a grown man's disillusioned meeting with the mincing figure of a headmaster he once feared and stood in awe of. I last saw Mr. Pulling this summer, and he is no less august or imposing than when I first saw him, as a fourteen-year-old, in all his massive, angular, self-assured, commanding completeness. He was six foot three, weighed, say, two hundred pounds; his light blue eyes penetrated you, and, incidentally, the room; his questions were kindly composed and patient, but there was an instant no-nonsense that prevented you, say, from suggesting impulsively that you both go out together to buy a popsicle. Anyone interviewed by Mr. Pulling was, so to speak, permanently interviewed by him.

Both of my brothers, who had graduated, were most enthusiastic about the school, though they spoke about it with that blasé moderation one expects from truly urbane teenagers. My brother John was passionate about sports, and Millbrook—much influenced by the British tradition—was heavy on sports, which were prescribed for everybody, every afternoon (oh, those endless afternoons). My brother Jim was interested primarily in nature, and he had discovered in Millbrook a man called Frank Trevor, whose insatiable interest in the animal and vegetable worlds greatly exceeded any interest in any other subject, save possibly the necessity that the United States go instantly to war against Hitler.

Now Mr. Trevor, R.I.P., also left his mark on the school. It is only fair to say that later in life he developed nervous difficulties, if that's what you call it when you arrive at a faculty conference with a demand to make, and with a loaded pistol in front of you. In any event, Mr. Trevor had a genius for evangelizing his love of nature and animals. To the horror of the younger members of the family, my father announced the summer before my matriculation that he, my mother, and the three oldest members of the family would be spending July and August in Europe, and that he had invited Mr. and Mrs. Frank Trevor to preside over the Sharon household (seven children, a governess, two nurses, two music teachers, seven servants, two grooms) during their absence. Mr. Trevor would teach us about nature. . . .

My father returned to find—somewhat to his chagrin,

we were pleased to note—that our property now harbored probably the largest zoo this side of the Bronx. The entire summer had been given over to making leaf impressions in white clay, building pens, and feeding snakes. And dinner conversation was usually on some such theme as how horses (which we loved) were actually responsible for more deaths than snakes (which Mr. Trevor loved), the poor little misunderstood creatures. It was not until much later, when I sat opposite him in class at Millbrook, disemboweling a pig, that it occurred to me that, unlike horses, no one attempted to ride snakes; and I like to think that Mr. Trevor more than any man developed polemical instincts in those of his students who, unlike my adoring brother Jim, believed that somehow our Maker had managed, in creating man, to transcend nature.

Sports, nature. What else?

Community Service. A sacred conception for "The Boss," as Ed Pulling was (is) universally known, a datum that had come quickly to the attention of Senator Moynihan. *Non sibi sed cunctis* was the school motto: Not alone, but together. As I reflect on this I find a latent inclination for collectivization there (Mr. Pulling is a liberal); but, really, it wasn't that. Mr. Pulling believed that by and large, boys who went to boarding schools were a privileged lot, and that privileged people must know about the needs of the community. The war was soon on us, and that meant that perforce we would need to perform such duties as the first generation of Millbrook students hadn't done—make up our own beds, clean the halls, serve the tables (there was no longer any unemployment, in that area or anywhere). And the war brought on such a scarcity of manual farm labor that we were asked to volunteer to pick apples in a neighboring orchard, at thirty-five cents an hour. It was a desperate dilemma for me every time, because I loathed picking apples, but I loved to smoke cigarettes, and in the isolation of a neighboring orchard one could do this with impunity. (Sixth-formers could smoke at designated times, twice a week. Boys caught smoking at other times were usually expelled.) A dreadful ritual of every Saturday morning, after a prayer and a singing of the morning hymn, came when the headmaster made the daily announcements. He would read out the names of the boys who were to report in the late afternoon to the Jug, as we called it, for commonplace delinquencies, like lateness or disorderliness. The miscreants spent their time picking up stones from one pasture, and bringing them together along a line where a stone fence would eventually spring up. The distinctive horror for me of landing in the Jug was that because it was scheduled late in the day on Saturday, it postponed, and even entirely threatened, my precious weekend at home. I remember Mr. Pulling's quandary when it was brought to his attention that the removal of stones as a form of punishment interfered with his concept of Community Service (one or more afternoons per week), during which other chores of public benefit were undertaken, e.g., Athletic Records, Biology Assistants, Bird Banding, Blackout Committee, Commons Room Committee, Confiscation Lockers, Electrician, Exhibits Manager, Fire Department, Flag Officer, Greenhouse, Meteorology, Receptionists, School House, Stable Assistants, Squash Court, Store Committee. He thought about it, and revealed his transformation of the Jug. So as not to contaminate the noble idea of Community Service, the Jug henceforward would be held not in the late afternoon, gathering stones for a new wall, but in the early evening, copying out the encyclopedia—during the hour the weekly movie was shown. I missed *Casablanca* on that one.

But it was the academic part of Millbrook in which Edward Pulling took the greatest pride. Up until the time I left (1943), no one who graduated from Millbrook failed to be accepted by the college of his first choice (my brother John's class: two to Harvard, five to Princeton, one Yale, one Rutgers, one University of Arizona). Granted, now and then a boy would be encouraged not to apply to too exalted a college. And it was only after reading the charming autobiography *Musical Chairs* by Schuyler Chapin, now Dean of the School of the Arts at Columbia University, that I discovered that the diploma ceremoniously presented to him on commencement day at Millbrook was merely a certificate of attendance.

But Mr. Pulling was deadly serious in the matter of academic excellence. Teaching senior English, he gave out his very first A in 1942. He took undisguised pleasure from any academic accomplishments by his students. I desired to pursue the study of Spanish, but since the language was spoken at home I was advanced. Never mind: Mr. Pulling directed his Spanish teacher to conduct a special class—for a single student. Under Nathaniel Abbott (father of the present headmaster) music was seriously pursued, through a student orchestra, a glee club, visiting teachers, trips to hear artists (I was driving back from a concert by Rachmaninoff when the radio reported an attack on Pearl Harbor). Although Mr. Pulling did not himself easily manage this, retaining a residual aloofness proper to his station and harmonious with his personality, he encouraged close relationships between the masters and the boys, like Mr. Trevor's with my brother Jim, John McGiffert's with my brother Reid (McGiffert would read aloud Reid's short stories to his guests), my own with Mr. Abbott (who took me to Tanglewood to hear Koussevitzky rehearse the Boston Symphony). By nature an authoritative man, Mr. Pulling nevertheless assembled a collection of young masters to whom he gave full rein. The wife of the teacher of Latin and football taught two of us (or attempted to do so) musical harmony. Henry Callard, the gentle assistant headmaster, beloved of all the students, was incongruously the chief disciplinarian. He taught American history, and by emulation he taught the virtues of Quakerism; he left to become headmaster of the Gilman School my senior year (*his* son is now the headmaster of Hotchkiss). Mr. Prum, from Luxembourg, taught the physical sciences and cultivated a kind of exaggerated, narcissistic authoritarianism. ("Sir, do you know the answer to Problem Five?" "I know zee answer to *oll* zee prroblems.") Mr. Hargrave Joyous Bishop, my dormitory master as a fourth-former, was an avid francophile. I remember, in conversations with my roommate, guessing at his age. We rounded it off at sixty-five. He was in fact thirty-five, and a fairly recent graduate of Princeton. His ecstasy came when French diplomats or artists would come to Millbrook to speak (Mr. Pulling had a way of drawing people to his school to perform)—preferably if they could speak only in French (to advanced French students), so that he could utter *"Tiens!"* every moment or two, signifying that he had understood everything. The patrician Arthur Tuttle, whose brother was master of Davenport College at Yale, taught math. A genuine highbrow, with the reputation of having a considerable private fortune; tough, but with a soft streak. Frederick Knutson (Latin, football) was so carried away by the military spirit of the war that he took to marching his athletes to the playing field in accents so martial they were not otherwise heard between Millbrook and West Point. One day my roommate Alistair Horne, in a yelp of enthusiasm, leaned out from our third-floor suite and in a perfect imitation of the Führer's (Mr. Knutson's underground nickname) accents, ordered, "ReVERSE, HARTCH!" whereupon half the undergraduate body reversed its line of march, all but mangling the Führer, who conducted a feverish campuswide investigation, but never found the voice of the impostor.

Alistair Horne would seriously study the martial ways of the Germans and the French. In those days he was also studious, but always there was room for the spontaneous outburst. It was his turn to wait on table, one day, and his fate to be assigned The Boss's table. As he put down the large platter of chow mein he managed accidentally to drip it right down the length of the headmaster's tweeded sleeve. The ten boys (ten to a table, one master) watched with horror at this slow-motion profanation. It was only after he had set down the platter that Alistair recognized the enormity of the offense. So he turned and said, "That's all right, sir. It won't hurt you *externally*." He smiled nervously, and went off to fetch a rag. Mr. Pulling's reaction to student insolence was not easy to predict, because there were insufficient instances of it to make for reliable statistical generalization. But he let this one go by.

Millbrook encouraged a civility among its students. There was practically no bullying, and when an instance of it was uncovered Mr. Pulling dramatically announced at the morning prayer session that he would close down the doors of the school rather than tolerate such stuff. The initiation ceremonies for new boys were theatrical enough to bring on a certain tension, but were absolutely painless. The Boss understood the need for traditions in a brandnew school, and egged some on, some more successfully than others. For instance, he would read the whole of *A Christmas Carol* to the entire school at the Christmas ceremony, to the progressive dismay of all who had heard the story once, or twice, or three times (there were six forms then). But, ho-ho-ho, he would persevere. His devotion to the war effort was such as to sponsor student vigils where, at night, we would strain to catch traces of German bombers, that we might report them to the military. The airplane identification training was turned over to Mr. Trevor, who proceeded in his most obnoxious way to require us to distinguish between miniature wooden Heinkel 111's and Messerschmitt 110's, in order to guarantee the security of Dutchess County. I took pleasure in telling him, after I had failed my third airplane identification test, about the lady who had won the prize in Great Britain by identifying the very first of the fabled Messerschmitt 262's—to the surprise of the community, given her notorious opacity at airplane-identification class—her instructor at one point exasperatedly professed her doubt that this student could distinguish between a kangaroo and a canary. But the R.A.F., on her advice, had risen, shot down the coveted fighter, and the mayor had given the lady a banquet and a huge silver cup. Now he asked her inquisitively what it was about the airplane that had distinguished it in her eyes? "Why," she replied, "at the identification class, the Messerschmitt 262 was the only airplane with a pilot in it!" Mr. Trevor was unamused.

Alistair was one of four English boys who had come to America to escape the blitz. The youngest of these was positively the most insufferable brat ever exported by the United Kingdom. Lord Primrose was about twelve, and I bear today on my right leg the scar from the kicking he gave me in the ice rink when I was ordered to fetch him in, he having decided to ignore the hockey master. Alistair Horne was from London, and we were drawn together as roommates in our sixth-form year. Neither of us was apparently judged by Mr. Pulling as of leadership quality, because we found ourselves, in our third-floor eyrie, in charge of only three younger boys, instead of the customary twenty; one-and-a-half-boys each, as we delighted in putting it. Alistair made me a bootleg radio (these were forbidden), and read widely. I am godfather to his oldest girl. He is among Britain's top historians. Between us we have published forty books.

Mr. Pulling contrived an agony I think altogether unique. Once a year, beginning in the winter term, every boy in

the school had to deliver a five-minute speech to the entire school. This was done either at lunch, after the announcements, or in the morning, after the hymn and announcements. Some boys would be physically sick before their turn came. Some would freeze, for agonizing moments, while schoolboys and masters stared at their fingernails. But The Boss was determined that any graduate of his school should know how to address a large group on the subject of one's choice (a typical topic: "The History of the Ford Motor Company"). I think it fair to say that the system seemed to work. That is, after three or four years of it a student accepted the ordeal as that, to be sure: but as an ordeal related to the coming of age, which came to me and my thirteen classmates, nine of whom survive, probably faster as the result of Millbrook plus a world war, than otherwise.

For those who grew up with Millbrook, indeed are older even than it, the school conjures up, as schools tend to do, a special image. Always there is the fragrance of the New England fall, and winter, and spring; the cider, the ice, the vernal torpor. Weekend dances with Ethel Walker students, hours of football practice, earning my first income by typing other students' papers ($1 per paper; grammar corrected, $1.25 per paper)—until The Boss discovered this, outlawed it as a "pernicious" habit, causing me to consult the dictionary, and to puzzle over the exotic use of the word; but, at Millbrook, we always knew that for better or for worse, if Mr. Pulling had said it, it was, *de facto*, so.

Nathaniel Abbott writes me, a few weeks after the article's publication, an appreciative letter and confesses the pride he takes in his son, the incumbent headmaster. "Upon our return, I looked back into my barrel of broken glass and came up with a music program, a copy of which I enclose for you to include with your memoirs." I examine a nicely printed four-page folder, and read the title page: "Millbrook School Music Department, Fifth Annual Concert, May 23, 1943." And on page 3, the musical day's affliction ♯8, "*Scherzo*, Mendelssohn; *Chorale*, Franck; *Country Gardens*, Grainger—William Buckley." I noted that my name appeared thrice more in the program: as a member of the Glee Club and of the Orchestra, and as Librarian for the Orchestra. I had forgotten I was librarian for the Millbrook School Orchestra, but then I suppose the datum is perishable.

When Reagan was inaugurated I made a rough resolution to write periodically, but with studied infrequency, to the President. I saw no reason to lose touch with a very old friend, and there is of course the collusive imperative: we are both engaged in the same business. I put it to him over the telephone during the interregnum, and he gave me the device to use to assure that a letter gets placed on his personal pile. I have used it sparingly, but frequently enough to maintain a tactile sense of communication. I write him now my own analysis of the Stockman business, and a sentence or two on the nature of my own misgivings about the economic program. I close, "Take care, and promise not to give away the Erie Canal. Remember, we built it, we paid for it, and it is OURS!"

The reference is to a public disagreement he and I had over the Panama Canal Treaty, which he opposed, in 1978. We debated in South Carolina, on television, for two hours. He brought along as his experts and interrogators Admiral Jack McCain, former Commander-in-Chief, Pacific (and an old personal friend); Roger Fontaine, professor at Georgetown; and Pat Buchanan, the columnist and former speechwriter for Nixon. I brought Admiral Zumwalt, former Chief of Naval Operations; James Burnham, the strategist and philosopher; and George Will, the columnist. Both teams had access to Ellsworth Bunker, who had directed the treaty negotiations, and the chairman was Senator Sam Ervin, who had presided over the Watergate hearings. It was a very successful encounter, for the reason that everyone who participated in the discussion had exactly the same priority of concerns. Here is where debates genuinely contribute to the public understanding. (I remember afterward, at the reception, getting the sad news that Hubert Humphrey had died.)

I think, ironically, that Reagan would not have been nominated if he had favored the Panama Canal Treaty, and that he wouldn't have been elected if it hadn't passed. He'd have lost the conservatives if he had backed the treaty, and lost the election if we'd subsequently faced, in Panama, insurrection, as in my opinion we would have.

Six months after the debate, getting ready in Pasadena to set out with Pat to dinner with the Reagans at Pacific Palisades, I was told over the telephone by my host that I was to tell the driver to proceed *very slowly* up the drive.

PRICE $1.00

FEBRUARY 17, 1978

THE
DEBATE BEGINS

NATIONAL REVIEW

Resolved:

THE PANAMA TREATIES SHOULD BE RATIFIED

REAGAN
VS.
BUCKLEY

"Why?"

"Never mind why, just do as I say," he teased.

So I did; and as we mounted his driveway the headlights shone on three successive cardboard signs, each four feet square, on the first of which had been etched in huge red crayon:

"WE BUILT IT!" Then,

"WE PAID FOR IT!" and, finally, tacked to the front door,

"AND IT'S OURS!"

I decided to add a P.S. to my letter. "Barbara Walters asked for my help in getting together one or two questions to ask you in the forthcoming interview [scheduled for Thanksgiving]. Here's one you may want to think about: 'When the Constitution made the President commander-in-chief, the Founders envisioned a man directing an army or a fleet, and the worst that could result was a lost battle, or war. But in a thermonuclear age, Constitutional authority seems to give the President the right to take steps that could result in the elimination of American society. Is it wise that a single man should exercise that much power?'"

Barbara had asked me the week before, while I was attending a party given by Roy Cohn and Tom Bolan in honor of Van Galbraith, who had been designated ambassador to France, if I had any thoughts on any questions she might ask Reagan, with whom she was scheduled to do an interview. I promised to think up two or three tough ones, did so, and phoned them to her last Sunday. But afterward it occurred to me that I shouldn't be in the business of ambushing an old friend, which is why I decided to relay the question to the old friend. In doing so I had no sense that I was emasculating the question. It would be a tough one to confront, whether on one second's notice, or one week's.

Frances told me over the telephone that the WNET people were anxious for at least a tentative reading on whether I'd take on the *Brideshead Revisited* assignment. I have tried to reach Alistair Cooke on the telephone, but got no further than establishing that he was somewhere in Vermont. I decide to go with it, and spoke with Sam Paul of WNET, whom I haven't met; he was to prove bright and amiable. I told him my schedule was pretty intractable, and arranged to view the entire series a week from Saturday in Stamford, and the following Saturday to tape the whole of the commentary. Having made the decision, I was glad of it; and all the more glad, ten days later, on seeing it whole, inasmuch as it seemed to me to have a most fearfully anti-Catholic impact. This was not so much intentional as intrinsic to the plot, written by someone with a transcendent, if misanthropic, faith in what he was up to. Having made most of the Catholics in his book personally insufferable, Waugh replied huffily to a critic by observing in a letter that "God . . . suffers fools gladly; and the book is about God." In any case, it seemed to me that if only for the sake of doing a little historical justice to the author's intention, it made sense to sketch in the background, to protect against any facile conclusion by the uninformed that the author was an anti-Christian fanatic—to which end I secured the help of critic and novelist Wilfrid Sheed, Hugh Kenner about whom I have written, and Peter Glenville, retired as a theater and movie director, a student at Oxford in the thirties, with whom Waugh once discussed a movie script. Weeks later, Herb Caen, the unbottled scorpion of San Francisco (for whom I have a fugitive liking) would write in his column how inappropriate was my own selection to introduce the series:

HOW LITTLE WE KNOW

SLICE OF WRY: Maxwell Arnold suggests that William
Buckley Jr., fairest flower of the right wing, is an
odd choice to act as host of the TV series based on
Evelyn Waugh's classic English novel, *Brideshead Revisited*. On Page 543 of *The Letters of Evelyn Waugh*,
we find the author writing to Tom Driberg on June 6,
1960. After congratulating him on a magazine article
about right-wing movements, Waugh asks Driberg,
"Can you tell me: did you in your researches come
across the name of Wm. F. Buckley Jr., editor of a New
York, neo-McCarthy magazine named *National Review?* He has been showing me great & unsought attention lately & your article made me curious. Has he been
supernaturally 'guided' to bore me? It would explain
him. . . . If anything can."

I wrote to Caen:

Dear Herbert: The item on *Brideshead*, Waugh, and me was understandable fun. Though perhaps a little skepticism would have been in order, even as I'd have shown skepticism toward any writer who pronounced that "Herb Caen is a bore." We are other things. The letter you quoted, Waugh-to-Driberg, was an inside joke. Waugh had just finished reading a book by me the last chapter of which is an attack on Driberg. Following the letter you quoted were several not listed by the anthologist Mr. Amory, for reasons unknown. Mr. Waugh also submitted a piece to *National Review* and wrote a book review for us. His last letter to me, I quote:

Combe Florey House
Combe Florey
Nr. Taunton
2nd April 63

Dear Mr. Buckley:
Very many thanks for *Rumbles*. [*Rumbles Left and Right* by WFB, New York: Putnam's 1962.]
Some of the essays were familiar to me from *National Review*. I reread them with the same zest as those which were new. You have the very rare gift of captivating the reader's attention in controversies in which he has no direct concern. I congratulate you on the collection. At your best you remind me of Belloc; at your second best of Randolph Churchill.
. . . Please accept my greetings for Easter (which I shall be spending in Rome).

Yours sincerely,
Evelyn Waugh

Herb, I thought the world of Evelyn Waugh, but sometimes when I think of what he wrote about me, I blush.

Yours cordially,
Bill

Herb Caen is not in the business of collecting personal
jokes at his expense, so the best he got around to publishing in his column was:

OKAY, fair's fair: The late Evelyn Waugh, author of
Brideshead Revisited, did once refer to William F. Buckley Jr. as a bore (Buckley is "host" of the Ch. 9 series
based on the book), but later, they became dear friends,
as befits two hard-working snobs. As for the series itself,
IT is a bore—just too excruciatingly dated for words,
my dear, and dreadfully close to self-satire. The clothes
are nice, though . . . (I speak as a Waugh fan. *A Handful of Dust* is his classic, whereas *Brideshead* is Waugh
at his worship-the-rich worst) . . .

Herb does not mind communicating with snobs, provided they are hardworking, and accordingly wrote me a
letter so pleasant it would have ruined his reputation if it
had appeared in his column. ("I envy you your equable
temperament. Perhaps that accounts for your good looks,
flawless diction and full head of hair. . . .") He enclosed
yet another comment on *Brideshead*, this from a nineteen-
year-old college student who looked at ten minutes of one
segment, then left the room, remarking, "What is this,
a kind of preppy *Roots?*"

Time, now, to focus on the speech, part of an all-day affair at the Waldorf sponsored by Yankelovich, Skelly and White, the well-known pollsters, the afternoon half of which was to be devoted to Business and the Media, with my twenty minutes the opening remarks.

I would make several points, beginning with the failure of the press to live up to its own critical criteria. This I'd illustrate primarily by examples taken from television. We published recently an account of the infrequency with which the television media mentioned deficit financing and non-productivity-related wage demands as factors contributing to high prices. CBS mentioned monetary policies only six percent of all the times it discussed inflation—Tom Bethell actually counted. During two years of television news, 1978–79, only five references were made to budget deficits (this would be in interesting contrast to the frequency of the media's stated concern after Reagan's program was inaugurated). I would discuss some of the planted axioms of liberal economics—for example, the unexamined philosophical premises of the graduated income tax. I would examine, also, the impact that that which is visualizable tends to have on the television news. It is much easier to convey the image of a single child or mother blasted to eternity as the result of the bombing in Vietnam than successfully to communicate the quality of life of Ivan Denisovich, multiplied by a factor of ten to fifteen million, in a camp to which CBS cameras have no access.

I completed my notes, and ate the perfect chicken sandwich Gloria brought me, with a glass of cool white wine. Pat came in, en route to her lunch, and we discussed the weekend plans, and she told me *now don't forget* that my black tie and cummerbund were in the pocket of my tux, and I promised I'd remember, and walked down the stairs with her, saw her out, and dangled for a minute over the harpsichord.

There aren't many running points of tension in my household, but one of them is that Pat persists in perching a half-dozen photographs on the harpsichord. The mere effort of removing these discourages thoroughly impromptu, three- or four-minute sessions on an instrument that, unlike the piano, really requires that it be opened up in order to do any justice to the subtlety of its tone. The instrument here in the hallway in New York belongs to the great Fernando Valenti, a Challis presented to him by his friends and students in the mid-fifties. It was proclaimed by him to be the finest Challis ever made, by that shy little harpsichord maker with Parkinson's disease who twice, before dying in 1974, came to tune and voice the instrument, both times before Fernando's occasional

recitals here. Valenti recorded over *eighty* long-playing records on this instrument, and gave it up only after fashion, with its iron foot (yes, it is so also in music), ruled that harpsichords shouldn't have a sixteen-foot register, which register permits the player to sound a note an octave below the note he is depressing. I stay out of the argument among the professionals and the theorists. All I say is that used correctly (as by Fernando), the sixteen-foot can achieve simply wonderful musical effects, and I do not doubt that J. S. Bach and Scarlatti, if they had heard the sixteen-foot (and it is not absolutely established that they did not), would have welcomed its discreet use, and perhaps even have specified its use, here and there. Recitalists at my apartment regularly use it.

Anyway, I must run. I went back upstairs, changed, Jerry got the bag. Soon I wormed my way through the Waldorf to the indicated meeting room, which was empty because the audience was listening to the luncheon speaker. It was ten minutes to two, and I was scheduled to begin at two. A hospitable woman with Yankelovich came and kept me company, and soon the audience of several hundred filed in.

They were to have heard Senator Bill Bradley at lunch, but he couldn't make it, and instead they listened to Richard Blumenthal, an attractive young Democrat, formerly U.S. Attorney in Connecticut. I was sorry I didn't hear him, or an earlier speaker, Michael Novak, a friend and contributor to *National Review*. I chatted with Mark Green, who would speak after me. He is a liberal activist, ten years with Ralph Nader (if you can bear it). He apparently bore it well because he is young, fresh, enthusiastic, and resourceful. That is the reason I use him with such frequency on "Firing Line," in the role of examiner. He is to follow me, I learn; and after him, Don Hewitt, executive producer of CBS's "60 Minutes." But in accepting the engagement my office warned my hosts that I

would need to fly out of New York right after speaking
(indeed, in a private plane) to meet a prior commitment
in Toledo. Everyone seemed in a good humor about this;
I was introduced, got up, and performed, my eyes carefully
on the clock.

I think this very important when there are other scheduled speakers. Once, in Philadelphia many years ago, Louis
Auchincloss, Ralph Nader, and I were scheduled to speak
between eleven and twelve, twenty minutes each, to the
annual booksellers' convention. We were begged to keep
our remarks to the specified time, as any failure to show up
at noon in the dining room would cause three thousand
soufflés to collapse, or whatever. Nader began. And spoke
for forty minutes. Auchincloss and I looked at each other.
I was scheduled as the third speaker, so I raised all ten
fingers, and he understood that each of us would cut our
prepared remarks in half. Not easy to do.

At the Waldorf the questioning was lively, and when I
left I had the feeling (I get this about half the time) that I
had given the audience meaty propositions, and had upheld
their plausibility during the question period.

Back in the car, I spoke on the phone with Frances most
of the way to LaGuardia. Little things, but they needed
attention. Mark Dichter, the cinematographer who last
summer sailed with us as far as Bermuda (from St.
Thomas) on the boat I chartered, needs a date to do joint
work on the documentary we have planned (OK to set up,
I tell Frances). It is a coincidence that that is exactly what
Allen Stanley needs, who is producing a documentary on
the earlier trip in 1975, about which I wrote in my book
Airborne (OK). Frank Mankiewicz wants me to go to a
luncheon for National Public Radio (there is a conflict,
but I could make it for the pre-lunch reception). John Fox,
who is working on a book about Whittaker Chambers,
needs some time (OK), and Molly Ingram of Holiday
Yachts wants to find out what we want in the way of food

during Christmas when we cruise aboard the *Sealestial* (answer: ask Pat).

The airplane, dispatched for me by a friend of the Friends of the University of Toledo Libraries, is a little Grumman, and the pilots are anxious to go, because there are heavy head winds, and I am supposed to be at a cocktail party before the dinner. The two pilots lifted the ship into the air, and during the next two hours my seat belt was never off. Reading was extremely difficult, and I was working on the research folder for the guest on one of two "Firing Line" programs that we would be taping tomorrow, namely John Brown, Governor of Kentucky. I don't get motion sickness (though I am careful never to say that I never will get it—I have seen too many virgins suddenly, inexplicably, collapse at sea), so the movement didn't upset me, it just made things difficult. Which is nothing to what I did to my hosts, two of whom were waiting at the airport most anxiously when we came in, almost an hour late.

They zoomed me to the Inverness Club, and I learned the background of the association that sponsors this annual dinner, devoted to maintaining interest in free library service under the patronage of the University of Toledo. My hosts (Mr. and Mrs. Leslie Sheridan) were wonderfully pleasant and good-humored, and, arriving too late for the cocktail party, I was taken to my seat, and wine was served. The dinner was very long.

I have often reflected on this. A secret ballot, I am quite certain, would reveal that ninety percent of those who attend large, festive hotel or club dinners, which are to be followed by speeches, would be infinitely grateful if the first and third courses were decorously pre-situated at their places, leaving to the waiters only the burden of bringing the main course. When I was not yet thirty, I spoke to the largest seated dinner audience I have ever addressed: sixty-five hundred Philadelphians who had attended retreats at St. Joseph's in the Hills during the preceding year. It was held at Convention Hall, the lobster salad was there when we arrived, and behind the bread plates, a raspberry tart, with a slice of cheese alongside. It remained only for the waiters to bring piping hot filet mignon, baked potato, and beans. Red wine was on the table in carafes. The speaking began forty-five minutes after we filed into the room, everyone satisfied. At least by the food.

The introduction took me by surprise. Most introductions are contractions of your Who's Who and/or the kind of thing one would expect if being nominated for President, in which, to use Mencken's metaphor, you are compared to the rising sun, the full moon, and the aurora borealis. In the professional fraternity of public figures I doubt there are many who are influenced in the least by such ritual sycophancy. It serves a purpose, of course, with the audience, particularly if it is an audience partly conscripted by the philanthropic nature of the event. It is pleasing for them to know they have come to listen to Shakespeare, or Abraham Lincoln. One does come upon, every five years or so, an introduction inherently interesting to the speaker, either because of the felicity of the composition, or the resourcefulness of the research. A historian at the University of Texas once introduced me to an audience of students by saying that he had done research into my family. I knew that my grandfather had been sheriff of Duval County. I knew that he had been a Democrat, knew that he had been a law-and-order sheriff. "But I am not certain that Mr. Buckley knows that his grandfather's allegiance to the Democratic Party surpassed his allegiance to law and order, because although Sheriff Buckley died in 1904, he voted for Lyndon Johnson in 1948." That was fun. Tonight the vice-president for academic affairs, English scholar William Free, began by quoting those nice lines of Pope: "Yes, I am proud: I must be proud to see/Men not afraid of God, afraid of me:/Safe from the bar, the pulpit, and the throne,/Yet touch'd and shamed by ridicule alone." It transpires that as an undergraduate at Yale Mr. Free had, along with a classmate, challenged me in a public letter. "The letter is long forgotten, but not the response. Whatever the merits of our arguments, the skill with which his were put taught us a lesson in humility that made a lasting impression." Free quoted Auden, and by now convinced me that his generous amiability concealed a continuing distaste for my views: "Time . . . Worships language and forgives/Everyone by whom it lives; . . ./Time that with this strange excuse/Pardoned Kipling and his views,/And will pardon Paul Claudel,/Pardons him for writing well." I'd need instruction in what exactly it is we're supposed to pardon Kipling for.

"The nation's best-known conservative man of letters unfolded a 'liberal' attack on sloppy rhetoric and collectivist economics Thursday night at the Inverness Club," the following day's paper related. "William F. Buckley, Jr., whose own prose has almost never been called sloppy—or liberal—regaled the annual dinner for the Friends of the University of Toledo Libraries with an hour of droll 'reflections on current contentions,' especially those concerning economic policies." There followed a gratifyingly accurate account of what I actually said, by a staff writer (Mr. Jack Lessenberry) of the Toledo *Blade*, though marred, I thought, by the subhead toward the end of the story, "Buckley Says Andrew Carnegie/'Was an Awfully Dumb Man.'" "Mr. Buckley, whose father was a millionaire oil magnate, drew his biggest laugh of the evening when responding to a questioner who asked him about Andrew Carnegie's theory that all inheritances be outlawed, so that the United States would be led by an 'aris

tocracy of talent, not of inherited wealth.' 'He was an awfully dumb man,' Mr. Buckley, who received $4,000 from
the library association for his Toledo speech, said."

I don't think I said that, or if I did I misspoke, as the expression goes, intending merely to say that the notion of
confiscatory death penalties was a very dumb *idea*. I went
on to say that F. A. Hayek, in his *Constitution of Liberty*,
insists most persuasively that if one came upon a society in
which no one was wealthy, that society would be better
off endowing one hundred people at random with a million dollars each than being without citizens with surplus
funds. One trouble with confiscatory death taxes, I explained, is that they would place a most unhealthy incentive on profligate spending in later years. Moreover, the
tribal instinct being what it is, many men work for their
families and children, and the idea that property once
acquired, i.e., after the tax has been paid on it, isn't one's
to disburse as one likes is primitive in its collectivist bias.
Something like that. Carnegie was in many ways an eccentric, but anyone shrewd enough to contrive the kind of
protective tariff that nursed his steel business along was
hardly dumb.

After it was over, a biographer of Ezra Pound with
whom I have corresponded wanted to take me off for a
nightcap, and I thanked him but begged off, because I had
to write my Friday column tonight, and dictate it to New
York before flying to Louisville tomorrow. I shook hands
all the way round, slipped out to the elevator, and opened
the door of my room.

The feeling, after lecturing, on regaining the occupancy
of one's own room is a delight whose resonances have been
insufficiently sung. The sheer relief of silence is a part of
the magic. The stillness of the surroundings. Pat packs me
a flask of vodka and little cans of grapefruit juice, and I
disrobed, poured a vodka and grapefruit juice, and, since

there is work to do, unzipped the typewriter, this without relish. I have in my briefcase the New York *Times* with the whole of Reagan's speech on disarmament, the European challenge, etc.; so I wrote my column under the title "The Year of Europe" and assessed, country by country, the probable reaches of the peace movement currently being encouraged (and in some instances, engineered) by the Soviet Union. "Mr. Joseph Sobran," I wrote happily, "the bright and witty columnist, has remarked yet one more terminological usurpation by the Left. To call those who, without compensating concessions by the Soviet Union, are prepared to dismantle our defensive arsenal in Europe members of a 'peace movement' would be to say that Neville Chamberlain led the peace movement in Great Britain during the late thirties, or that Henry Wallace led the peace movement during the forties. The Soviet Union has from now until mid-1983 to ascertain exactly what will be the consolidated picture within Europe on the designated eve of the deployment of our Pershing and Cruise missiles designed to counteract the Soviet weapons." My pitch was: that we must hold absolutely firm on the matter of deployment of the theater nuclear weapons. I argued that Soviet leaders would make no substantial concessions unless they judged as resolute our determination to deploy the missiles, and Europe's disposition to accept them.

Having twice checked the alarm clock, because I am due at the airport at 9 A.M., I read something about somebody and, turning off the light, remembered to count on my fingers the five decades of the rosary, a lifelong habit acquired in childhood, and remembered about half the time. That half of my life, I like to think, I behave less offensively to my Maker than the other half.

Five
FRIDAY

Leslie Sheridan rang that he was downstairs and ready to convey me to the airport. I had breakfasted, talked with Frances, and decided there would, after all, be time to telephone in the column from Louisville before the (12:30) deadline, so I left. In the car, we chatted and Leslie pronounced the previous evening a great success, which was nice to hear, though in fact the preceding evenings are always pronounced great successes, hosts being as nice as generally they are. At the field it was cold. I greeted the pilots and said I hoped the air wouldn't be as choppy as yesterday's, and got a reassuring reply. The flight was about two hours and I dug into the portfolio on the other television program, this one having to do with busing as an instrument designed to effect school desegregation, or integration. It had been a while since my mind dwelled on the subject, and there was much to catch up on.

We flew at about 7,500 feet and encountered little turbulence. There was snow as we came over Cincinnati, and I remembered that extraordinary fortnight fifteen years ago. I had been scheduled to speak one night in Louisville, but the pilot landed the plane in Cincinnati because of bad weather in Louisville, and I took a 110-mile taxi ride, arriving in Louisville forty-five minutes after my speech was supposed to begin. One week later (what are the odds against such a thing?) I was scheduled to speak in Cincinnati and the airplane landed in Louisville, requiring me to take a 110-mile taxi ride to Cincinnati, breaking into the banquet room after some of the guests had simply given up.

When I arrived in Louisville, the car from the local television station whisked me off to the Galt House, where the young, attentive manager reminded me I had been there a couple of years before. The hotel in question is sort of Diamond-Jim-Brady-Western, and in my huge suite, thirty-two Muscovites could have been housed.

Warren Steibel, who, when the program is taped outside New York, generally gets in a day ahead to supervise technical arrangements, rang me before I had even sat down, and I told him to come on up. Warren has produced all but the first dozen or so "Firing Lines"; we have been everywhere together, and I have long since developed a huge admiration for his professional competence and a special gratitude for his knowledge of my own (by no means eccentric) likes and dislikes (foremost among the latter, to be made to arrive at a studio much before the technicians are

ready to roll). He gives me a rundown on the schedule. The first show will be with the two professors, on the busing question. The second show will be with the governor. A hundred-odd supporters of the station will compose the studio audience, and after the second show there was to be a reception, but that reception would last no more than forty-five minutes, guaranteed. After that, Warren had promised our hosts, I would read several commercials calling for local support to the station. Then we would be whisked away to the airport, in plenty of time to catch the 6:30 flight back to New York. Did I need anything?

Just the time to finish my research, and type out the two scripts. But I took Warren's telephone numbers—he and his assistant, George, need to be at the studio several hours ahead of time, to arrange the setting and practice with the technicians.

I telephoned my office, and dictated the column into the recording machine. Moments after hanging up, my brother Jim reached me by phone from Washington. He dined last night with Clare Boothe Luce, and she professed her indignation at the *Time* mag story, and it was left to Jim to ask me whether I thought a call from her to editor-in-chief Henry Grunwald was in order. God no, I said; surprised, actually, that Clare had made the offer, having on more than one occasion heard her express her powerlessness at *Time* even when Harry was alive and running things, so mighty was the fortress separating Henry R. Luce, editor-in-chief, Time Inc., from Harry Luce, husband of Clare. Probably the gesture was a mere act of civility, even as it may be difficult for a congressman not to *offer* to look into the matter if he finds himself spending an evening with an old friend whose grandmother didn't receive her last Social Security check. Jim agreed, and the social circuit is completed.

It was only a quarter to twelve, but I was suddenly

ravenous and ordered a hamburger and a beer. I ate the
hamburger while still standing, because I had given myself
a minute to read the front page of *The Wall Street Journal*,
which was spread out on the desk. I gulped down a glass
of beer, unzipped the typewriter, and spread out my research. Then I was hit—it happens sometimes—with a most
awful, undeniable, need for sleep. In the Infantry, during
the first hour you march for fifty minutes and then take a
ten-minute break. In succeeding hours, the break is reduced
to five minutes. The question, back in 1944–45, was always
whether to smoke a cigarette—or attempt sleep. Half the
time I would sleep; and ever since I have had no problem
at all in sleeping for ten minutes. The alarm on my clock
isn't calibrated finely enough, so I set it for fifteen minutes.
I was instantly sound asleep, and woke before the alarm
went off, substantially refreshed.

For reasons I haven't fathomed, the half hour to forty-
five minutes I give to writing out the introductions to
"Firing Line" guests, and making notes of questions from
the material previously researched, I continue to find the
single most taxing activity I engage in. I don't know why
this should be so. My introductions follow an uncom-
plicated formula. If the guest is vastly illustrious, his
identity is given in the opening paragraph. If less than that,
the whole of paragraph one is devoted to the issue being
discussed during that hour. The whole of paragraph two is
devoted to a biography of the guest. There is then a one-
sentence mention of the examiner, with the promise that
he will be introduced more substantially "in due course."

The examiner has been coached by Warren, and his instructions are simple. 1) He must stand, at the outset of
the program, behind his lectern, so that the camera can
bring him in when I mention his name. He can then sit,
but 2) he must, beginning after thirty minutes, watch me
for any sign that I am about to introduce him, because

when that introduction is performed, 3) he must be back at his lectern.

I introduce him sooner, or later, depending on several factors. If the guest is dull, I bring in the examiner early, for relief. If the guest and I are in substantial agreement, I bring in the examiner early. Or—if the guest is brilliant, but I feel that the right moment has come for a change of gears—then I bring the examiner in early. But as a rule of thumb, the examiner comes in fifteen minutes before the hour's end. His instructions are to take his time in phrasing his questions, from which he should not endeavor to conceal his own bias, but not be preachy. Finally, he should ask questions not only of the principal, but of me. My introductions close with a phrase that has become standard: "I should like to begin by asking [Mr. Blow] why [he believes the earth is flat]?"

I devoted the hour to composing the introductions, and to making my notes, then I changed my clothes and, as Warren directed, reported down at the lobby at exactly 2:45, where the kind lady from the studio was waiting; and we said goodbye to the Galt House.

The studio appeared busy. Like most studios, it comprises mostly hallways and small rooms, and people in a hurry. I was made up—years ago Warren told me sternly never to forget to instruct unfamiliar technicians to put makeup on my hands, because I bring them often to my cheeks, and awful visual anomalies happen when chalk-white hands come up against ruddy brown cheeks.

The studio was full of WKPC's guests, and I walked over and greet my own guests, who were already seated and plugged in. I sat down, a technician clipped the tiny mike to my necktie, applying an inch of adhesive tape to cause the electric wire to set out vertically toward my waist, and I checked the little stopwatch on my clipboard, which George has handed me. It is pre-set so that when it reaches zero, the show is ended, fifty-seven minutes and twenty seconds after the music begins. On the table to my right is a digital stopwatch, a reserve in case my regular stopwatch stops working (this happens, curiously, a half-dozen times per year). "QUIET IN THE STUDIO!" Then the monitor is seen 10-9-8-7-6-5-4-3-2-1. Then the music from Bach's Second Brandenburg, while the viewer sees the opening credits. I look down at my notes. I begin talking when the music stops playing, which it does after about thirty seconds. . . .

MR. BUCKLEY: It's been a long time since we have visited on this program the question of busing as a means of effecting interracial comity. The issue appears to rise to high pitches of noisy advocacy, both by those in favor and those opposed, and then to recede from the headlines, at least for a while. To the end of determining what's up in the busing world, we have two distinguished scholars here in Louisville, one of them also an attorney, to report on the question.

Willis Hawley is the dean of Peabody College in Vanderbilt University, where he is a professor of education and political science. Professor Hawley received all three of his degrees at the University of California at Berkeley, after which he taught at Duke and at Yale, settling down finally at Vanderbilt. There he has undertaken the principal responsibility for a government-financed study entitled "The Assessment of Current Knowledge About the Effectiveness of School Desegregation Strategy," a massive document stretching to nine volumes, for which an alternative use would be to throw these volumes at teachers or students who disagree with their findings. These we will discuss presently; suffice it to say for the nonce that they would appear to endorse busing in virtually every respect.

Professor Robert Sedler, really, goes further. In a recent law article he advocated a construction of the Fourteenth Amendment to the Constitution which would in effect abolish the traditional differential between *de facto* segregation—that is, such segregation as occurs when all the kids in the neighborhood simply happen to be of a single race—and *de jure* segregation, where schools are segregated as the result of machinations of the school board. Professor Sedler teaches at the Wayne State University Law School, having before that been with the University of Kentucky Law School. He is a most active litigant, having figured in a number of constitutionally prominent anti-segregation cases. He has written a number of books, including, after three years as a professor at Addis Ababa in Ethiopia, a book called *Ethiopian Civil Procedures*, published shortly before Ethiopia gave up civil procedures. He has written profusely for the law journals.

[There are generally no examiners when there are two guests.]

I should like to begin by asking Mr. Hawley whether the views or findings of Arthur Coleman were examined in your lengthy report?

[I was off to a bad start.]

MR. HAWLEY: James Coleman?

MR. BUCKLEY: Arthur, I think his name is—is it James? It *is* James, isn't it, yes. [The two big names are *James* Coleman, and *Arthur* Jensen.]

MR. HAWLEY: James Coleman has written a great deal. I'm not sure what you have in mind.

[I have in mind leading him to a quote from Coleman, but I'm not yet ready to use it. I give him a hint.]

MR. BUCKLEY: '78.

MR. HAWLEY: The white flight issue, yes, of course. Mr. Coleman, as well as most other scholars who have studied this question, have found that school desegregation brings about white flight from public schools under certain circumstances. I don't think there's much debate about that. The question is whether that *needs* to happen, whether it can be reduced and whether the long-term effects—

MR. BUCKLEY: [attempting levity] Mr. Sedler could pass a constitutional amendment against it, couldn't he?

MR. HAWLEY: [smiling] He's not the only one who would like to do that. But in general I'd say that the folks who point to white flight as the most serious problem of school desegregation generally overstate the effects of desegregation in that regard. There are lots of things going on in the country that would otherwise explain whites leaving public schools.

MR. BUCKLEY: I didn't actually have that finding [the problem of white flight] of Mr. Coleman primarily in mind. I had [another finding] the summary of which, in his words, is, "There are as many cases where achievement levels decline as where they increase; thus, the notion that black children will automatically increase their achievements in integrated schools is shown to be false." Had you [sarcasm] forgotten that one?

MR. HAWLEY: No. Mr. Coleman didn't himself do that study. He reported on a study that was published in 1975, which in turn dealt with the studies up until 1973. More recent evidence shows, to the contrary, that school desegregation in most instances brings about positive consequences for minority children with respect to academic achievement. Indeed, I think there is considerable consensus among scholars on that question. The only issue, I think, about that has to do with whether those effects occur throughout the school period or whether it's primarily an early school effect. We find that the effect is primarily in the early grades.

[Coleman had affirmed the work of another reliable scholar, but it is left sounding as if Coleman had been relying on stale studies.]

MR. BUCKLEY: Is David Armor a considerable scholar? [He was the author of the study in question. A Harvard Ph.D.]

MR. HAWLEY: He is. He has not studied this question. That's not his particular area of expertise. [I am left in doubt now. Coleman was quoting *some* study, and I thought it was Armor's. Perhaps it was Jensen's. But I had better go on the offensive rather than take a chance dropping another name.]

MR. BUCKLEY: Is your definition of a particular area of expertise somebody who agrees with you?

MR. HAWLEY: No, of course not [he laughs], but in this case it's a question of who is studying the issue.

MR. BUCKLEY: Is Tom Sowell [useful here: the black economist who has done trenchant work in sociology] a considerable scholar?

MR. HAWLEY: He is, but he has not studied the effects of school desegregation on children.

[A wise old bird. He's not going to volunteer the name of the author of the study. I decide to make light of it all.]

MR. BUCKLEY: I think you're saying it's Greek, and that I can't win. [The allusion is to the old story about the white voting registrar administering a literacy test to a Negro. In Greek. The Negro studies the text and says: "It say no Nigra's goin' to vote here today."]

[It is time to turn to Mr. Sedler, who begins by saying that his interest is not so much in whether blacks profit from integrated schooling as it is that the two races should study *together*.]

MR. SEDLER: The primary justification for school integration in my view, both from a constitutional and from a policy standpoint, is that it brings black and white children together during the educational process, teaches them how to live together in a multiracial society and a multiracial world. . . . When black children go to school only with other black children and when white children go to school only with other white children, neither black children nor white children, in my view, learn how to function as effective adults.

MR. BUCKLEY: [I need now to spear the philosophical point.] I think your views are extremely interesting, but I'm sure that you, as a lawyer, would upbraid me if I failed to ask whether your views are constitutionally relevant?

And so it goes. Mr. Sedler wishes to make the point that if equality is written into the Fourteenth Amendment, then you have got to effect equality, and one way is to require integrated schooling. Mr. Hawley is happiest talking about the sociological advantages—empirically demonstrated, he insists—of integrated schooling. I am left arguing that the sociological proofs are at least ambiguous, and that to read equality into the Constitution via the Fourteenth Amendment as authorizing compulsion is an invitation to the ideologization of an instrument that was devised as a compact between *free* people. The program was pretty good. Everyone got a chance to say what he wished, and there was a sense of consummation after the hour was over.

Warren (who is a massive physical figure) beckoned to me imperiously from the door of the studio and such a signal from him, so unusual, signified a crisis of sorts. (*The*

governor's secretary called! The governor has been im-
peached! Can't possibly make it!) and so I went directly to
him, forswearing the conventional little disengaging chat-
ter with my guests. He had a piece of paper in hand, and
told me that the President was trying to reach me on the
telephone. The floor manager ushered me into his office. I
dialed the White House. The operators there are renowned
for their general knowledge and tact, but I announced myself in the obvious way: "This is . . . I am returning the
President's call." They then ask what number you are
calling from, and one must suppose this is to guard from
someone at Elaine's restaurant going to a pay phone and
hiccoughing that he/she is Henry Kissinger/Jacqueline
Kennedy Onassis. I reply that the call was placed to my
office, giving that number, but that I am in Louisville,
Kentucky, giving this number. In a few seconds the operator advises that the President is tied up, but could he
reach me in about a half hour? I say that unhappily he
can't, forswear saying that the President will understand
that the show must go on, and say simply that an hour-
long television program will begin in about five minutes,
but that I can call back then. Another silence, and then I
am told that an hour from now would be just fine.

This communication was hardly extraordinary, involving merely me, a phone operator, an assistant, and the
President. But the resources of presidential communications systems are not to be underestimated. When
President Nixon decided, ever so cautiously, to back the
candidacy of my brother Jim for the Senate in 1970, Mr.
Nixon disclosed his plans to me in the Oval Office, and in
an extensive conversation advised me that he would have
the Vice-President identify himself in some way with Jim,
notwithstanding that the incumbent running against Jim,
Charles Goodell, was the Republican nominee and Jim was
running as a conservative, under the banner of New York's

Conservative Party. Ten days later, the chairman of the luncheon in New York, at which Vice-President Agnew was to speak and my brother to be present in the audience, called to question me on whether the Vice-President was merely to be seen shaking Jim's hand (Version A), or whether the Vice-President in his speech was actually to say quote unquote how glad he was to see James Buckley in the audience (Version B). The chairman refused to go with Version B unless the White House explicitly cleared it.

So, I called Bob Haldeman at the White House—but learned that he was in Spain, with the President. I asked then for presidential assistant Peter Flanigan, who thinks on his feet as fast as any man alive, so that in ten seconds I was able to describe the problem. "Can you hang on a minute?" he asked. Certainly. Well, it took closer to two minutes. Flanigan was back on the line. "We'll go with Version B." "Great," I said. Wondering whom he had talked with, I remembered that, in addition to Haldeman, John Mitchell had been in the Oval Office when Mr. Nixon had disclosed his plans. "Who'd you check with—Mitchell?" I asked. "No. I checked with Haldeman. He wasn't sure, so he asked the President." It is well known that George Bernard Shaw, on being informed of the discovery that the speed of light is 186,000 miles per second, commented that this was the most obvious lie he had ever heard. GBS wouldn't have been so skeptical if he had listened in on that conversation.

It was time to go with John Y. Brown, Governor of Kentucky. A delicate matter in introducing him was how exactly to handle the presidential business. Some of my guests on "Firing Line" have been presidential nominees, some have been candidates for the presidency, some explicit con-

tenders for the candidacy, some inexplicit contenders for the candidacy, some have simply been known to harbor a quiet conviction that all the reticulated factors argue their presumptive qualifications. It is in this last category that John Brown fits, and therefore in introducing him you do not wish to shove him farther up on the scale, as this might require him to make disavowals uncomfortable to him, and disrupting to the viewer, who may have tuned in to have a look at someone who might yet be President.

So, in my introduction, I handled this by saying, ". . . [Governor Brown] is most conspicuous for identifying himself with the need to bring to state government the approach of business. Moreover, he has taken this position while simultaneously serving as a) a Democrat and b) a Democrat who is widely interpreted as profoundly believing that his nostrums for the state of Kentucky ought not to have a mere one state as their beneficiary. He would, or so it is assumed, consent to serve as President of the United States."

So we go into the whole matter of the extent to which government is "business." I remind him that his own father once said that "government is not a business," and he replies that a *knowledge* of business is *always* revelant, and I counter that mental homes, for example, don't lend themselves to strict business accounting, and he said that really I've got to understand that *everything* lends itself to business analysis; for instance, he asked the head of the Kentucky Council on Higher Education a while ago how much does it cost per student per year in Kentucky colleges? And he *didn't know*—how do you like that? So I say the measurement of cost can't *always* be relevant, look at Karen Anne Quinlan, and he says it is *always* relevant, even if you aren't *guided* by it, and for instance Ronald Reagan's background had nothing to do with business, and that is one of the reasons why Reagan isn't really equipped to do everything he might do as a leader, and I say well, Pericles, Napoleon, Lincoln, and Churchill didn't have a business background, and they did all right, and he says wouldn't they have done *better* if they had had business experience?

And so on. He is an engaging man, and along the line it occurs to me that the effort to get him to intellectualize his point is a) not working; and b) that its not working could well be testimony to the effectiveness of such a man, whose skills and concepts are in every sense practical. John Brown bought the Kentucky Fried Chicken business from the white-suited Colonel for peanuts years ago and built it into a national compulsion. He makes, and stresses, a further interesting distinction, namely that men engaged in businesses they do not own haven't anything like the kind of concern for economy exercised by men who do own their own business; and this I do believe, a point that did not escape James Burnham's notice when he wrote *The Managerial Revolution*.

It was over, and I went out dutifully to call the President. But he was still tied up, so I went and mixed with the audience—alert, sophisticated folk, mostly middle-aged. A young woman accosted me as "Uncle Bill" and kissed me, and held my hand, and I was garrulously dumbstruck until the lady with the station asked, amiably, "When did you last see your goddaughter?" Suddenly I recognized that it was Howard Hunt's daughter Lisa, and indeed I hadn't seen her for several years. I get to meet her husband for the first time; and then Warren is there, telling me please to come quickly to the telephone, and for the third time I was back in the office, and the telephone operator said would I hang on for a minute, which I do, and presently my old friend the commander-in-chief was on the line.

He wanted, he began, to thank me for my letter. That was not the letter I just finished writing, but one about a month old. I told him I just finished writing him a fresh letter, and I mentioned, to be concrete, the Barbara Walters bit, and we discussed for a moment or two the appropriate answer if indeed she decides to ask him that question next week (she didn't). He told me he has just come back from an exercise with George Bush, a war game in which the enemy launches from the Caribbean. That, he said, would give us three to eight minutes to launch back. I said the

Founding Fathers could hardly have imagined a plebiscite on whether to do so in the time involved. I then told him Ron and Doria had enjoyed *Nicholas Nickleby*, and he said he knew that already, and thanked for asking them, and I told him Christopher, my son, had enjoyed the movie at the White House. I thanked him for calling, told him to give my love to his wife, while promising, at his request, to convey his to Pat, and I told him I knew how busy he was, and we said goodbye. A social call.

I have several times reflected on something my old friend Frank Shakespeare once told me. He was then the head of the United States Information Agency, and I had agreed to serve as a member of its Advisory Commission. Frank took me to the Oval Office (my first view of it). Henry Kissinger was the fourth person there, with Nixon, and the exchange went on for about fifteen minutes when Dwight Chapin (appointments secretary and dirty trickster) entered discreetly and handed the President a note. I instantly inferred that this was the procedure by which guests were signaled to leave, and was therefore surprised when Nixon said to Chapin, "Tell him to wait just a minute," after which he resumed his conversation with me. Upon the termination of the point he was making, I rose, said the usual thing about how busy the President was, we all shook hands, and I left.

Walking away from the White House, Frank told me that I had violated protocol. "The way it works is *you* never terminate a session with the President, *he* terminates it. As long as he says nothing abortive, it signifies that he wants things to continue as they are, and the tradition is that we are all there at the pleasure of the President." I can understand that. I mean, there are no intellectual difficulties here, are there? But I still think it makes it easier for a President, or for the King of Siam, if you initiate the mo-

tion to go. After all, there is nothing to stand in the way of
his overruling you. Reagan, for example, could have said,
"Hang on, there are a couple of other things I want to talk
to you about. Do you think we should go to war against
Libya?"

In any event, I returned to my goddaughter. Governor
Brown, who has been mixing gladly with the little crowd,
was saying good night. We shook hands, he invited me to
be his guest at the Kentucky Derby, and the technician is
telling me that they are ready to shoot the commercials.
There are four of them, all to the effect that contributions
to WKPC, or participation in its forthcoming auction,
make possible such interesting programs as "Firing Line."
One filler has to be read a second time, "because [the
stage director shook his finger] you said the auction lasted
six days, but it lasts *eight* days." I looked at the script that
had been handed me, where indeed it said *six* days, but what
the hell, I go again. I bound then from the chair, and Warren and George are waiting, as is the car, so we say hasty
goodbyes to everyone, and I sank back in the seat. Warren
says we're in plenty of time. George was in the front seat.
We discussed the shows, lightly. Soon we were at the airport, and while Warren lined up to check in at the ticket
counter, I went to the telephone to speak with Pat to tell
her we were at the airport, that I'd eat something here,
never mind holding anything for me at Stamford. She said
she would record the seven o'clock news for me, but she
had forgotten: Is the videocassette antenna switch supposed to be *off* or *on* when one records?

George and I sat in the little pizza-type restaurant and
ordered for ourselves and for Warren, but before we were
served a flustered Warren came with the news that our
flight had been canceled. We held a quick summit, and the
three of us separated, Warren to see whether there were
means, via another city, to get another flight; George to

make local overnight hotel reservation in case all else failed; I to go through the Yellow Pages and look into the possibility of a charter. Warren doesn't like little planes, and lately I've agreed with Pat not to fly in planes that don't at least have two engines and are pressurized. Sometimes (as in the Grumman) I waive the latter provision, but not the former. It took me about twenty minutes to establish that it was not feasible, on such short notice, to arrange a charter at acceptable prices. It took about the same time for Warren to establish that there was no acceptable way of traveling commercial so as to get to New York tonight, and to make fresh arrangements for the morning—and George had us booked at the Executive West Motor Hotel near the airport.

I escorted my bags to my room, phoned Pat, and descended instantly to the dining room. It is quite unexpectedly posh, with a menu—including things like pheasant, snails, and pigeon—you'd expect at some of the Ritzes, or at Brideshead. Warren and I agree that it's always hell not to Get Back Home, but that if one absolutely *has* to be grounded, it is good to be grounded *after* the television shows have been recorded, when it is still *early* in the evening, when the next day is *Saturday*, and when you are booked on a nonstop the following morning. And so we whiled away an hour eating and drinking (not bourbon, though this I must surely do when I go to the Kentucky Derby).

I thought, on reaching my room just after nine merely to read; to leave alone my wretched briefcase. I'd already called Pat, and she has called Jerry to tell him what time tomorrow to meet me. I needn't use the telephone at all. I returned to *Gorky Park*, dazzled by the familiarity the author shows with life and habits in Moscow; but my mind wandered.

Exactly the same thing happened to me ten years ago; both were unprompted, although its having happened then makes less than unique its happening again now: I resolved here and now that I would experiment, once again, with a journal, a book-length work about the events of a single week as it unfolded. The present contract with my publisher called for me, during February and March, to bring together another collection, something I have been doing every three years now for nearly twenty years. I don't know why I have so little appetite for doing a new collection this year—there is plenty of material. The last time I did a collection (*A Hymnal: The Controversial Arts*) I logged, roughly, the time it took me to assemble it, and was disagreeably surprised to find that editing a collection requires more time than I spend writing a novel or (most of) my nonfiction books. It wasn't that I resented the time, or wished to abridge it; rather I had a strong feeling that *Cruising Speed*, which chronicled the events of the first week in December 1970, had in my judgment succeeded in exploring an unusual device for autobiographical revelation —easier to execute and, in some ways, potentially more revealing than the more comprehensive conventional treatments.

("Don't you think it a bit much to write an entire book devoted to the events of a single week?" the TV interviewer had asked when *Cruising Speed* was published, to which I replied, "I don't know. John Keats devoted an entire ode to a single Grecian urn." Funny.) But I remembered that ten years ago in my mind I fashioned right away a set of self-imposed rules. I must look, when I am back in Stamford, at *Cruising Speed* to see whether I remembered them exactly, but I think I do, think they were reasonable for that book, for this one, and for others that may come from other writers.

One such ground rule was that there was to be no coyness in the matter of who-do-you-know. For instance, it would after all have been unusual if I *hadn't* seen a great deal of Ronald Reagan over the years. When I first met him he was heading up Democrats-for-Nixon, but actually was heading up a movement that evolved as the practical political counterpart of *National Review*—nice zeugma, that. There must be no concealment of our friendship, yet no exaggeration of our political relationship. I have asked him less than a half-dozen favors in twenty years, and most of these had to do with *National Review*. (One not in this category was that he consent to be interviewed by Truman Capote on the subject of capital punishment; they became friends.) Two remain confidential. And he has asked my direct help, or advice, only two or three times. I realized that the only way to handle Reagan in the book is exactly as is relevant during events of the week in question.

A second rule: All correspondence mentioned must either have been seen, or replied to, during the week being written about. But where it clearly makes sense, flashbacks are okay. And finally, at a very important personal level, somewhere—right now, as a matter of fact—the point must be made that nothing can be deduced about people not mentioned, by the fact of mentioning those who are. My affection for and reliance on given human beings might be central to my life—and their names might not appear here, where anyone's appearance is circumstantial.

All of this went through my mind in less than five minutes, and I was pleased at having made a fruitful commitment. But I decided not to say anything to anyone about it, not for a while, as it's always possible I'd change my mind, though unlikely. I won't say anything even to Sam Vaughan of Doubleday, who is coming to lunch tomorrow. I went back to *Gorky Park*.

Six

SATURDAY

I ordered breakfast at 6:45 and it came at 7:25, as I was starting out the door. I gulped down a piece of toast, left the coffee, and went to the lobby, where Warren and George were waiting, and into the commutation bus to American Airlines, scene of so much commotion just twelve hours ago. Aboard the plane, George was squirreling away the two tapes of yesterday's shows, Warren was reading a big fat novel, I sat down with the Louisville paper and, before I was through with the first page, I fell asleep. We were almost at LaGuardia by the time I awoke.

It was cold and gray, and as we arrived in the baggage area the familiar face of Jerry wasn't there, and that was almost unprecedented. I went to the pay phone and dialed the car's telephone. The receiver at the other end was picked up and answered by an excited monosyllabic *Bukeeee*—Jill's name for me. That meant that Jerry was somewhere between the parking lot and where I am standing. It being a Saturday, he has riding with him his brain-damaged daughter Jill, age nineteen, who cannot verbalize, but who loves the company of her devoted father, and also loves Rowley. She is sitting in the car and has answered the telephone. Before I hung up, Jerry had materialized. We made the routine exchange: he gave me the keys to the car, and I gave him the checks to my bags. Carrying my typewriter and briefcase, I said goodbye to Warren and George and crossed the street to where the car was regularly parked.

I greeted Jill, who sometimes responds—always while looking out the window—inserted the ignition key and turned it on, which activated my telephone. I dialed Pat and she told me that David Niven was already there (he would stay the weekend), and to hurry home. Jerry came with my two bags and handed me a package of mail from Frances, and we headed for Stamford. I raised the glass partition, Jerry turned on the radio, and I my tape recorder.

A young lady who works in the White House news

summary room is doing a report on "*our* President's leadership style" and wants an interview with me. "My roommate works for Jim Wright (Dem.) and when she starts gloating sometimes (like when Robb won the election [as governor of Virginia]) I just start reading *National Review* and everything seems to get back to the proper perspective. . . ." I tell her to let me know when she's coming to town.

The next business was a little tricky, but everything is a little tricky when you are dealing with artists.

A few weeks ago I got the most awful news, from Tom Wendel in San José: that our friend Fernando Valenti had been told by the doctor that he had cancer, and that the affliction was terminal; indeed he had probably only six months to live, unless he consented to radiotherapy of some sort, in which case brief remission was possible, but not probable. I wrote instantly to Fernando, whose personal life has been very sad, and also passed the news along to a few friends. He and Rosalyn Tureck haven't been friends, exactly (it's "Dr. Tureck" and "Mr. Valenti"), but they respect each other.

Fernando has played the harpsichord at our annual staff Christmas party every year for seven or eight years, and it happened last year in December that Rosalyn was in New York. I airily asked her one day if she would like to come to the party and she said sure. A day or two later I mentioned this to Fernando, and he said honest injun, he would rather she *didn't* come, but that he didn't want to tell me the reason. *So*, rather apprehensively, I asked Frances to call Rosalyn's secretary and gently to disinvite her.

So why hadn't he wanted her there?

Six weeks later he wrote her a letter from California giving the reason. "Just a brief note of apology for something that has been crunching on my mind for several weeks! It

was indeed I who suggested to Bill Buckley that it might be more discreet *not* to invite you to our Christmas concert this past December 11. My thought was that, whereas Bill himself has unwaveringly exalted tastes in music and probably has a special record player piping the Goldbergs into his bathtub, the vast majority of the audience for these Christmas parties tends to feel seasonally festive and much more in the spirit of bourbon-and-soda than of Bach-and-Scarlatti. Of course, I have never been able to convince him of this, not in years and years. All six Partitas, forty-two Scarlattis, and the Chromatic Fantasia for an 'encore' are *still* his idea of the most jovial possible Christmas.

"As a means of partially getting my own way, I contrived to play some rather clever (not as 'clever' as they *could* have been, however) arrangements, by an old acquaintance of mine, of folkloric and semifolkloric tunes (mostly Irish) into the movements of a suite (*Allemande, Courante*, etc.). For some reason, having always heard *you* at your best, I harbored the notion that such outright horseplay would be somewhat beneath you and I would rather have had you present when I was really going to tear into something. Later on, the implication of a total lack of sense of humor on your part struck me as unfounded and unchivalrous."

The ending of the letter was as rococo as anything ever executed by Scarlatti: "Accordingly, I am writing you this note of apology. Please believe that it is I who have been the loser. By a misguided thought I deprived myself of the honor of your presence at our little concert, as well as the pleasure of seeing you again after so many years."

Now on receiving this, Rosalyn wrote to thank Fernando for his "charming" note of apology. But, she said, what's this all about her not having a sense of humor? She didn't get that *at all*. "Therefore, it is beyond my imagination to guess what has led you to your comment, and would appreciate an explanation."

In due course I saw Fernando out in California, and he mentioned to me that Rosalyn was "mad" at him, but that was life. I thought no more about it. But when I told Rosalyn about Fernando's illness, she told me she would write to him immediately, even though he had written her a *very* unpleasant letter after his Christmas concert. Now Rosalyn, I said, I am *quite certain* that Fernando would *not* have written you a *very unpleasant* letter. Absolutely positive.

So now Rosalyn writes, "I enclose copies of a couple of letters that may interest you. These form the reason for my comment . . . to you about Valenti." And she adds, "My heart goes out to him. I hesitate even to ask how he is, because I fear so negative a reply. However, I hope he is not suffering."

So now I undertake to heal the breach and dictate: "Dear Rosalyn: I think it clear that you simply misunderstood Fernando's letter. What he intended was to communicate that he at first thought you might be embarrassed by one or two liberties he proposed to take in giving the staff a little horseplay on the harpsichord. On reflection he recognized that you would have entered into the spirit of the season and forgiven the levity. I thought the letter a tribute to the respect he feels for you. But enough of that. . . ."

I tell you . . . After some experience, I think it's a good idea not to invite one artist to an event featuring another artist, at least not one held at home. It is simply embarrassing to elaborate on why this is so. So just take it from me.

Senator Orrin Hatch wants to know whether I will write a column about his Community Home Health Services Act. "By the turn of the year 2000, the number of Americans sixty-five years and older will have increased by thirty-five percent." The problem of the aged simply hasn't been corporately addressed.

In a book (*Four Reforms*, 1973) I proposed that all young people graduating from high school be encouraged to give a year's time to helping to care for the aged. The libertarian enzymes in me caused me to recommend that the custom be gradually institutionalized by the straightforward device of having leading private colleges refuse to accept entrance applications to freshman year except from students who had done one year's social work. I'm told the idea was actually taken up (however briefly) by the authorities at Harvard, but sank. To launch it, you would need four or five of the most desirable—or, more accurately, most desired—colleges to act together on the idea, so that the isolated college taking the initiative wouldn't simply lose out to the competition. If Harvard, Yale, Princeton, Columbia, Cornell, Brown, and Dartmouth were to issue such a declaration, effective say for the freshman class of 1985, the idea would get off the ground. . . . I promised Orrin Hatch to do the column.

Gertrude Vogt, who was my secretary forever until Frances came (1968), and to whom I dedicated *Cruising Speed*, writes from San Francisco, where we recently visited. She complains that the New York *Times* arrives irregularly, and I urge her to complain directly to New York, as they are very good in these matters, no doubt animated by the sincere conviction that people who don't get the *Times* regularly simply don't function very well. It is a matter of patriotism, really, isn't it?

A youngish man who wants to join the Council on Foreign Relations has one of those nice-type problems. You see, his roommate at Yale was *the current president of the Council on Foreign Relations*. But ever since Watergate and Abscam, things like this have to be handled with the *utmost* delicacy and regard for punctilio. So he makes an appointment to meet me, so that I can size him up, so that I can, after talking to him for twenty minutes, write a letter to the membership committee, which is, in effect, run by the president, so that I can inform the president of the Council on Foreign Relations what his ex-roommate is like. But I do the whole performance without cracking a smile, even though the president of the CFR is one of the most amusing, and easily amused, persons in the world. I manage to chronicle in my recommendation that "an index of [the candidate's] lovable perversity is that on leaving New Haven he turned right, rather than left." I think he'll be all right.

I tell a nice man in Fort Lauderdale who wants me to put out a collection of my journalism that in fact I have put out a lot of collections.

The chairman of the Board of Trustees of the Associates of the Yale Medical Library writes a charming letter asking me to be the speaker at their annual function. "Unfortunately, our purse is small and the honorarium consists of only one hundred dollars and carfare." I was reminded of my friend Erik von Kuehnelt-Leddihn, the hardest-working man I have ever met, who has struggled all his life with poverty while writing, lecturing, translating, in a dozen languages. Ten years ago he was asked by the Harvard International Relations Council could he please give an address to some large assembly at Cambridge, which he managed to do by taking a 3 P.M. plane from Chicago, and a midnight plane back to Chicago to meet his morning engagement. A few weeks later he received a check for twenty-five dollars. "So, I returned it, wiss a leetle noht. I said: Eef thiss iss intended ass a fee, it ees not enough. Eef thiss iss intended ass a teep, I do not take teeps." That sounds snotty, and I think I make it plain to the good doctor that my obligations to *National Review*, with its annual loss in the several-hundred-thousand-dollar range, require me to give priority to commercial dates; all of this I explain as courteously (and factually) as possible. But I should have leveled with the doc and suggested that he do away with the hundred-dollar business, and merely stress the honor of it all. It would be wonderful to be able to speak only to those assemblies that, for whatever reason, particularly appeal. And, preferably, to audiences of one hundred or fewer.

We are all familiar with the saw about the criminal evidence seminar in law school where suddenly someone enters with a popgun, fires it at a startled student in the front row, and bolts out the window; after which the professor asks the class to set down a record of what happened, what the fellow looked like, where he came in from, where he went out, etc. The fun comes in reading out loud the papers, which tend to disagree on almost all particulars. A lady writes that she is outraged because of the "exchange of sick humor" between me and the person I was speaking to on "Firing Line." "[You] intimated that perhaps it was not such a bad thing to be disabled because of all the benefits which would accrue from the federal government. I recently became disabled because of multiple sclerosis and have great difficulty walking a short distance. I can assure [you] that money does not help the agony of disability. I was deeply offended by [your] cruel and stupid exchange." In such matters there is no need even to go and look at the transcript. Some things you know simply *cannot* be, and this is one of them; so I write: "I cannot imagine my saying anything that *suggested* that people gladly become handicapped. You must have misunderstood me," and console myself by thinking of the law professor's experiment.

The current issue of the *Authors Guild Bulletin* reveals that its editor, Stuart W. Little, is resigning. I met him first when my brother Jim brought him down from Yale, as the imposing chairman of the *Yale Daily News*, in, oh, 1940, when I was fourteen. He has been the compleat writer: drama critic, book reviewer, speechwriter, editorial writer, biographer. And his son Christopher, a gifted professional photographer and human being, came with me on a trip across the Atlantic on a sailboat, a venture chronicled by me, with photographs by Christopher, in my last book, *Atlantic High*. I write Stu, who has not disclosed his plans, wishing him well.

A friend with contacts within the academic community of the University of South Carolina asks whether, in the event the invitation should be forthcoming, I would accept an invitation to be the commencement speaker, and receive an honorary degree? Oh dear.

In the past I have generally said yes to such invitations, but experiences a year ago at Vassar and this year at William & Mary have rather thoroughly affected my attitude.

I was invited in March to deliver the commencement address at Vassar; I accepted (my wife and a sister were at Vassar), and many weeks later saw for the first time issues of the Vassar newspaper. After a few telephone calls with the president of Vassar, I made my decision and wrote to her a letter I gave to the New York *Times*, parts of which received considerable publicity.

"The majority of the senior class of Vassar [this I learned from the Vassar paper—53 percent of the senior class asked that the invitation to me be withdrawn] does not desire my company, and I must confess, having read specimens of their thought and sentiments, that I do not desire the company of the majority of the senior class of Vassar. Really, they appear to be a fearfully ill-instructed body, to judge from the dismayingly uninformed opinions expressed in their newspaper, which opinions reflect an academic and cultural training very nearly unique—at least, in my experience. I have spoken, I suppose, at five hundred colleges and universities in the past thirty years, and nowhere have I encountered that blend of ferocious illiteracy achieved by the young men and women of Vassar who say they speak for the majority of the graduating class and, to some extent, say so plausibly by adducing the signatures of the majority of that class in their recall petition. One professor of English writes to the newspaper, 'It was Buckley who offered pridefully in those days the caste of mind and insinuating attitudes toward academic which intellectually veneered the crudities of Joe McCarthy, and in so doing, fueled McCarthyism at its most virulent pitch with respect to the academic community.' That the man who composed that sentence should be teaching English at Vassar rather than studying it suggests that Vassar has much, much deeper problems than coming up with a suitable commencement speaker."

At William & Mary earlier this year no recall petition had been circulated, but protests were vehement, occupying most of several issues of the student newspaper, and there were threats of protests during the ceremony. I thought of simply pulling out, which Pat wanted me to do, but decided finally to go ahead, and see what happened. However, I resolved also both to seduce and challenge the graduating class. I asked Tom Wendel, who is a professor of colonial history at San José State University and one of my oldest and closest friends, if he would collect for me some anecdotes involving William & Mary, which he did, around which I constructed an introduction calculated to immobilize active protest, without committing sycophancy. . . .

Mr. President, ladies and gentlemen of the graduating class:

A couple of weeks ago I was talking to the Prince of Wales [Message: I manage to get around even without William & Mary], who earlier that day had received the hospitality of this institution [Message: W&M knows how to be hospitable—e.g., to British royalty], which he characterized as quite wonderful [Message: obvious].

I suggested to him that the geographical location of William & Mary symbolized the realization of the perfectly appropriate relationship between the American people and a British monarch. Williamsburg, after all, is equidistant from Jamestown—the point at which the British elected to establish a North American Empire—and Yorktown, the point at which the North American Empire made conclusively clear to the British that they had gone too far [Message: there is such a thing as going too far].

At Williamsburg a fortnight ago history suggested that the proper relationship between America and Great Britain is halfway between servility and hostility. Friendship and courtesy among equals [Message: I extend the metaphor of how behavior should be governed].

Besides, William & Mary's charter should have prewarned his Royal Highness that he would be well treated. Your charter speaks of founding a college "to the end that the church of Virginia may be furnished with a seminary of ministers of the gospel and that the youth may be piously educated in good letters and manners" [There, my message is now plainspoken]. We all realize that any attempt to teach virtue has got, in this imperfect world, to be asymptotic: one never quite achieves the goal. And by no means is this always the fault of students. Professor Edmund Morgan [of Yale; who would also receive an honorary degree], in whose company I am honored to find myself [my near embarrassment was hilarious. I had taken Wendel's quotation attributed to Edmund Morgan as the work of an eighteenth-century American historian, and had so written him into my speech. When I found myself, at dinner the evening before, seated next to Edmund Morgan I had to search out and destroy the first page of three copies of my address, thoughtfully handed out earlier that afternoon], recorded in his classic *Virginians at Home* the commentaries of a shrewd observer during the last decades of the colonial period, namely that he had known "the professors [of William & Mary] to play all night at cards in public houses in the city and often seen them drunk in the streets" [Message: my compliments on the one hand to those faculty members who had also written in to protest my appearance; and a reminder to the students that I know that their elders can also misbehave].

But Williamsburg was to go through a great deal, particularly during the Revolutionary War and immediately after it. Bishop Asbury, the great circuit rider, noted in his journal on December 11, 1782, "I rode to Williamsburg, formerly the seat of government, but now removed to Richmond. Thus the worldly glory is departed from it. As to divine glory, it never had any. The place has suffered and is suffering: the palace, the barracks, and some good dwelling houses burned. The capitol is no great building and is growing to ruin. The exterior of the college not splendid; and but few students. The bedlam house is desolate, but whether none are insane or all equally mad, it might perhaps be difficult to tell" [Message: W&M has had a, well, interesting history, in which other evils have figured than miscast commencement speakers].

All institutions have high and low days. So is it with commencement speakers. What should our posture be? Surely, also, somewhere between servility and hostility [Message: I intend to be friendly and courteous, but that's it]. What rule should govern their attitude toward honorary degrees? [Message: this is for those of you who wrote in to the paper suggesting that I be okayed as a commencement speaker, but that the offer of an honorary degree should be withdrawn.] A pragmatic one, surely. Nicely expressed by Professor John Kenneth Galbraith, who told me that his policy with respect to honorary degrees was to have one more than Arthur Schlesinger. My policy in commencement addresses is straightforward, namely not to let words come from my mouth which I would be embarrassed to utter before my colleagues at *National Review*, who are my chosen colleagues [Message: I'm not going to depart from my chosen positions . . .]. Because, of course, to do otherwise would be to beguile and cheat the student body, which it would be infamous to do on the day you complete your formal education and matriculate into extra-academic life [. . . and you shouldn't want me to]. It is also important, I think, to acknowledge that there is no law that says that commencement speakers are any better, or any worse—that they utter nobler, or less noble thoughts—than student speakers. I remember about ten years ago serving as commencement speaker at Gettysburg College. The student speaker who preceded me arrived at the lectern with two differently pitched saxophones strapped around his neck. He spoke about the complicated interrelationships between truth, justice, peace, beauty, and love. Each time he completed one of his dozen formulations, he would put one or the other saxophone to his lips, striking a single note which he understood to be the musical equivalent of the harmonious interrelationship he had verbally constructed. His exegesis lasted forty minutes [Message: students can also be boring, and obnoxious]. That evening, short on cosmic material, I wrote a newspaper column describing the tortured afternoon. Three days later I received an indignant letter from the president of the graduating class advising me that in *his* opinion my own address had been no great shakes. Allowing me to make the obvious reply —namely, that I was hardly surprised, since after all

Gettysburg owed its reputation substantially to its historical underestimation of great orations. I note from the *William & Mary Quarterly* a dispatch published in August of 1798 as follows: "Our noble President was burned in effigy in Williamsburg on the fourth of July by the students of William & Mary College." The President in question was, of course, John Adams. At any rate, if you proceed to burn me in effigy after I am done, you will demonstrate that I and John Adams have yet one *more* thing in common.

Well, it worked. The audience was calm, and appreciative. But what a lot of *work*. Pat Moynihan, who that same year had had an experience at the University of Pennsylvania equivalent to mine at Vassar, called me up when he read about my withdrawal to say grouchily, "Do those little bastards [the demonstrators] think we have nothing else to *do* with our Sunday afternoons?"

I write my friend that I will need to know that the invitation incorporates accepted procedures of student democracy at the University of South Carolina. Hell, it's their commencement.

We have pulled into my driveway, the weeping willow trees on my right, the scrubby little apple trees on my left, and Jerry stops, as ever, opposite the garage study, which is where I leave my papers. He then drives on to the main house with the bags, and I walk there. As I climbed the stone steps the sea became fully visible, looking gray and gusty. Burlap bags cover Pat's huge pots and the plants they harbor. I opened the main door and felt the warmth of the heating and of my home, and David Niven bounded over and we embraced, French-style, and gabbled on as we walked into the sunroom.

Though the talk is full of levity, all is not well. David was last here three weekends ago. He had set out the following Monday on a pretty grueling ten-day trip to promote his novel *Go Slowly, Come Back Quickly*, just published by Doubleday, already a best-seller in England and destined for best-sellerdom in the United States. I had noticed then that he wasn't in full control of his speaking voice. Saturday night we showed him the tape made the preceding spring when he appeared as master of ceremonies at the fine two-hour Hollywood tribute to Fred Astaire. We had seen him in Switzerland before and after the Astaire business, and he had told us he had had a most fearful time controlling his voice, so much so that at one point he was not sure he would be able to go on. So we listened intently as we viewed the videocassette, in David's company (he had never seen it), and although he did sound a little laryngitic, the problem was not distracting to the viewer. But three weekends ago he'd had clear difficulty in enunciation, and was so worried about it that he reduced his liquor consumption from his normal three glasses of wine per day to a single glass; this, though, had made no difference. He had told Pat and me that the doctor in London had deduced that it was a plain matter of physical fatigue (he had been working very long hours on a movie) and that after the lecture tour was over he was heading for Acapulco and there, as a guest of Loel Guinness for ten days, he expected to recuperate fully. So now I listened to him attentively as he described his travails on the promotion circuit, to see whether in fact he had licked the problem. He hadn't; and soon we were speaking about that frankly, and inquisitively; such an exchange as is possible between close friends.

At that moment the bell rang, and Sam and Jo Vaughan came in. Sam is incapable of arriving anywhere without great parcels of gifts, which he now distributed, including the first copy of my new novel, *Marco Polo, If You Can*. Pat had come down, and in the bustle we managed to hang the coats, and the lot of us went back, through the living room, to the sunroom. Sam is David's publisher as well as my own and, a description I used once in *Cruising Speed* about another friend, quite simply a bird of paradise. It is not known how anyone can manage to be as attentive as Sam is to his friends and authors, and not infrequently one qualifies as both. His notes are bright, cheerful, witty, inventive. He is, for his authors, a *presence*. There is nothing more important to an author; and David, who went from another publishing house to Doubleday in part on the strength of the liking he took to Sam, agrees. David hadn't before met Jo, petite, pretty, bright, easily amused, attentive in just that winning way that permits nuanced conversation. She has been suffering from a bad back. I have chronic sinusitis, Dupuytren's contracture, and skin cancer, so I suggested that we devote three minutes to our several physical complaints, and then shift to sublime subjects, like David's and my books. Pat celebrated this by distributing bloody marys, which she makes with one-half bloody mary mix, one-half beef broth (necessarily Campbell's beef broth, even when Jack Heinz is being served). And at just that moment Van Galbraith comes in, apologizing that wife Bootsie can't come. Van and David and I have experienced years of each other's company in the Gstaad area, to which Van began bringing his family for skiing vacations over ten years ago, and so it is in the nature of a reunion. The company was already hearty, but the supplement of Van Galbraith raised it very nearly to the level of hilarity, and the conversation bubbled along.

Van leaves tomorrow for Paris, where he will be the freshly invested United States ambassador. Three weeks ago he paid me a nice compliment and his expression of the favor was conveyed with marvelous obliqueness. He told me that the swearing-in ceremony at the State Department had now been fixed for November 13, that about one hundred friends and family were coming in for it, that the ceremony would take place in "one of those ornate places over there," that the procedure was that Bill Clark, Deputy Secretary of State, would preside (Al Haig would be out of town); Lee Annenberg, the chief of protocol, would administer the oath. "Then there's a speech given about me, a personal speech, and I wonder if you'd give it, although don't go out of your way, maybe the date's no good." I checked and it was okay. Ten minutes on Van Galbraith . . .

A year ago I had sat through the three and one-half hours of raw film taken by Mark Dichter and his assistant, who had accompanied Van and me and four other friends on a sailboat. We sailed from the Virgin Islands to Bermuda, and then on to the Azores, and to Spain. But the cinematographers were with us only on the first leg (the idea was to produce a documentary). I dimly remembered that two or three minutes of the two hundred I had seen depicted Van in an argumentative mood with Dick Clurman on the matter of working for the government, Van going on about the sheer futility of the exercise. So I called Mark. Mark, would you do me a *great* favor . . .

It took a great deal of arranging, and the State Department people were at first a little sluggish, but soon got into the spirit of the thing. Unknown to any of the fifty-odd government officials and hundred-odd guests of Van, when they promenaded into the elegant Franklin Room, was that a huge television screen had been hidden behind an oriental screen in the corner of the large room. Hidden also was a television videocassette player into which the three minutes of incriminating film had been inserted. So that when the signal was given by me from the lectern, the

lights would suddenly dim and the crowd, standing, would hear Van's voice, turn around, and see him sitting, dressed in shorts and polo shirt, in the cockpit of a sailboat, barreling over the Atlantic Ocean, and giving his views of government service in language appropriately salty. Oh, the thought of it that day was almost too wonderful to endure. When I arrived at the State Department, Van greeted me, while his aide, in on the plot, winked, which meant everything was going well; and we went and chatted with Bill Clark for a few minutes until the ceremony was scheduled to begin.

It was all very solemn, and before my eyes my old friend suddenly became, by act of Congress and of the President of the United States, ambassador to France, successor to Benjamin Franklin. I was then introduced for the traditional personal tribute . . .

Secretary Clark, Jim [brother James, Under Secretary], Ambassador Galbraith, ladies and gentlemen.

It is characteristic of the personal courage of Ambassador Galbraith that he should have deputized me to speak on this solemn occasion. Courageous because I have known him for many years, and very well.

But then I have been told that the ceremony here today, to the extent that I figure in it, is *intended* to be highly personal. This was said to me by no fewer than three State Department officials, from which I deduce that there was some active concern in these parts that I might take the occasion to recite my *Weltanschauung*. To do so would be in the tradition of those journalists who do not report events without giving historical background. We recall that the lead sentence in the London *Times* announcing the declaration of war against the Kaiser began: "Back in 1870 . . ."

Well, if it is to be personal history, so be it.

Back in 1947, it happened that I won the only election I ever won. I remember having called my brother Jim, at the time a student at the Yale Law School, while I was a freshman in the undergraduate school. I had expected that the voting for the chairmanship of the *Yale Daily News*, which election was traditionally carried out one year before assumption of office, would be close. Since Jim had been an officer of the newspaper, I asked him whether it would be ethical for me to vote—in the unsigned ballot we each would insert into the basket —for myself. Jim, then as now, believed in deliberation; but told me that Yes, he thought this could be done discreetly, and in good conscience. And so the following day I folded the piece of paper with my own name written on it and dropped it in with the other twenty or thirty. A few minutes later the incumbent chairman emerged, and announced that I had been elected the chairman of the *Yale Daily News* for 1948. He paused dramatically and smiled, adding, "I am pleased to report that Bill was elected unanimously."

We moved, a few of us, from that chamber to the nearest watering hole, which was Deke fraternity house, and there a blond, heavyset fellow sophomore accosted me to ask, with what I came to know as characteristic curiosity and ebullience, just what was the hilarity all about? It is something of a poetical miracle that exactly thirty-five years later, I should be involved in a situation that calls for at least as much hilarity. The similarities are almost perfect. It is rumored that Van voted for himself. And the President has told me that the vote for Van was unanimous.

I have not confided to the President, or to Secretary Clark, or to anybody, I guess, my special knowledge of the general and orderly deliberation given by Van Galbraith to the hypothetical possibility of joining the government.

It happens that in June a year and a half ago, when the President was still only a candidate for the Republican nomination, Van and I were together, as I am happy to say we have often been, on a sailboat. I have in mind a conversation we had about two hundred miles south of Bermuda, heading first for that island, then on to the Azores, then to Spain. There were six of us doing the sailing and the navigating. The day was blue, the wind brisk; we were an entire happy day removed from a sloppy and emetic little storm that had dogged us for forty-eight hours. As we were eating lunch, one of our company, Dick Clurman—former head of correspondents for Time-Life, and former Commissioner of Parks and Cultural Affairs in New York City—was arguing the nobility and inspiration of public service. As I remember I was somewhat skeptical, adhering to a rather dogmatic position that there was a deep and instinctive antagonism between service in the private and in the public sectors. Van, if I remember, joined in expressing skepticism of a sort, reminiscing briefly about his single experience in public service, as aide to a Secretary of Commerce in the Eisenhower administration. If memory serves, the conversation was not extended, lasting only for three or four minutes, but the banter did indicate something of the mood of the freshly installed Ambassador to France, back in the long ago, when there was another President in the White House, and when the only immediate problem Van Galbraith faced was whether the navigator would succeed in guiding the boat to Bermuda. . . .

[At this point the videotaped section came on the screen. It showed the ketch in full sail, Clurman and Galbraith heatedly arguing in the cockpit, Galbraith insisting that working for the government was generally pointless. He recalled his own experience as a legal aide to the Secretary of Commerce under the Eisenhower administration. The last words the audience heard him utter were: "Don't you understand, Dick, most of the people in Washington are *assholes*." The crowd roared, the screen went blank. . . .]

For the first years of their marriage, Van and Bootsie lived in Paris. They came back, briefly, to America for a year in New York, after which they were gone again, this time to London, where for a number of years he pursued his professional career [as a banker-lawyer], traveling frequently to New York and spending his vacation periods for the most part in Switzerland, where on his first visit I took him skiing for the first time. As I think back on it, if I were to add the distances we have sailed together to the distances we have skied together, it is probably safe to say we have, by wind and gravity, circled the globe.

It was at law school at Harvard that Van first interested himself in the politics that make the world go round, so very eccentrically. Soon he became conversant with the principal engines of political behavior, and with those forces that have pockmarked this century. I remember once, in 1957, when we found ourselves in Baltimore to serve as ushers at the wedding of a friend, and in the morning I thought impulsively to visit Whittaker Chambers in Westminster, one hour away. One would not take just anyone to that reclusive eyrie in western Maryland, but I took Van there with full confidence, and we stayed two hours. A few days later I had a letter from Chambers. He began it, "I liked Galbraith at sight. This happens so seldom with me that I wondered why it happened. As I listened to him laugh, watched him study the titles of my books, watched his mind fasten on one or two points of no great importance in themselves, but somewhat as an ant, at touch, clamps on the rib of a leaf that may be littering its path, I liked him better. I decided that what I liked was a kind of energy, what kind scarcely mattered. One of our generals was once being ho-ho-hearty with the ranks, as I understand generals are sometimes, especially if newsmen are present. He asked a paratrooper, 'Why do you like to do an insane thing like jumping out of airplanes?' The paratrooper answered: 'I don't like to, sir, I just like to be around the kind of people who like to jump out of airplanes.' I felt something like the paratrooper about Galbraith. . . ."

His friends, for whom I speak, would agree that his qualities are special. Everyone who has known him is more cheerful for the experience of having known him. The French will find him, in his official capacity, in no sense different from how they found him in private life fifteen years ago. He is hospitable to every kind of ambiguity, charitable in his constructions of human behavior, but entirely convinced that the Lord has provided man with a fundamental apparatus by which we distinguish between what is right and what isn't; and convinced that the challenge to right thought and right conduct was never in history more menacingly threatened. I can imagine no presence in Paris more distinctively American than Van's, because jaded and worldly men will see in him the storybook American, the man of spontaneity and steadfastness, of innocence and wit, of flexibility and purpose. It may seem somehow wrong, in these circumstances, to congratulate the French people, but exactly that far I am prepared to go, confident as all of us who have known him over the years are, as also those of you in government who have known him over the years or have come recently to know him—Al Haig, Bill Clark, Bill Draper, Tom Clausen, Tom Enders, Jim Buckley, Jack Maresco, my son Christopher—that his presence as his country's ambassador will inform and refresh, yet another installment in the apparently endless repayment of the debt we incurred when, as a young and struggling republic, we welcomed the arrival of Lafayette. I join you all in wishing him and Bootsie a great and fruitful adventure, in the service of our beloved country.

I hadn't seen Van since the swearing-in, which he now described to everyone at lunch in hilarious detail, and I told the guests that I had the videocassette at hand, so we trooped into my music room that looks out over the sea, drew the curtains, placed the big television screen up, and ran Ambassador Galbraith's Atlantic Charter. That reminded David of a story in which *he* was caught up in mad social embarrassment, but he said Pat and I had heard it, but I made him tell it, and his old vocal powers came through.

It was a couple of years ago, and the dozen tables, at one of those palaces around Buckingham, were set for six people each, and David found himself seated opposite the Queen of England, and on the Queen's right an elderly duke-type, full of whiskers, who approached David most affably while the Queen was in animated conversation with the man on her left. The duke said to David, "I say, Niven, have you seen Tommy Phipps in New York lately?"

"Well yes," said David.

"How is he?"

"Well, I saw him just a week ago, and I said, 'Tommy, how are you?' And he said, 'Well, I fall down a lot, and cry a lot, but otherwise I'm fine!'" The duke roared.

At which point the Queen suddenly turned and said, "What was that, Mr. Niven?"

Well, David said, there was no *way* such a story could be repeated and made to sound funny, but neither was there any way to deny the Queen's request, so he had said, "Well, ma'am, there's this man in New York, a friend of uh"—but David hadn't of course caught the duke's name, so he nodded with a bright smile—"a friend of some of us over here, and he said to me"—David said he was growing more and more desperate in the foreknowledge of the absolutely certain failure of his story—"and he said to me"—David's voice here trails off slightly—"that he feels fine except he falls down a lot and cries a lot."

"Oh dear!" said the Queen. "Poor man!"

But, said David—and now he stands up. He usually does, from sheer excitement, when he really gets going—the duke then said, "Ah, Niven, it's been a long, *long* time." And, not having any idea who he was, David could only

say, "Yes, it's been a long, *long* time!" And then he said,
"But it was a *memorable* day, Niven, a memorable day."
"Yes," David had said in desperation, "it was *certainly* a
memorable day!" Whereupon the duke said, "I know we
haven't seen much of each other in recent years, Niven,
but I *always* tell my friends I was very proud that you
served as best man at my wedding."

It was all great fun, and we went in to eat one of Pat's
incomparable meals, with Julian (whom Pat met, years ago,
as the chef on the boat in the south of France that David
and Hjordis Niven had chartered) introducing something
(I forget what) brand-new as dessert. We went into the
living room for coffee, and Gloria told me that "el señor
Valenti" was on the line.

I hadn't talked to Fernando since getting his news and I
dreaded this conversation, though Tom Wendel had informed me that Fernando had finally agreed to submit to
the radiotherapy and that the neck tumor—though not the
primary tumor, which they hadn't succeeded in locating—
was responding. We spoke in Spanish for a while, as over
the years we have got into the habit of doing (Fernando's
father was Spanish—the doctor to the King of Spain). Fernando has a way of inducing great melancholy by ostenta-
tious levity. But he told me he had decided to spend Christmas in New York, the doctors willing, and that they would
give him their decision the following week. I told him I'd
have his plane met, and Jerry would take him to Barbara's
apartment (Barbara, Fernando's former wife, was ill in
southern California, and had turned over her apartment
to him). Fernando asked what was I doing this year about
a Christmas concert? I told him that I had assumed right
along that he would not be in New York, and that even if
he was, he would not (I must get just the right word here)
"feel" like playing. But I hadn't wanted to engage another

harpsichordist (Judith Norell, also a fan of Fernando, sweetly volunteered) on the grounds that it would sound too much like king-is-dead-long-live-the-king, so I had arranged, via Michael Sweeley who runs Caramoor, the great summer music festival at Katonah, New York, to bring in a choral group. Fernando said he thought that was fine, and anyway he wouldn't be reaching New York until five days after the scheduled concert. I told him I'd continue to pray for his recovery, and went back to the living room.

The weather had suddenly turned bright, and I asked if anyone wanted to walk. Van said he had to go home and attend to last-minute business. He and David arranged to disport in Switzerland in December, as Van would continue the skiing vacations with the children in Gstaad (he had solemnly explored the question whether the French would resent his going to a Swiss resort).

Sam and David and Jo were dressed in overcoats, I handed around walking sticks, and as we set out I thought, Why not take them and show them my new boat? We could then take our walk around Yacht Haven. They thought this a capital idea, so we got into the Volvo and five minutes later stopped outside the pier, one of thirty or forty, where my little (36-foot) sloop was squatting, along with three or four others whose owners had decided, as I had, to winter in the water.

It was very cold, but the sun had come out, and as I stepped into the cockpit and diddled with the combination lock I got a second capital idea. I said, Hey, let's take a ten-minute cruise! They said fine, though I think I detected just a trace of hesitation in Sam, but taxing him on this a few minutes later, he countered by saying that he was trying to reflect on whether Doubleday's insurance policy permitted the publisher and two authors to go out in the same hull.

In a minute the little diesel was purring, the dock lines were released, and then with David handling the bow line and Sam the stern line, off we went. At first I hadn't thought to raise the sail, but I decided I'd show them, as we headed south toward the harbor entrance, with the strong wind coming in from the west, how wonderfully easy it was to handle the genoa with the roller furling device. So I turned the wheel over to David, got the winch handle, and lo and behold the genoa was out, and we were bouncing along at six and a half knots. Oh how exhilarating the sailboat is! I thought about the mainsail, decided against raising it. A practical problem was that the temperature was so cold, one's hands had to be stuffed into one's pockets every minute or so. Poor Jo looked frostbitten. Without just a little crew drill, better stick to the genoa.

So we raced out, about a mile and a half, just outside the harbor, and they marveled at the seakindliness of the vessel, which seemed to iceskate over the waves. Then we turned around, and headed back, and en route I gave excruciatingly detailed instructions on how to effect a landing. And there was never a prettier one than this, as the boat came to a dead stop just by its pier and was promptly snubbed down at either end by David and Sam. I told them that the very next time I sailed to Spain, I'd take them along. We walked back to the car, and of course Pat was furious on learning that we had been out sailing, declaiming at vigorous length that obviously Sam shouldn't be head of Doubleday Publishing if he permitted his *most valuable asset*, David, to go out in midwinter with the madman she was married to. All this was great fun, but Sam and Jo had to drive back to New Jersey, so regretfully we saw them off. David said he would take a little nap, and I got into the car and drove to the Radio Shack a mile or so down the line, because I need to have a present for James Burnham's birthday party tomorrow, and it occurred to me that perhaps a few of those television games would entertain him. He has always liked games, and with that mind of his, which framed *The Managerial Revolution* and *Suicide of the West*, good as ever in brief moments but, since the stroke, incapable of retention, perhaps engagements on the television screen—some solitaire, some he might play with his wife Marcia—might be just the thing. I scooped up a few and drove back. It was dark now, and I parked opposite the study and groped my way in. I turned on the light and checked the temperature—forty-five degrees, so I turned on both the gas heater and the electric heater, and in ten minutes it was sixty-five and I had an hour in which to go back to the mail.

Sophie Wilkins, my beloved friend, scholar, translator, writes the most complex, ornate, profound, erudite letters I regularly get, and it is always a little dismaying when I answer them because there is never the time, and often not the resources, to do them justice. Today she comments on an essay Jeff Hart has published in *National Review* in which he gives an account of hearing four poets while studying and teaching at Columbia: Dylan Thomas, W. H. Auden, Robert Frost, and T. S. Eliot. Her own memory of Eliot's performance (she was then departmental secretary for the English Department) was sharply different from Jeff's. "The 'show,'" she wrote, "was so dramatically the exact opposite of the Dylan Thomas event, somebody should really make a movie on the basis of my description: the Great Dead Poet, looking totally mummified—well, he was [now] happily married and had gained weight, as Jeffrey Hart says. He looked like a well-upholstered package—flanked by *two* undertakers in dress uniform (penguins): Jacques Barzun to the right of him, Lionel Trilling to the left of him. I didn't even hear the introduction, it was given in such hushed tones, appropriate to the funereal occasion. Then the GDP at last was stood up behind the lectern and proceeded to read, indeed, indeed, work that had been the great excitement of myself and schoolmates in high school, a quarter of a century ago! 'April is the cruellest month . . .' Yes, to be sure, but the way it came across was that he was basing his appearance solidly on the past. Normally a poet gives you a little work-in-progress, something you haven't seen yet that he needs to try out on a live audience in a live voice—and he reeled it off in the spirit of those ancient, scratchy, flawed Caruso records: mechanically, with the whole afflatus of infinite boredom he was entitled to feel at such reiteration of what had once been a bombshell. Not one living word came out of him, in that dead voice (the poet was dead, the man had probably never been so happy, and I did not begrudge him that; he had certainly earned it). But to read Jeffrey Hart's pious conclusion, 'Eliot *was* the West that night.' Yes indeedy, but if so, he was burying us more effectively than Khrushchev ever could, burying us from the Inside, beginning with himself. Just thought you ought to know."

Sophie then harked back to Edgar Smith. She is grateful that Warren Steibel does not intend to portray her. He is planning a movie based on the killer who had persuaded WFB of his innocence—who in turn mobilized rescue missions—which in turn got the conviction upset—which in turn got Edgar out of jail on a second-degree plea—who in turn five years down the road tried to kill another woman, was caught (WFB turned him in), tried, at which trial he confessed his guilt of the first crime, convicted, and sentenced. Sophie had befriended Edgar during his long spell in the New Jersey Death House and had edited his extraordinarily successful autobiography, *Brief Against Death*. The whole business got fresh publicity when, shortly after

Abbott's release, which had been effected by Norman Mailer, Jack Henry Abbott resumed killing. The theme played was that writers tend to exhibit a weakness for killers. There was Norman Mailer, sponsoring Jack Henry Abbott. William Styron had had a similar experience, as had William Buckley with Edgar Smith. A critical distinction is finessed here: I thought Smith innocent, Mailer knew Abbott to be guilty—indeed, Abbott never said he was not.

Anyway, Warren has assured Sophie she need not be portrayed in the movie. I write: "Dearest Sophie: I for one am glad to coexist [with you]. But then many of such matters as you raise I have never given conscious thought to, and of course I'm not so sure whether that is good or bad. Your wonderful recollection of Eliot and of Thomas elated me, but I don't think I'll pass it along to Jeff, for the obvious reason. As for Edgar's situation, I am happy you are reassured by your meeting with Warren. Occasionally he talks to me about the film, but by no means systematically. It occurs to me suddenly that somebody has got to play me. I hope he will find someone who looks very innocent. . . . All love."

David Belin was the principal staff lawyer during the Warren investigation of the Kennedy assassination, and was chief counsel for the committee, headed by then Vice-President Nelson Rockefeller, looking into the CIA. He wrote what was taken to be the definitive book on the assassination (*November 22, 1963: You Are the Jury*) in which he said that there was simply no proof that anyone else was in on the killing. He dined with me last week, coming in from Des Moines, to ask my help in getting a publisher to bring out a twentieth anniversary (of the assassination) book that would dispose of all the grassy knollers that have cropped up over the years. In the course of the evening he complained about the Des Moines *Register*'s tendentious handling of a UAW strike of the Delavan

Corporation, and I told him I didn't know about the news editor of the *Register*, but had had dealings with the editorial page editor whom I found to be a humorless hypocrite who wrote prose heavier than lead. Now he sends me a detailed account of what happened at Delavan, and the failure of the *Register* to report it fairly. I thank him, and ask him to let me know when he is ready for me to approach the book publishers.

Twenty-five years ago I drafted a form note that continues to go out regularly to readers who let lapse their subscriptions to *National Review*. The text hasn't changed, and a surprising number of people reply, giving the reasons for dropping out (mostly it is eyesight, or cost; occasionally, acedia). The circulation department routes to me especially provocative letters, negative or affirmative. Some of these I acknowledge. Mr. Bob Wyche of Tyler, Texas, was *horrified* at his delinquency. He teaches government. "On the second day of school, government classes came to life as they viewed and interpreted all of the political cartoons printed in *National Review* over the summer. I took all of them, ran them through the Thermo-Fax, made transparencies of them, and projected them onto a screen with the overhead. Why, then, had I not renewed my subscription? Mere neglect and procrastination. Enclosed is my check for a renewal. Thank you for writing." So I thanked *him*.

A Harvard student sends me a copy of the first issue of a conservative highbrow paper the dissidents [Harvard-Radcliffe Conservative Club] are putting out, and I acknowledge it. "There's good writing in it, but it suffers desperately from typographical drabness. I would be glad to make you a gift of our [*National Review*'s] art department to effect a more challenging design, if your people are interested. Let me hear."

Professor Marion Levy, chairman of the East Asian

Studies Department at Princeton, writes me provocatively, asking why I even bothered to chide Fr. Timothy Healy (president of Georgetown University) for his rather unbalanced treatment of the Moral Majority. He wishes Fr. Healy had read "one of the great books of the twentieth century . . . Eric Hoffer's *The True Believer*. Had he done so, he would be well aware of the fact that the new righteousness [that Healy deplores] is quite consistent with a very strong strain of what he refers to as 'western religion' which I would prefer to call Judeo-Christian religions since I think both the singular number and the geographical adjective are misleading in these respects. Indeed the new righteousness has a broad level of consistency with a major element in many if not all religions, despite the fact that many of us would prefer to emphasize quite different aspects of religious belief. It always surprises me that it should be regarded as cynical to point out that we use the term 'bestial' to describe a type of conduct that is characteristic of no beast save *Homo sapiens*. One doesn't have to be Hobbesian to be aware of that aspect of history.

"But then (dare I start a whole paragraph with such a phrase in writing to thee?), I think most people are wrong in their apprehension of what our problems are. I think the main problem we face is coping with very high levels of interdependency. People in general have never been very much interested in freedom and have accepted very high levels of authoritarianism and hierarchy quite easily if it was visited in sufficiently local forms. People have not in general felt that he or she governs best who governs least but only that he or she governs best who governs most locally. I do not think Hobbes was right in holding over us the threat that life would become solitary, poor, nasty, brutish, and short. For us it is far more likely to become crowded, affluent, nasty, brutish, and long. Can people adjust as well to longevity, affluence, and peace as they have in the past to shortgevity, poverty, and war? In these respects the Japanese may give us a better basis for hope than most other people in the world."

Professor Levy enclosed an extraordinary correspondence with a fellow professor at Princeton (whom he had never met) in which the other professor quite huffily rejected a manuscript by Levy alleging it to be insubstantial in quality and vituperative in tone. Seasoned editors reading it would mostly, I think, agree that the professor-editor simply didn't enjoy being chewed up by Levy, never mind that his journal is called *democracy*— "democracy" (small "d") as in "Amerika." I keep running into a good deal of glumness on the question whether self-government is here to stay. I reply briefly to Professor Levy, though other than to wonder at the bad manners of the professor-editor, I don't get into the substance of their quarrel.

Ira Cohen, co-executor with me of Harry Elmlark's will, sends me the *Publishers Weekly* review of *Marco Polo*, tells me he has damaged his ankle, and that his wife, who went to Vassar with mine, liked my sailing piece in *The New Yorker*. I promise to send the book when it materializes, and tell him I have now the picture of Harry's ashes being scattered in the Sound.

A gentleman from Massachusetts tells me he has come upon a copy of the *National Review Reader*, 1957, a volume of material published in *National Review* during its first year of life, and is willing to sell it to me. "On the inside page is the following in original handwriting: Ex Libris Mrs. Albert J. Beveridge, Gratefully: Wm. F. Buckley Jr., Suzanne La Follette, Frank S. Meyer, L. Brent Bozell, James Burnham, John Chamberlain, Willmoore Kendall, Whittaker Chambers." My goodness, what I made my poor colleagues do. That was the first year we sent out a general appeal to our readers for funds, and everyone who came in with one hundred dollars or more got what that year I called "an exiguous token of our esteem," a phrase that has stuck, as in, "what's the exiguous token this year going to be?" I had forgotten I asked everyone to sign all those books individually. I tell Mr. Wilkinson thanks, but the volume is not worth a lot of money.

I have been trying for about ten years to arrange a day when I could accompany Bill Rickenbacker, my old friend and sometime colleague, to Pittsburgh. He goes thither when the great resident organist, Paul Koch, performs on the famous Beckerath organ at St. Paul's Cathedral. Last week I asked Frances whether I was free on April 27th? "Dear Bill: I could weep. I was moving in on April 27th only to find out that I am (once again) m.c. at the American Book Awards. Is there a date in May?" Bill (son of Eddie) is one of those terribly rare people simply drenched in talent, which he has not—is "merchandised" the right word? Linguist, writer, economic analyst, humorist, pianist, pilot. He is living now in Massachusetts, on a farm, writing pastoral monthly letters, analyzing stock trends, practicing the piano, teaching Latin to a neighbor's son. What does it matter, to merchandise one's gifts? Is a better word for it "advertise"? Surely if you spend three hours a day practicing the piano, you will want to play for somebody? Or if you paint all day long, show—even sell—your pictures? And if you write, don't you wish that others should read what you write, and shouldn't you therefore seek publication?

Is it a matter of style? Self-pleasure is heady stuff, but isn't it (the commercial aspect of it all to one side, the need to provide for oneself and one's family)—antisocial, in the grave sense of desiring not to share? What are a man's obligations, if any, to the New York Graphic Society's representative who approaches him for permission to reproduce, and offer prints of, a painting by Leonardo da Vinci which he owns and which is heretofore unphotographed? Is it all a matter of style, or in part a matter of style? Some pleasures cannot be shared, but must one seek to share those that can, which includes insights into right reason?

A young (eighteen) lady I have never met has come to New York to attend a modeling school, and never since Helen left Sparta was there such maternal grief, notwithstanding that her mother approved her daughter's mission in principle. The mother has corresponded with me for years, is wonderfully witty, emotional, literate, and writes to beg me *not* to see or communicate with her daughter for a couple of months lest this stimulate homesickness; though it is never made clear just how I could stimulate homesickness by visiting with somebody who doesn't know me. Anyway, I write her now—"Is it safe to make a lunch date in March after our return [from Switzerland]?"

To Keith Mano, whose book *Take Five* I have just completed reading in galleys, I write:

Dear Keith: Well, I've read the book. The copy I took with me on the trip was inadvertently left in San Francisco, so I had to wait until Sam sent me a replacement. I don't doubt that it is a work of genius. The reader (this reader) is struck more by the phrase-by-phrase energy, ingenuity, insane exuberance, than by the narrative dynamic. That may hurt, I don't know. It may be deemed just too powerful. One can only hope, at this level—I have no faith in my powers to predict commercial success. Certainly it will, once and for all, distinguish you as a total master of the language. That I should figure in this book [*Take Five* is dedicated to me], so prominently, and so affectionately, is quite the nearest I'll ever get to achieving temporal immortality. There is no way to thank you for this, except to insist that you should know the measure of my gratitude, and to accomplish that will require a lifetime. Affectionately, Bill.

An editor for E. P. Dutton sent me the galleys of Wilfrid Sheed's brief book on Clare Boothe Luce, asking for a jacket blurb, which I send him:

Dear Mr. Corn: I have read the book you sent me by Wilfrid Sheed, on Clare Luce. It is a work of art, the more impressive for the remarkable job it undertakes, namely to draw a full portrait of one of the truly remarkable women of the century, such that neither admirers nor critics will feel scorned. I would not have thought it possible, but then this tends to happen every time I pick up a work by Sheed. Sheed on Clare Luce is a juxtaposition insanely felicitous, and I congratulate you for whatever role you played in bringing this about. Yours faithfully.

Three weeks later I saw Bill Sheed during the *Brideshead* screening, and it transpires that Mr. Corn is no longer with Dutton. He neither acknowledged my blurb nor passed it along to his successor; no doubt a clerical oversight. The book is everything I said about it.

To my son Christopher I write:

Dear Christo: Ken Galbraith called, about this & that. Has just returned from an extensive trip to Japan, which is why he hasn't read your book [*Steaming to Bamboola*] which, however, he is taking with him to Chicago this weekend and will have read not long after you get this note. He called to my attention something he thought faintly alarming, a sentence in the publisher's covering letter that came in with the manuscript. The phrase in question (which he quoted from memory) apparently says of you that "he wrote much of the best seller, *Airborne.*" He feels that the publicist is here implying that you wrote other than the sections attributed to you; i.e., that you ghost-wrote much of *Airborne.* Perhaps it would be wise if you called the relevant creature at Tom Congdon's and had him/her read you the phrase in question to see if Ken is correct, in which case you can use your own judgment as to whether any correcting statement should be sent out to those who have received your book, or whether it suffices merely to alter the line in future uses of the point. All love.

Later I saw the blurb, and Ken had made more of it than it spoke. Christopher goes to such extraordinary lengths to play down any ties with me that would conceivably be thought to be parasitic that he came as close as he ever does to being miffed by this, but quickly the misunderstanding was straightened out.

The sequel to all this was amusing, because almost two months later Ken Galbraith still hadn't read Christopher's book, which is most awfully unlike him. Christopher had no intention of pursuing him, but I thought to goad him with a telegram, which I did five days before our scheduled television debate at Harvard on Reagan's economic initiatives. "DEAR KEN: TELL YOU WHAT. IF YOU'LL READ CHRISTOPHER'S BOOK, I'LL TAKE A DIVE ON THURSDAY. BILL." The communication was transcribed with some difficulty by Kitty (Mrs. G.) because she didn't know the expression "to take a dive." I was not surprised that within twenty-four hours Ken had read the book and called me to dictate a plug for it. I was agreeably astonished, sitting in Ken's living room with a half dozen of his friends, after a most spirited debate, to hear Ken bring up the subject of Christopher's book and regale the company with praise for it, followed by the statement that he considered Christopher one of the "top half-dozen writers of his generation." Ken can be very generous. To be sure, this usually happens with other people's money. But he is personally as generous a man as I have known.

Pat has rung the intercom. David is up, and they are watching the evening television news. Do I want to join them? Yes.

There were just the three of us at dinner, and David spoke of the demonstrations going on in western Europe, and of his conviction that it was wrong to read anti-Americanism into them, and I more or less agreed. After dinner I showed him a most wonderful documentary film. The principal figure in it is Philip Weld, for whom I have developed a considerable attachment notwithstanding that I have seen him only twice. I met him years ago through Herbert Kenny, the poet, critic, longtime book review editor for the Boston *Globe* (he is now retired), and one of my oldest friends. Weld was then active as the publisher of several newspapers, including the Gloucester (Mass.) daily, and his avocation was sailing on multi-hulled vessels, i.e., catamarans and trimarans.

Last spring Herb acted as intermediary in two situations, which came together quite coincidentally. I had heard from a friend in Boston that the *Globe* was publishing my newspaper column very irregularly, and I feared that this must be because of a hostility to me by its new editorial page editor, Martin Nolan. I have never met Mr. Nolan, but I remembered reading a reference to me by Nolan a year or so before, so I fished it up, called Herb, and told him I proposed to write to Tom Winship (the editor and Herb's former boss); which I did, sending along a copy to Herb.

Dear Tom: A friend who lives in Greater Boston and is therefore one of your subjects wrote me a letter rather more detailed than the usual letter on the same theme, complaining of the virtual disappearance of my column in the *Globe*. But this correspondent was more concrete than others I have once or twice called to your attention. He said that Mr. Martin Nolan feels a considerable hostility to me. You can of course surmise that I thought this inconceivable, and so wrote to ask my correspondent where he got such an idea, and to my surprise he wrote back immediately giving his evidence. He pointed to an article published in *The Washingtonian* in December of 1977, an article which I had seen, but forgotten. It was a profile of George Will, involving interviews with several of his professional colleagues. The relevant passage is: "I think he [Will] is . . . a real conservative, a first-rate thinker, the best thing to happen to commentary here in a long time. You don't get too many Ph.D.'s humping around in daily journalism, you know. He's not a cheap-jack careerist like Buckley, who spent so much time trying to justify the Nixon administration." When I saw this back in 1977 I hardly questioned Mr. Nolan's evaluation of George Will—after all, I had appointed him Washington editor for *National Review* some time before Mr. Nolan ferreted out his talents. I was, however, surprised to be labeled a cheap-jack careerist at the service of Richard Nixon. In August 1971 I convened an influential group in New York City which issued a statement publicly suspending our support of Nixon (front page, New York *Times*). In December 1971 I announced my support of the maverick candidacy of John Ashbrook against Richard Nixon. In February 1972 I alone (I think) of the seventy reporters following Nixon in China categorically criticized Nixon's behavior, and the Shanghai Communiqué. In March of 1972 I declined in a personal letter to Nixon reappointment as a member of the U.S. Advisory Commission on Information. In December of 1973 I called for the resignation of Nixon. In January 1974 I recommended to my brother in the Senate that he do the same, which he did in March. To suggest that I was a Nixon careerist under the circumstances would seem to reveal more about Mr. Nolan's familiarity with the writers he speaks about, than about my record with respect to Nixon.

The question of course arises whether someone who spoke in such heavy terms about me is likely to exercise disinterested judgment in evaluating my copy. You and I have been friends for a long time, and you and your colleagues (I enclose an example) have from time to time been very generous in your evaluations of my writing over many years. Harry Elmlark was, understandably, devoted to you, and if he were alive, I'd have tossed this mess at him, knowing he would deal with it.

I guess what I need to convey is: 1) I don't want just the Boston *Globe*'s money, I want its reach. 2) I recognize that it is the preeminent paper in the area, but I would settle for other papers rather than merely be paid, while the column, week after week, is shelved. 3) It isn't reasonable to suppose that an editorial page editor who was willing to be quoted in 1977 to the effect that I am a cheap-jack Nixon careerist is likely to be balanced in his evaluation of what I have to offer. Under the circumstances, I would like to petition for one of the following: a) a policy decision on whether the *Globe* wants my column—defined as, does the *Globe* want, not merely to buy my column, but also to publish it, say half the time; or b) a release, which would permit Universal Press, without any prejudice to its other features, to withdraw my feature from the *Globe* and sell it to other papers in territory now reserved by the *Globe*.

And how are you otherwise? Always with warm regards.

To this, Tom Winship replied:

Dear Bill: As you might suspect there is a big difference of opinion here at the *Globe* over columns. There are those who are rooting for you because they like your literate and perceptive analysis of current events. On the other side, are those who view your columns differently. If the situation remains unchanged and your column is seldom used in the *Globe* during the next few weeks, we will release it to the syndicate for possible sale elsewhere in our territory. Indeed we are required to do so under a consent agreement with the Justice Department. What say if either you or the *Globe* bite off the matter of Buckley in the *Globe* by June 15? All the best, Tom.

In turn, I answered:

Dear Tom: Fair enough. And if we have to unplight our troth I will give you a free subscription to the *Globe*'s successor so that you can continue to be enlightened. Warm regards.

Herb told me he had sent a copy of my letter to Phil Weld, in part because they are very close friends, but also because Phil likes my stuff, has for years been a director of the *Globe*, and is a friend of Tom's and Nolan's (it would probably be safe to say about Philip that he is a friend of everyone he has ever met). At just about that time, Herb

wrote and asked if I would be willing to write an introduction to Phil's forthcoming book *Moxie*, an account of his extraordinary one-man race across the Atlantic, Portsmouth to Newport, in which, at age sixty-five, Philip Weld set a world record for single-handed-sail speed across the Atlantic. I said sure, and am glad I did, because the book is superb.

In due course I received an answer from Nolan, to wit:

Dear Mr. Buckley: The problem here is not any "considerable hostility" which I have for you, because I have none. Rather, I count myself among the admirers of your earlier work. That work was characterized by a vitality and diligence that I have not seen lately. If any three of your columns were as well researched as your letter to Tom Winship was, we'd all be better off. Many columnists, including George Will, whom we both admire, now write twice weekly. That schedule allows a more discriminating choice of subject matter and more time to write. The vague deadline offer by Tom in his letter to you of June 15 might give you time to decide whether you wish to rearrange your schedule. That would have a bearing on your column's appeal for us.

> Sincerely yours,
> Martin F. Nolan
> Editor, Editorial Page

The character in my novels, Blackford Oakes, has in him a streak of self-indulgence of a most masochistic character. I confess I have it too. I remember as a young adult reading *The Postman Always Rings Twice.* There is a scene there where the man and the girl, fleeing the cops in their car, have an accident, crawl out of the wreck in the woods, the police not ten minutes away and closing in; and suddenly his lust overwhelms him and he says to himself, I must have her, *I simply don't care* what the consequences are. Blackford Oakes is a schoolboy (in novel number 1) about to be flogged by a British headmaster to whom decorum means everything and the absence of the deferential "sir" a sin of nearly mortal proportions.

[Scene: the headmaster's library. Oakes has been prepared by the assistant, and lies over the end of the sofa, rear end, unclothed, upward. The headmaster, seated, is reviewing the Delinquencies Register.]

Dr. Chase spoke for the first time.

"Oakes. O-a-k-e-s. I have a good many complaints here about you, Oakes, though I have not previously acted on any of them. My mistake, I can see now. Tell me, sir, have you ever been beaten?"

Blackford was hot now not only with fear but with rage. But he knew that nothing—no threat, no punishment—would deprive him of the imperative satisfaction of answering curtly. "No," he said.

The same demon overcame me and so I wrote out a letter that could only have the consequences of getting me fired from the *Globe*.

Dear Mr. Nolan: I have not approached you with a request that you appraise my work (we both know you are free to discontinue your purchase of it at any time). If you wish to evaluate it, I suggest you put in to review the seventh volume of my collected columns which Doubleday will bring out next year.

Yours faithfully.

It did, of course, lead to cancellation; but having ruined poor Phil Weld's campaign of conciliation, I had to tell him the truth, which was that the writing of that letter left me with a fierce Johnsonian joy. He was very kind about it all; indeed so was Tom Winship who in due course wrote:

Dear Bill: I feel badly. First, why haven't I written sooner? It's not my style to let unhappiness go by without direct communication with you. I lay that to my innate sloppiness in matters about my desk and upon too much travel of late. I also feel badly that we have come to a parting of the ways. I frankly didn't think that I should throw myself across the railroad tracks so early in the game of Marty's regime as editor of the editorial page. I urged him to keep Buckley in the *Globe* family because you write so very well. I did not go beyond that. I do value our friendship and I trust that it will survive this bump in the road. Happy sailing.

Best regards.

To which I replied, in part, "By no means should this interfere with our personal relations. There is always the alternative that you should become the publisher of the Boston *Herald American* [which had picked up my column]. Or would that be asking too much? With warm regards."

In planning the documentary, Weld had shown wonderful enterprise by getting six hot boats, with skippers of different personality stripe, and rigging a camera before which the contestants soliloquized once or twice a day. The resulting collage of fun, rage, desperation, danger, and fear, with wind, seas, calms, made for the most exciting sea documentary I ever saw. And David, viewing it, agreed. Incredibly, the networks didn't buy it, though CBS Cable did. It is unmistakably a classic.

The documentary finished, Pat said she was tired and would go straight to bed. I asked David if he would like to take a Jacuzzi. We went down to the cellar, and in ten minutes the Jacuzzi pool was full. From it I can look out over the white marble to the exquisite thirty-foot-long pool, with the Robert Goodnough mosaic, reds, golds, blues, yellows in infinite complexity of shading, beginning at the near end, slithering away to the far end, and rising up

the whitewashed stucco wall, lit by pool lights and, at the
far end, recessed lights that come on to the desired bright-
ness: the whole a beautiful shimmer of colors bouncing off
an overhead mirror that runs the length of the room. It is
the most beautiful indoor pool this side of Pompeii, and
from time to time I would leave the Jacuzzi and plunge
into the water, wonderfully bracing at the seventy degrees
I keep it, and with the flick of a switch, the far end of the
pool begins to throw water out at you through an under-
water jet, the effect being that you can swim as if you had
an entire ocean to traverse. Then back to the Jacuzzi; back
to the pool. We dressed, turned off the music, and David
said he felt a lot better, and I agreed, and we said good
night.

Seven
SUNDAY

I rose early because the day would be crowded, so I took my breakfast downstairs, leaving Pat asleep. The Sunday New York *Times* was there, and I had to be ruthless, rationing myself to a mere half hour with it—I'd catch up later. The sky was bright, light blue, the sea a leaden blue, the early sun provocatively incandescent, the wind vigorous and steady. From the veranda, I could make out the skyline of New York. That kind of clarity comes only a half-dozen times a year. I headed to the study to do more correspondence before Mass.

An irritating letter from the "entertainment editor" of the Eagle Publishing Company of Pittsfield, Massachusetts. So much so that it almost certainly bounces off an interesting row I had with the paper's editor years ago. I decided to refresh myself on what had happened before framing my reply.

It was way back in 1969 that I wrote to:

Lawrence K. Miller, Editor
THE BERKSHIRE EAGLE
Pittsfield, Mass.

Dear Mr. Miller:

I should have thought that you put a high enough value on your readers to protect them against columns written by a "notorious anti-Semite." In the event that that isn't the case, you are less fastidious than I am. Because I would not want to be associated with any newspaper disposed to tolerate among its regular writers a notorious anti-Semite. Under the circumstances, (a) you should fire me because you believe the characterization of me by [the columnist] George Connelly (your issue of October 6, 1969) to be true; or (b) you will disavow the charge and apologize for having printed the libel, and perhaps take the opportunity to say what is your policy toward columnists who pass their libels through your pages; or (c) I shall—just to begin with—instruct my syndicate to withdraw my column effective immediately.

Yours faithfully, Wm. F. Buckley, Jr.

Dear Mr. Buckley:

Thank you for your letter of October 13 addressed to Lawrence K. Miller. In response thereto, the marked item enclosed was appended to the October 20 column of Professor George G. Connelly.

Yours obediently,
Robert B. Kimball
Assistant to the Editor

Enclosure: "Apology. Prof. Connelly, in a column of Oct. 6 based in part on an article by Gore Vidal in the September issue of *Esquire*, imputed anti-Semitism to William F. Buckley, Jr. Upon examination of all available evidence . . . an apology is tendered Mr. Buckley on behalf of our columnist and this newspaper—Ed."

Dear Mr. Miller:

I note that not only are you too busy to prevent your columnists from submitting libels, you are also too busy to take the time personally to apologize to the victim for publishing them. I note also that the normally verbose Mr. Connelly is suddenly struck dumb, leaving it to others to apologize to me on his behalf.

I am not disposed to have dealings with such people: not even professional dealings. On the other hand I do not wish to satisfy myself at the expense of such of your readers as desire to read my column. Under the circumstances, I shall continue to send you my column on the regular basis, on the understanding that you will not henceforward pay any money for it. I shall myself absorb the cost of mailing. Perhaps you and Mr. Connelly can meet and giggle together at this demonstration that crime can, after all, pay.

Wm. F. Buckley, Jr.

They continued to run the column for a while, sending the regular monthly check, which I instructed the syndicate not to cash. (It was on the order of twenty dollars a month.) After two or three months they dropped the column, sending along a letter to Harry Elmlark, the syndicate's president, to the effect that they would not accept it free of charge. Dear Harry. The idea of *not* cashing a check was theologically alien to him. And then to lose a customer—because his syndicate wouldn't take that customer's money! It was too much; but Harry decided to show fortitude, and decided also to tell me, three or four times a week, how strong and loyal he had shown himself to be during his tribulation.

So, years later, Mr. Wiseguy writes me. His references are to a form letter sent out over my signature by an organization known as Friends of Firing Line, whose executive secretary is Mrs. Norma Woodley. Her principal concern is to raise money for local sponsors of "Firing Line," and to send out occasional promotional bulletins. The *Eagle* gentleman writes:

Dear Mr. Buckley: In reply to your letter of October 22, thank you for your good wishes and for notifying me of the beginning of the 16th season of "Firing Line," whatever that is.

As for having Mrs. Woodley "help you in any way she can," thanks again but no thanks.

I am also pleased that you are helping Bell and Howell sell so much of whatever it is they sell. [The reference escapes me, but it isn't worth calling Norma.] Do I detect a little touch of Reaganomics there?

If you by chance run across Warren Steibel, please give him my regards and tell him it's been too long between drinks.

I am glad that you and I have become friends after all

these years. It will give me an opportunity to find out if your dinner parties are really as much fun as all the columnists say.

With best wishes.

I decided the letter was tasteless enough to warrant a riposte.

"Dear Mr.——: Your answer to my form letter was unnecessary, though perhaps in a corner of the world so provincial as to deem it amusing to feign no knowledge of 'Firing Line,' you actually thought the letter personal, which if it had been, it would have been quite differently composed. Yours faithfully."

My notebook tells me that we decided at the last editorial conference that we could not continue to use as our economics editorial writer someone who had gone to the Treasury Department. I write to him to explain why, and I hope he understood, though I received no acknowledgment of the letter.

Ken Galbraith called me last night on a delicate matter. While he was serving as ambassador to India, his children became very close friends of the children of Ali Bhutto, at the time a high government official in Pakistan, whose fortunes subsequently declined, indeed so sharply that early in 1979 he swung on a noose, executed by General Zia. The objective is to effect a little relief for one of Bhutto's daughters, an activist whose detention has been in rather harsh circumstances. Ken is scrupulous in advising me that there is no imputation, explicit or implicit, of injustice in the detention, merely a request that it be done more clemently—perhaps house arrest? All this I convey to Under Secretary Jim. Jim is the State Department's overseer in Pakistan matters, and recently concluded some sort of an arms deal involving many millions of dollars, in return for which, echoing the left-wing press, his children began referring to their father as "The Merchant of Death," as in: "Ma, is the Merchant of Death home for dinner?" Perhaps it would have happened anyway, who knows, but five weeks later Bhutto's daughter was taken from prison into house arrest.

I write a memo to Rick Brookhiser. A dozen years ago we received a manuscript composed, or so the covering letter informed us, by a fourteen-year-old schoolboy in Rochester who protested to the authorities in his school that the other side of the story was not being presented on the scheduled Vietnam Day.

The piece was astonishingly literate—wry, even—and jaunty rather than merely cheeky. We published it. And kept an eye on the author, who went on to Yale where he experienced the single disappointment of getting one B plus (all his other grades were A's). He came to us for summer work, and then we offered him a job after he graduated. He took it, on the understanding that in one year he would leave to go to law school. Soon Priscilla and I conspired together; I lunched with Rick and told him that if he would give up law school, we would in one year promote him to senior editor, the youngest in *NR*'s history, and labor to pay him a living wage. His productivity, efficiency, and versatility have become legendary. He has been temporarily assigned the job of executing long-range editorial projects, and I write him a memo: "Apropos the feature project business, I should think a massive piece on the Catholic Church and pacifism should be considered, in the light of the predicted result of the bishops' conference this coming week. See the Op-Ed page 'Jubilant Declaration' in the New York *Times* by the Catholic pacifist."

Mr. John Crane writes me from Washington, Virginia, to tell me that Dr. Franklin Littell is probably acting hypocritically in his capacity as Chairman of something called Christians United for American Security, which has just taken out a full-page ad objecting to the proposed sale of AWACS to Saudi Arabia. How so? Well, says the correspondent, Franklin Littell is a secret agent of Israel.

"Since I am familiar with Littell's past secret employment and Littell's strong anti-Arab views, it seems to me reasonable to suppose that this ad in the Washington *Post*—which must have cost many thousands—was financed by 'friends' of Littell, if not entirely, then at least in part. . . . I don't object to a lobbyist lobbying if he does it openly, but I HATE hypocrisy—and wolves wearing sheeps' clothing."

Franklin Littell! Dear me. Dr. Littell is a jerko I ended up suing a few years ago, for comparing me with Ribbentrop, and saying, among other choice items, that I made my living by lying and cheating. The lawsuit was against him and the Macmillan Publishing Company, which had published the libels in a book called *Wild Tongues*. Littell, a church historian by profession, had previously headed an organization discreetly funded by the Democratic Party some time after Barry Goldwater ran for office, which organization did its best to depict many conservative activists as fascistic.

I had begun by asking Macmillan for an immediate retraction, and for reimbursement of my legal expenses, which at that moment could not have been greater than a few hundred dollars. Macmillan replied by telling me that they themselves didn't believe a *word* of the unpleasant charges made by Dr. Littell, but that their devotion to the First Amendment made it impossible for them to apologize, or to remit lawyer's charges.

Mr. C. Dickerman Williams, my attorney and surely

my most distinguished friend, told me his advice under the circumstances was to proceed with the suit—"It will only last a couple of days" was his guess, based on his familiarity with the defense and his general experience of libel law.

What happened was both painful and amusing. The district court judge before whom the case fell had, it happened, been nominated to his position by my brother Jim, then junior senator from New York. But Jim's modus operandi in the matter of court appointments had been impeccable. He had appointed a panel of distinguished lawyers (C. D. Williams was its chairman) who made nominations whenever there was a vacancy, nominations based on manifest qualifications. Without exception, Jim forwarded the panel's nominees to the President. The judge now volunteered to excuse himself, but Littell and Macmillan said: No, they trusted him, he should try the case (a jury had been waived).

The judge in question was a youngish man with a brilliant record. If memory serves, he had been first in his class at Harvard twenty years before. But such was the attention he had evidently given to learning the law, he did not have time to learn much about certain other things. For instance, when my attorney began by denouncing Littell's comparison of me with Ribbentrop, his honor asked who Joachim von Ribbentrop was? During the ensuing four or five days, at about two or three thousand dollars per day, we were conducting a seminar on recent European history for the benefit of the judge. On the afternoon of the fifth day I got a telephone call from the president and unmistakable boss of Macmillan, Mr. Raymond Hagel, who said he would like to see me, how about breakfast, before the trial resumed that day? Fine I said; and the next morning in my apartment I was face to face with one of the world's premier salesmen.

This is bloody ridiculous, he said; it's costing us both a goddamn fortune. Besides, you won't win, because *New York Times v. Sullivan* protects us.

I replied that *New York Times v. Sullivan*, while it shifted the burden of proof where public figures are concerned from the suee to the suer, hadn't in fact repealed the laws of libel, to which he repeated that it was ridiculous, that Macmillan would *clearly* win, and he didn't care about Littell, Littell was Littell's problem, and anyway Littell was probably judgment-proof.

Well, I said, we'll just have to see how it goes.

And so he said, Look, just to *prove* to you that Macmillan doesn't believe all those unpleasant things about you, we'll *publish* your next book!

That statement marshaled every arrogant corpuscle in my system, so I said look, Mr. Hagel, your telling me that Macmillan would *consent* to publish my next book is like your telling me Macmillan will agree to accept a gift from me of fifty thousand dollars, since I figure that's what a publisher typically makes off one of my books. He stood up, strode over to within three inches of me and said: Okay, tell you what. We'll publish your next book and the first fifty thousand dollars we make off it, we'll *give* to you.

But—he added quickly—for the sake of our general reputation, we'll have to give it to you in a nonconspicuous way. So I said, well, you could buy fifty thousand dollars' worth of advertising in *National Review*. Yeah, he said, we could. He called his office to get some figures, and I mine to get some. Ten minutes later we had a deal, and a half-hour later my lawyer told the honorable court that the case against Macmillan had been settled; and one year later Macmillan published *Airborne;* and, for a lovely spell, *National Review* looked like a house organ of Macmillan, so heavy was our advertising schedule.

Littell was then defended, free of charge, by Macmillan's public-spirited lawyer, and found guilty by the judge on three counts; the lawyer appealed, two of the three charges were thrown out, the third sustained, and I got a check from him for a thousand dollars or so.

So now he's into AWACS. I told my correspondent that if indeed the government of Israel is paying Dr. Littell to argue their line, Dr. Littell is a crafty old bird, because the rest of us do it for nothing.

I acknowledged a witty letter from John Burton, professor at the School of Business at Columbia, who is president of the board of trustees of Millbrook School, about my Millbrook piece. "All of us," he writes ironically, "who had felt the gentle whimsy of Frank Trevor's tongue, the self-effacing modesty of Ed Pulling, and Xavier Prum's uncertainty about mathematics answers could relate to the characterizations which you drew so well."

For maybe five years in a row I found myself seated, by coincidence, at the annual Al Smith Dinner on the dais next to Carlos Romero Barceló, who was then the mayor of San Juan and is now Puerto Rico's governor. He was wonderfully obliging a couple of years ago when I went to Puerto Rico to do two "Firing Line" programs, and now he has written to ask me to draw attention to the anomalous impact the President's proposed tax reforms would have on Puerto Rico. I wrote a column based on his analysis which now I send him, thanking him.

Kevin Starr is a Harvard Ph.D. in American history, a man of great shyness who gives play to a romantic spirit in a column he writes for the San Francisco *Examiner*. Last week, dining at Trader Vic's in San Francisco with friends, I bumped into him, but in one of those awkward situations where, although both of us were seated in the same extended seat, as in a church pew, conversation was not possible. I wanted to make it clear that I regretted this. I wrote him so.

Jameson Campaigne, Jr., who heads up Caroline House, a small publisher, and who I've known for twenty years, reaching back to when he was fifty percent of the conservative student body at Williams College (the other one came to *National Review* to work), wants a blurb for a book which I simply haven't time to read, so I beg off. His letter contains also a proposal that at *National Review* we amass some of the apocalyptic statements being made about what's going to happen to the world under Reagan, and publish them a year later. "The feature might have a salutary effect on these fellows, in addition to being highly entertaining." His P.S. is, "Mightn't 'lagniappe' be a good substitute for 'exiguous token' in your next fundraising letter?" Actually, I don't think so. Because a lagniappe is not necessarily a token of *esteem*. It is simply a gratuity.

My watch tells me it is almost time for Mass, so I rung the kitchen and told Gloria we must go in five minutes. I write to Cheever Tyler in New Haven, the chairman of the *Yale Daily News* a half-dozen years after I served, and the most active trustee of the Yale News fund and related activities, a charming and witty attorney. "Dear Cheever: My son Christopher is to be the featured speaker at the 4th of December *Yale Daily News* dinner, and under the circumstances I have decided to invite myself to that dinner. Question, could I have the pleasure of your company? The proceedings I am told will not be long. If that is agreeable, we might meet for drinks ahead of time. Advise." It turned out that he would be out of town. Moreover, Christopher subsequently confessed that my presence might make him a little (more) nervous, so I didn't go.

Gloria sat in front with me, Rebeca and Olga in the back seat. Gloria's beautiful nineteen-year-old daughter has a weekend guest, and one of them will need to ride in rear of the station wagon, sitting on one of the boat cushions back there, but they insist they will *both* do this, so I let them in through the back and we drove three miles to

St. Catherine of Siena in Riverside. To St. Catherine of Siena because there is a most beautiful service there at 10:30, to be sharply distinguished from most Catholic Masses since the awful events of Vatican II. I must not go on about it, because I have written on the subject, and it only makes me weep. But I have privately offered as final proof of the existence of God that Evelyn Waugh was struck down fatally after Mass on the Easter Sunday immediately before the procedure was instigated in which one is instructed, at one point in the service, to shake hands with the parishioner on your right and on your left; and in due course, the one in the pew ahead, and the pew behind. Before long Catholics at Mass looked as though every one of them was running for public office. The thought of reaching over, hand outstretched, and running into Evelyn Waugh . . . I don't know how exactly he'd have handled it, but I remember that on one occasion when Hilaire Belloc came to New York he stood during the canon of the Mass, as is the habit on the Continent. At which point a deacon shuffled over to him and whispered, "We kneel here, sir." Belloc, his hands on his missal, turned calmly and said, "Go to hell." The deacon, startled, said, "Oh, I'm so sorry! I didn't know you were a Catholic!"

The singing at St. Catherine's is utterly beautiful, the music marvelously selected, and, given the acrobatic compulsion to bob up and down every few minutes, it is actually possible, in the interstices, to worship the Lord, even while wondering why He permitted them to take from us the Tridentine Mass in Latin.

The sermon, on the other hand, was provocative, in the unendearing sense of the word. The impression is widely held that Sunday mornings, for Catholic communicants, are devoted to homilies on abortion, or on communism, or on civil disobedience, or on whatever was the issue that figured most prominently in the week's news. It happens that this isn't so. For instance, I have yet to hear a sermon on the subject of Ireland—not one. And I have heard only two on the subject of abortion, one on the subject of the Vietnam war. Today's was by a visiting bishop from South Carolina who talked about justice, and soon one realized he was talking about social justice. I thought it worthwhile to write down (in the back of my prayer book) one or two of his points, perhaps for use in a column.

For many years I have pronounced to myself the traditional words, no longer recited by the priest when placing the host on the tongue of each communicant. He used to say, and now I say it for him, "*Corpus Domini nostri Jesu Christi, custodiat animam tuam, in vitam aeternam, amen.*" May the body of our Lord Jesus Christ safeguard your soul through life everlasting, amen. I long since concluded that no other verbal sequence comes as close as this in documenting human equality. The same words, for prince or for pauper; reminding us, young and old, healthy and sick, rich and poor, of our common dependence on our Maker.

Many years ago I was struck by a passage in one of the marvelous novels of Bruce Marshall. I had thought it was from *The World, the Flesh, and Father Smith*, but having now chased it down I find it was from *Father Malachy's Miracle*, one of the great *tours de force* in modern literature. In the first chapter are these wonderful paragraphs, which, I think, say it all on the subject of equality:

A fat man climbed into the same compartment as the little clergyman, a fat man with a face that was so red and pouchy that it looked like a bladder painted to hit other people over the head with at an Italian carnival.

He sat down, or rather threw himself down, in the corner opposite the priest and began to read a pink paper in which the doings of horses and erotic young women were chronicled at length. He was followed by a middle-aged woman who had a peaky, shiny nose with a funny little dent in the middle and whose hat was one of those amorphous black affairs which would have been, at any moment, out of fashion in any country.

The priest was distracted from his meditation. It was impossible, he told himself, with a wry little mental smile, to think competently of the Father and the Son and of the Holy Ghost proceeding from Both, with such a bulging, red face in front of him and such a peaky, peering woman placing her parcels here, there and everywhere. How hard it was, here below and with the material and the temporal crowding out the spiritual and the eternal, to love one's neighbour, how hard and yet how necessary. For the soul behind that bulging, red face had been redeemed by Christ just as surely as had his own, and Our Blessed Lord, while He hung on the cross, had seen the funny little dent in the middle of the peaky, peering woman's nose just as clearly as He had seen the broad, bland visage of Pope Pius the Eleventh, and so merciful was He, loved it just as much. And yet it was difficult to imagine bulge or dent in heaven unless, among the many mansions, there were one which should be one-tenth Beatific Vision and nine-tenths Douglas, Isle of Man. Of course, if it came to the point, it was difficult to imagine the majority of contemporary humanity in any paradise which did not syncopate Saint Gregory, and whose eternal sands were without striped bathing tents and casinos.

He closed his eyes again. If he must love his neighbour he would love him without looking at him. He closed his eyes, and not only did he close them, but he kept on repeating the reflex action in his brain so that, with the bulging red face and the peaky, peering woman, away went the compartment, the train, the station, the world; and, as Scotland went swinging after Scandinavia and Spain came scampering after and Australia flew to join the stars, he was alone with God.

A great nothingness was before him, a great nothingness that was Something, a great nothingness that was All; and in the warm freedom from the tangible he knew his Saviour and was absorbed by Him.

I am glad I found the passage, having remembered exactly only the sentence, "If he must love his neighbour he would love him without looking at him." But the radiance of the whole thing cries out, and the great mysterious dilemma is made plain.

In explaining something to Olga on the drive back it becomes relevant to know the Spanish word for "flesh," which I suddenly can't remember. So I ask Maria—and she can't remember, though she spoke not a word of English when, at age five, she arrived from Mexico. I get terribly exasperated, and Gloria and Rebeca offer several substitutes, none of them correct, so I find a circumlocutory way to tell Olga what I had in mind to relate—about how, in the Catholic Mass, the species were united for hundreds of years, with only the priest taking both the bread and the wine, representing, or more accurately incorporating, the flesh and the blood; whereas of course now in many churches anyone who desires it is also given the chalice from which to take wine. I reflect that it is the failure to come up with the exact word you wish that can result in tiring one so awfully when using a foreign tongue. Consider, for instance, forgetting in English, let's say, the word "apple," and trying to communicate, let us say, that "fresh cider is made by crushing apples." I will find myself, in my desperation, saying some such thing as, "fresh cider is made by crushing the fruit that Eve gave to Adam." After a while that kind of thing tires you, as it must the listener. The alternative is to change what you intend to say, so that when you come to the thought that fresh cider is made by crushing apples, you find yourself saying that fresh orange juice is made by crushing oranges, but then you have to figure out a way to relate *that* to the jug of cider being sold at the side of the road that launched you into this discussion in the first place.

Always they thank me when I stop the car and let them out, and always I say, "For nothing," which is exactly accurate. I let the girls out of the back of the station wagon and then get into the driver's seat again, because I must go to see Tom.

Tom Hume is in the hospital, having suffered a stroke that paralyzed his right side. It happened six weeks ago, and this is my third visit, having learned of the stroke from Tulita, his wife, only a fortnight ago. Tom and I were at Yale together. He is the architect of my music room, of our beautiful bedroom that looks out over so considerable an area of the sea, and of my swimming pool, though this he did not complete, having left to join a large firm of architects in New York City. We share also an enthusiasm for the sea, and Tom is as experienced a yachtsman as anyone I know. A month before his stroke we set out, with Van Galbraith and Danny Merritt and Reggie Stoops, in *Patito*, to take her to Newport where she would undergo refinements. We left at six in the evening and reached Newport at 10:30 in the morning, a distance of about 135 miles. We really *flew* to Newport that night, with absolutely relentless, but even-handed, winds all the way, coming in from the south and permitting us to exit the Sound at maximum ebb tide. Tom is tall, handsome, muscular, thin. He doesn't drink. He hasn't smoked for several years.

Why a stroke? No one knows, of course. The competent Tulita, having brought up six children, now works for Channel 13 in New York, but substantially she has become a therapist, wholly confident of Tom's recovery.

They were both in his room, and it's better that way because Tom couldn't talk, though one had the feeling that he can understand. His eyes were luminous with his extraordinary intelligence, and every now and again he essayed a phrase, but it usually reduces, smiling, merely to "shit," a word for some reason he could utter with abandon and security. His right arm is lifeless and he has been practicing pencil strokes with his left hand. I dumped on him last week a supply of oils, brushes, and crayons. He is extremely artistic, but I note he hasn't broken them out—probably trouble concentrating. His ambition, Tulita tells me, is to go from the therapeutic center, to which he will be taken in several weeks, right to his desk at the office—say in six months. Let us pray. I told him I had done just that at church, and he didn't say shit, because he is himself a believer (his uncle founded Canterbury School; his cousin is head of St. David's in New York). In fact, it was he who told me about St. Catherine's, many years ago.

By the time I arrived home, Jamie Niven, David's son, had arrived at the house, with wife Fernanda and two little daughters, and there is general conversational levity. Jamie is larger than his father, heavier, and more opinionated. He is in business, doing well, and has become a wonderfully well-informed conservative, traveling a nice distance from back when he wasn't eating grapes for Chavez, but I don't like to tease him about that because I once did, and I hurt his feelings. Pat and I were at their wedding and they are both sprightly and companionable people. At lunch, I forget why exactly, the subject of accents came up, and we succeeded in getting David to go right down the line, and he was successively a Cockney, a Yorkshireman, a Scotsman, a Dubliner, Gary Cooper, Johnny Carson—I have never known anyone with superior mimetic skills. He has to fight a little against whatever it is that is bothering him in the throat, and he tells us this, but manages, and with evident pleasure. The little girls are enthralled.

The great surprise came immediately after lunch. Christopher arrives—unannounced, unexpected. He had come up the night before for some function or other in New York, and now he was here with Leslie Dach, who had been his first roommate, during freshman year at Yale, in 1970. Christopher is a little overweight, is still wearing that cursed little mustache (why is it that it would never occur to one to refer to David Niven's "cursed little mustache"? or Clark Gable's?). He brings into the room freshness, affection, and informality. His mother forces food and drink on both of them, and we go for coffee and the kind of hopscotch conversation by which, in most social exchanges, you find out about things. It is quickly established that Christopher needs to return to Washington that afternoon, and in a sense that is a relief, because I would hate it if he could stay and I could not, which I cannot. In mid-coffee I got the same idea as yesterday, which had proved so pleasant. I approached him out of earshot of the others and whispered:

"Sail?"

He looked at his watch. He has not been to Mass, and four o'clock is the last service. I guaranteed him that I'd get him back in time. I dashed to the telephone and contacted Danny, and of course he is raring to go—we'll pick him up. So, with Jamie, we set out, and for the fun of it I have activated my stopwatch—eight minutes from the moment we switched on the starter in the car to when the *Patito*'s lines were cast off. We were under power for fifty yards before reaching the channel. Then—no amateur night here, with Danny and Christopher so thoroughly familiar with the boat—three minutes later we were under full sail, blasting out of the channel at full speed.

It is as bright as it had been early in the morning, cold and fresh. There were only two other vessels visible in a harbor crowded with sail and powerboats during the summer, and we felt the keenness I felt yesterday, though today the boat is more maneuverable; indeed, with a crew conversant with its paraphernalia, there is little you can't do quickly. In my schooner *Cyrano* it required fifty-five seconds at full motor power (the sails furled) to return to where you were, and during those fifty-five seconds a passenger aboard *Cyrano* drowned in the Hudson River ten years ago. *Patito*, under power, can jump through hoops, this because the rudder is broad and juts back well away from the keel center. We stay out for only twenty minutes, during which Christopher catches me up on this and that. I am highly excited over his forthcoming book, having now read the manuscript and marveled at the skill of the book's conception and execution. I dislike its title (*Steaming to Bamboola*) as much as Christopher does, but the publisher is absolutely stuck on it, and for once, Christopher's defenses are worn down. He enjoys being the speechwriter for the Vice-President, but tells me that unlike those speechwriters who complain that their material is severely edited, *he* complains that his is virtually unedited. Christopher has become extremely fond of George Bush, and his only complaint is that some days he reaches such a pitch of exhaustion that on getting home he can't even summon the energy to eat, so achingly tired is he. That's the kind of life that leads to lots of junk food, he volunteers, advising me that he is going on a diet (he is about five pounds overweight).

We got back by a quarter to four and, reaching the house, I embraced my son, because I won't be here when he returns from church, and he speeds off. There are two large cars in the driveway. One will take the Nivens and Pat to New York, Jerry will take me to Kent, Connecticut, for Jim Burnham's seventy-sixth birthday. I called Marcia this morning and told her that there simply wasn't any way that Pat could come, as she would be working all evening at Seventy-third Street preparing the lunch tomorrow for George Bush, with twenty corporation heads invited. Marcia said how sorry she was, but that she understood.

I had brought up a dozen different wines from the cellar, and Pat had wrapped each one festively in different-colored paper, and the lot of them were now in a big basket, together with the video games I bought yesterday. I said goodbye to Jamie and Fernanda and the girls, and for David a bear hug—I would see him next in Switzerland. I'd see Pat "before midnight if I'm lucky," I said as we kissed. I walked then to the study, and Jerry helped me stash my papers into the car.

More correspondence. Gus Renson, a retired mechanic-engineer of vast erudition, Belgian, opinionated, and a compulsive correspondent whose letters are charming and informative, wishes to quarrel over the portrayal in *National Review* of the battle of Yorktown. I thought it entirely reasonable to refer him to Professor Thomas Wendel, who wrote the piece, but now he tells me that I share with Wendel a "common francophobia," which is the first I've heard about *that* phobia of mine. But I'm glad Gus got into the subject because I subsequently discovered an interesting linguistic anomaly. Webster's Third defines francophilia as being "markedly friendly or attracted toward France or French culture or customs," whereas anglophilia is given as "particular unreasoned admiration of or partiality for England or English ways." This would suggest that Webster's Third suffers from a little francophilic-anglophobia.

Harvey Shapiro of the New York *Times Book Review* has asked me to write a hundred words about "the book I wish I had written." I almost always agree to do anything Harvey asks, for reasons obvious and not so obvious, and I go along with this, but with mental reservations, because what the hell, I mean, how do you handle such a subject? I resolve to do it by taking liberties, so I write, "When I consider how my light is spent, ere half my days, in this dark world and wide, I lament that I did not compose the message by which John L. Lewis advised the American Federation of Labor of the direction in which he elected to take the UMW. 'We disaffiliate.' To make it all the more beautiful, it was written in pencil, on wrapping paper. Aaargh! as Swinburne would say." (Harvey called Frances later, apologized, said my contribution was too offbeat—everybody else had actually mentioned entire books—and would I understand if he didn't run my contribution, which I did.)

Lewis Feuer sends me an account of the odd association of the Frankfurt Marxists with Columbia (University) Liberals, an association effected, incredibly, by no less than President Nicholas Murray Butler, back in 1932. I speculate that perhaps it was the pronounced conservatism of Butler that led him to tender the Marxists the bizarre invitation to set up shop at Columbia.

Playboy has a new mag called *Playboy's Fashion for Men* (I learn), and it apparently intends to go for the non-skin-flick-fashion–general-interest types, and the proposal is that I submit to the "main interview" for their Spring 1982 edition. "I realize that you rarely comment on this subject as a rule, but as you can see from the enclosed interview, we try not to limit our conversations only to fashion. Our first interview subject, Cary Grant, discussed his own perception of style and changes in films, among other areas; in the enclosed issue, pitcher Jim Palmer talks about his experiences with Madison Avenue and in the major leagues in addition to personal style. Since you exhibit quite a distinctive style, going back to your reminiscences of prep school and Yale, we'd like to use your personal tastes and observations as a basis for discussion and go on to the changes in Washington over the last administrations. . . ."

Frances had mentioned this letter over the telephone when it came in (I was out of town) and I told her I smelled a repeat of my situation with the conventional *Playboy* interview of ten years ago, when, upon being propositioned, I asked the managing editor how much I would be *paid* for submitting to a *Playboy* interview, and he practically fainted: we don't *pay* people we interview—to which the obvious response was, But *you* want to interview *me*, *I'm* not asking you to interview me; and finally we settled on three thousand dollars, which was by no means excessive, because one of those interviews takes hours upon hours upon hours, and leaves you with thousands of words to edit. The notion that I would be qualified to say anything at all interesting about fashions, even in a conversation en route to Reagan's deficits (where I knew the interrogation would soon lead), amused me. My wife is marvelously dressed, and I love it so—in fact she is in one of those permanent international best-dressed women categories—but I more or less wear more or less the same thing.

My father-in-law, who was a great big gruff no-nonsense tycoon with a nice, but generally inaccessible, sense of humor, went down for his breakfast one morning in Vancouver in his vast house to find the paper laid out for him as usual and his picture on the front page under the headline that he had been voted among the ten best-dressed men in Canada. That was bad enough, but what really did it was the caption: "Austin C. Taylor—Sartorial

Gem!" It was, Pat says, two weeks before he would consent to go downtown. I answered *Playboy* with a single sentence, "To proceed with the planned interview I would need an idea of the questions you propose to ask, and the fee you propose to pay." I am in favor of philanthropy, but feel no impulse to exercise that imperative for the benefit of Hugh Hefner.

A woman writes in a) to ask my opinion of the Ulster problem, and b) to complain about Frances Bronson. She had telephoned to get a quick fix on a) above. "In your absence, I spoke to your Executive Secretary, Frances Bronson. I believe I broached a sensitive subject with this person who went on to give me her personal opinion, one I did not ask for. She was insolent and rude. Her final insult was to pull the plug on our conversation." On the bottom of the note Frances had scrawled, "Bill— My [English] accent offended her: I was not insolent—just said a very complicated issue, etc.—f." "Dear Mrs. O'Connor: It is conceivable that you know more than I or my colleagues about the public issues involved in the crisis over Northern Ireland, utterly inconceivable that you should know more than I after thirteen years of professional intimacy concerning the manners of my secretary Miss Bronson. I can only conclude that the sensitivity in the case of the first issue leads to bad judgment in the second. . . . With all good wishes."

A woman is writing a book to be called *How You First Heard the News: The Reaction of Others Around You*. She desires my memories of where I was and what I did when JFK was assassinated, and tells me she already has responses from Arthur Miller, Ralph Bellamy, General Westmoreland, Henry Cabot Lodge, Isaac Asimov, and so on, and while I think free-lancers should be encouraged I tell her I'll comply when she tells me she has a book contract. That disposes of eighty percent of requests.

Dick Wheeler, back in the early sixties, was the proximate cause of a recurrent professional nightmare. He had graduated, achieving singular distinction as a columnist in the undergraduate paper, from the University of Wisconson at Madison, and at the time was employed as an editorial writer on the Oakland *Tribune*, working for William Knowland. I was scheduled to debate at Berkeley in a large auditorium at eight with a professor of politics on the general subject of congressional investigations, and Dick and his wife had me up to their apartment for dinner with a few guests. As the clock approached the hour I kept making gestures, wondering whether we shouldn't leave. Don't worry about a thing, Dick kept repeating—"it's only a few blocks."

Well of course, *it* happened. Traffic jam. And at twenty minutes *after* The Hour I dashed out of the car and started to run in the general direction of where I assumed the stage was—hard to reach because the external passageways were like those in bullfight arenas, or Madison Square Garden. When I arrived I was breathless, and the speaker, although scheduled to speak second, was already well embarked on his speech (the assumption was that I had taken ill, or whatever, and would not be turning up). Everything got progressively worse. I simply couldn't *hear* the speaker from where I was seated, and so began to edge my chair away from what I assumed was a dead acoustical spot. The effect must have been Buster Keaton-droll, because the audience clearly thought I was attempting to ham things up. By the time my opponent had finished, I didn't have the least idea what it was he had said, and in the scheduled colloquy, from which I hoped to reconstruct his line of analysis, he grandly waived his right of examination, leaving me with *nothing* at all to react to. The nightmare is of running through endless hallways, making the wrong turns, even as I try desperately to find the stage door.

Our friendship survived, and now Dick tells me he is working for a little publishing house in South Bend, and has joined an Anglican parish, one of whose ministers is Fr. Gerhart Niemeyer, age seventy-four. Gerhart became a priest a year and a half ago, and I flew to South Bend to witness what must have been the single most beautiful ceremony I ever attended. For days I was struck by the vision of my old friend, a self-exile from Hitler Germany, a devoted husband and father, a man of huge intellect and humor, who decided at age seventy-three theologically to go all the way, so to speak. I see him, dressed in white surplice, prostrate before the altar, or standing and reciting his part of the priestly colloquy with the bishop:

. . . As a priest, it will be your task to proclaim by word and deed the Gospel of Jesus Christ, and to fashion your life in accordance with its precepts. You are to love and serve the people among whom you work, caring alike for young and old, strong and weak, rich and poor. You are to preach, to declare God's forgiveness to penitent sinners, to pronounce God's blessing, to share in the administration of Holy Baptism and in the celebration of the mysteries of Christ's Body and Blood, and to perform the other ministrations entrusted to you.

In all that you do, you are to nourish Christ's people from the riches of his grace, and strengthen them to glorify God in this life and in the life to come.

My brother, do you believe that you are truly called by God and his Church to this priesthood?

ORDINAND: I believe I am so called.

BISHOP: Do you now in the presence of the Church commit yourself to this trust and responsibility?

ORDINAND: I do.

BISHOP: God and Father of all, we praise you for your infinite love in calling us to be a holy people in the kingdom of your Son Jesus our Lord, who is the image of your eternal and invisible glory, the firstborn among many brethren, and the head of the Church. We thank you that by his death he has overcome death, and, having ascended into heaven, has poured his gifts abundantly upon your people, making some apostles, some prophets, some evangelists, some pastors and teachers, to equip the saints for the work of ministry and the building up of his body.

*[The bishop lays hands upon the head of the ordi-
nand . . . the priests who are present also laying on their
hand.]*
THE BISHOP: Therefore, Father, through Jesus Christ
your Son, give your Holy Spirit to GERHART; fill him
with grace and power, and make him a priest in your
Church.

The notion of the subordination of the mind to God
continues for me to beg for recognition as the final wonder
of the world. In *The Constitution of Liberty*, F. A. Hayek
cites the Jesuit oath of St. Ignatius Loyola as the most extreme form of intellectual self-mortification, utterly incon-
sistent with the very idea of liberty; but of course he begs
the point, which is that it is only through the ultimate exercise of the free will that one abandons it, with the faith
that that act will bring on a special harmony, such as the
life of Gerhart—scholar, father, husband, musician, mor-
alist—has incarnated. I thank Dick for sending me the news
of the fiftieth anniversary of the Niemeyers' wedding, and
congratulate him on his new professional association.

It was dark, but although the road narrows and there are
three turns to remember to make, I don't think to tell
Jerry how to go because his memory of anywhere he has
ever been before is indelible. James and Marcia Burnham
have lived deep in the woods, three miles from the village
of Kent, since forever, as far as I know, and it was here
that as a supplicant I came in 1955, to ask him if he would
join the editorial staff of *National Review*. Although by
manner retiring—shy even; withdrawn and a little formal—
he was an intimidating figure. Valedictorian of his class at
Princeton, professor at New York University at age
twenty-four, author of texts in philosophy, Trotskyite,

a contributor to *Partisan Review*, celebrated author of *The Managerial Revolution*, a born-again conservative, premature anti-Communist, and then those three seminal strategy books on the struggle for the world—the strategic confrontation—ending with *Suicide of the West* (1964). For twenty-three years he had come in to New York every week for two days to serve *National Review* as senior editor, strategist, adviser, a mentor to all who experienced him. And then, returning on the airplane from the debate with Reagan on the Panama Canal, in a matter of hours he lost eighty percent of the vision of one eye, and ninety percent of the vision of the second—"macula degeneration," they call it, and there isn't anything you can do about it. This brought his resignation from *National Review*, but not the end of his afflictions: a year later a stroke, from which it was assumed he would not recover.

He did, but imperfectly. An evening spent with him yields no intimation that he is hindered. An evening which, however, the next day he will not predictably be able to remember. I turned the twenty-fifth-anniversary dinner of *National Review*, at which everyone was present *except* Reagan, into an impromptu (brief—I spoke about him for only three or four minutes) testimonial to Jim who, seated between Henry Kissinger and Clare Luce, rose—silver-white hair, glasses, shy appreciative smile, a wonderfully distinguished scholar and patriot—and acknowledged a standing ovation; and the next day he did not know that the affair had taken place. Although the *following* day it might re-enter his memory. Yet in conversation one does not notice anything awry. He became fifty-eight years old on the day John Kennedy was killed, and today he is seventy-six, and Marcia is celebrating the birthday in their Pavilion as they call it, an attractive stone one-story structure, separated from the New England rabbit warren where they live and suitable for parties and grandchildren; and there are a dozen old friends, including Priscilla, and champagne.

The conversation is animated, and Jim accepted gracefully all the little presents, and fussed about a bit to make certain everyone was happy and comfortable; and I notice that everyone who addresses him does so at the outset with deliberation, until satisfied that the speed of the conversation doesn't in the least distract him. The dinner was served buffet style, and we chatted away, and Marcia—still blond and Scandinavian and trim—made a toast to her husband in her characteristic reserved public style (*"Nobody was ever loved the way I was loved by Jim,"* she wept over the telephone the day after the stroke, when she thought Jim would not survive) and Priscilla, always shy on her feet, gave a marvelously eloquent, brief, aphoristic tribute to the man who shared her office at *National Review* for almost twenty-five years. Others are heard from, but it is important in such situations to guard against valedictory inflections. Soon after dinner I told Marcia that Priscilla and I simply had to go, because we must travel two hours to New York. In two cars, because Pitts needs her own in the city. I said goodbye, and made my way down the flagstones to Jerry. The night is very dark, but the occasion was very happy, Pitts and I agreed in whispers.

We are only eight miles from the house I grew up in, in Sharon, but the route does not take us by, and in any event I'll see it next week, because although it is substantially gutted, we are meeting there for Thanksgiving, preserving the family tradition. Gutted because five condominiums will exist where once a single family (to be sure, of ten children) was housed. Priscilla and (sister) Jane will each have one, and the large Spanish patio is intact, the colonial façade untouched. I wondered whether I would have to fight sleep, but the briefcase was full and I went back to it.

Sam McCracken is assistant to the prickly and brilliant president of Boston University. When Sam was a professor of Literature and Humanities at Reed College we corresponded, and en route to his new assignment several years ago he stopped by, a tall imposing blond man, married to a beautiful woman. The evening was slightly distracted by Sam's having just then gone off a regimen to which he had stuck for something like eighty days—no food, no wine. Objective: forty pounds. This was the night to celebrate, and accordingly he drank innocently huge glasses of Jack Daniels which my wife kept bringing him, and which he consumed as casually as if they were Dr Pepper. I looked with progressive astonishment at this Rabelaisian prodigy, who spoke, although there is a slight stutter, in such lucid and rhythmic language, and wondered how it was all biologically possible.

I had, before dinner, bathed one of our dogs, whose collar was now lying on Pat's beloved black slate coffee table, and Sam, punctuating a point about the irresponsibility of those who drive without attaching their safety belts, snuffed out his cigar conclusively—inside the dog collar, rubbing the cigar zestfully into the slate. Just for old times' sake, I sneaked a look at Pat (Mrs. McCracken was out of the room), whose first instinct was to scream; whose second instinct was to rise and go fetch a large ashtray; but who with habitual speed recognized that to place an ashtray alongside the dog collar would betray the hallucination, and embarrass Sam. A couple of days later, he wrote that he had had a strange sensation upon breaking his diet—that his wife told him he had had too much to drink, but that he felt just fine. I have felt fine about him for years, and read with admiration his frequent essays, mostly in *Commentary*, but occasionally in *National Review*.

Sam writes, "The author of the devastating send-up of Kennan in the current *New Yorker* is *aut WFB aut diabolus*. Marvelous! Your hand has not lost its cunning. If you publish it in your next collection, please take care to spell the name K+nn+n. Juries are likely to come down hard on rich men they think have abridged the rights of simple retired diplomats."

I read George Kennan's piece, and I must admit Sam has a point. "I have never been an advocate of unilateral disarmament," Mr. Kennan writes, "and I see no necessity for anything of that sort today." But having said that, K. goes on to say that the mere *existence* of nuclear weapons is the important datum, more significant by far than the question of who has dominion over such weapons. We should do away with ours. "I would feel the future of my children and grandchildren to be far safer than I do at this moment;

for if there is any incentive for the Russians to use such weapons against us, it surely comes in overwhelming degree—probably, in fact, entirely—from our own enormous deployment of them."

Uh-huh. And the use of bacteriological and chemical weapons by the Russians against Cambodians and Afghans came because of the enormous deployment by Cambodians and Afghans of bacteriological and chemical weapons; built with chopsticks. Oh dear, and George Kennan is such an intelligent man, and such a nice man. Well, let's hope he's right, that the Soviet Union will never use its weapons. "I suppose we can only pray that he is correct," I write Sam, "and giggle, just a little—as you authorize us to do—at his pretty little simplifications." An odd word to use to describe Kennan, but what's the right one in the circumstances?

I acknowledge with thanks lawyer Del Fuller's update on the appeals motion against the idiot commission in California that, overturning its own examiner, has ruled that the Bohemian Club in its summer encampment has to hire women. To the end of establishing that the non-hiring of women during the two-week encampment has nothing to do with sexual bias, I and (former) Governor Pat Brown were asked to go to San Francisco to serve as witnesses, and we were subsequently pleased by the thoughtful verdict of the examiner, handed down in due course, that men's highly private clubs can, without committing unlawful sexual discrimination, employ only men where the sex of the employee is relevant, as clearly it is in situations where, among other things, men wander about six hundred acres without much attention to dress. I congratulate Del on his brief, though frankly it has gotten so technical (like so much of the law) that it has become difficult for mere laymen even to follow the arguments.

I had it down to thank Professor Tom Sowell for his extraordinary performance on "Firing Line," defending the principal discoveries of his book, *Ethnic America*. Harriet Pilpel, so marvelously talented, riding the crest of so distinguished a career, is a love, and bright as a whip, but so frozen by liberal ideology that sometimes she simply ceases to *think!* As when, examining Sowell, she said: "Are you telling us that labor unions impede the progress of blacks and that you are therefore *against* labor unions?" To which he answered coolly that he had *not* been asked whether he was in *favor* of labor unions, he had been asked what were *some* of the impediments to *black* upward mobility. Sowell (himself black) radiates the most naturally aristocratic hauteur of anyone I've had on "Firing Line" since Giscard d'Estaing, ten years ago. Sowell suffers socially from his apparent apostasy from the black movement, as does the black economist Walter Williams, who having analyzed the minimum wage laws pronounces them an important factor in black teenage unemployment. The slightly underground crack these days is that Tom Sowell and Walter Williams have a private covenant, never both to ride in the same airplane.

Will I write a plug for Espygrams? "You are probably wondering what an Espygram is." Well, yes. "An Espygram is a verse or limerick written by Mr. Espy." Now if only the lady from Clarkson N. Potter, Inc., Publisher, had left it at that, the meaning of Espygram would be instantly communicable. But she goes on. "The reader figures out the missing words by using the context of the verse, the rhymes, and the number of letters in the words as clues. Espygrams are entertaining and challenging, and we've found that once people get the hang of doing them they can't stop."

I looked, and had no trouble whatever in stopping. One of them did, however, catch the eye, to wit:

In sleep, salacious Incubus
And Succubus make __ __ __ __ __ with us.
Now I suggest they wouldn't bother
If in our __ __ __ __ __ they __ __ __ __ ' __ each other.
Perhaps they're mutually __ __ __ __ __ __,
Or, odder still, have never mated.

Your job would be to come up with respective fillers, all using the same letters: *dates; stead; teas'd; sated.*

A first-year student at the graduate school of business in Cornell has thought deeply about a career in business—and wants out. He wishes to become a journalist. There are so very many of these who come to us. And our responses are always so dismayingly discouraging. *National Review* is a *tiny* editorial operation, and its actors are technicians of highly developed skills. Besides, young people coming to *NR* get very little experience in writing, because the stuff that's published is, almost all of it, written either by the resident pros, or by outside pros. There are of course exceptions, Brookhiser the most recent. For a while I thought we were running a finishing school for apostates (Garry Wills, John Leonard, Arlene Croce); but somehow the impression persists that all magazines have a half-dozen post-college-age positions available to anyone with a little talent. The same old story.

Norma Cox Woodley, who as I have said runs the Friends of Firing Line, is trying to raise the money from the Chase Bank to pay for the big upcoming Harvard debate on Reaganomics, but there is a problem here. The Chase people insist that Milton Friedman must be one of the actors. No Friedman, no grant.

I think it's probably true to say that no one in the world knows *both* Ken Galbraith and Milton Friedman better than I do (read carefully: *both*), and I should therefore be ideally situated to bring them together. But Galbraith says no: "Milton is a better debater than I am and I'm a better writer than he is." Well, that's a good answer.

Would Milton have agreed? Well, no. Because *he's* mad at Ken, because he says Ken *deliberately* misrepresents him —e.g., by continuing references to Milton's antagonism to the poor, such characterizations as make Milton really *quite angry*, because Ken knows *goddamn well* Milton's not unfriendly to the poor and Milton knows *goddamn well* that Ken Galbraith doesn't really think he's unfriendly to the poor. . . . I try to explain that that's just the way Ken is— I mean, he's perfectly capable of saying on network TV that Buckley is in favor of plague, poverty, and atomic war; and what if *I* adopted Milton's sensitivity, how then would *I* get along with Galbraith? That, Milton tells me, is *my* problem.

I know when things just aren't going to happen, and I'm not going to get Galbraith and Friedman on the same program up at Harvard, and I'm not going to ask them to do it as a personal favor to me, which maybe would, maybe wouldn't, move them. So I write to Norma: Couldn't she possibly talk the Chase people out of their insistence on Milton? I rattle off other names she might hold out: Laffer, Bleiberg, Baker, Dole—right down the list. (The answer would be: No.)

Mr. W. M. Woods of Oak Ridge is a man given above all other things to precision of thought, language, and calculation, and he is greatly upset by a letter writer to *National Review* who has defended the Post Office's insistence that it needs a nine-digit code. Because that gentleman miscalculated the number of discrete zip codes that this would permit, Bill Woods undertakes to set us all straight. . . .

"Mr. Fifield is guilty of applying a perfectly good formula for permutations to the wrong problem. His formula gives the number of permutations of ten things taken nine at a time where none of the things is repeated. In the context of nine-digit zips, it is of course permissible to repeat any of the decimal digits as many times as desired, up to nine.

"In that context, $P_r^n = n^r$ precisely.

"There is a way of calculating the number of distinct nine-digit zips that a child can understand. (I tried the problem on a bright third-grader. He had the correct answer in a few minutes.) In any sequence of consecutive integers, the number of terms is equal to the largest term minus the smallest term, plus one:

"$999,999,999 - 000,000,000 + 1 = 1,000,000,000$ (that's 1 billion).

"To put this in perspective, there are about 222 million people in the U.S. With a nine-digit zip, each person could have his own unique number, and so could each cat, dog, and pet canary. Mr. Fifield, what are those lines by Pope? The ones about that Pierian spring?"

You can bet your bottom dollar that Mr. W. M. Woods knows what are those lines by Pope. (The ones about that Pierian spring.) I thanked Bill Woods, as I have so often over the years, for one thing for teaching me how to use "exponentially" exactly right, and also "parameters."

Happily, we are in New York. Jerry knows exactly what approach to take, depending on the hour. It is only just after midnight, and five minutes later we pull up. I told Jerry 9:30 tomorrow morning, and thanked him.

Pat was still up, working at her desk. Come, she says, and have a look at the dining room. I followed her, and she walked in and turned on the lights.

It is really quite beautiful. Everything is set for the Vice-President and the twenty diners. The flowers, the china, the wineglasses, place settings. The picture lights

give the tables a wonderful radiance. I reproach myself that men tend not to focus on the amount of time these things take. A cliché, mostly because it's used in sly discharge of an obligation never taken up, which would be to remind oneself of the amount of time these things all take.

We went up, wearily, to bed.

Eight

MONDAY

I must write my column early, because *National Review*'s editorial conference is at 9:45. Ordinarily it would be on Tuesday, but this being Thanksgiving week it is, in the idiom of the shop, a "short week," because the printers take Thursday off. Pat was already awake when the alarm rang, so my breakfast is brought in, and she yielded me the *Times*. Already I have decided on the subject matter for the column. I can use the notes on the sermon yesterday at church, so I read the paper without that search-and-destroy feeling that so often propels me. I left for my little study just when the telephone rang for Pat's first morning call. I am privately convinced that Pat is a kind of social electronic ganglion, through whom half the people in New York transmit to the other half. Maybe she is a human microchip? I must dilate on that.

I discuss the bishop, and sermons in general. Sermons are really more a Protestant than a Catholic cultural staple. "It was not until Vatican II that a general scolding was given on the subject, the homily being prescribed as integral to the Mass (I wrote). Daily Masses habitually omitted it altogether, and many churches suspended the sermon entirely during the summer. It was thought rather an accretion, and it does not really surprise that the greatest homilist of the nineteenth century, Newman, came in from the Anglican Church; and of the twentieth century, Sheen, Sheed, the first achieved his reputation speaking not in church but over the radio, the second as a street-corner evangelist."

I was halfway through my column when the office phone rang and Helen (our switchboard operator) told me it's the Vice-President.

"Let me tell it to you fast, Bill, I can't come."

I try to absorb the shock as he speaks. But, come to think of it, he is actually telling me what I just finished reading in the huge headlines this morning, for some reason without thinking that it hazarded in any way the movements of the Vice-President of the United States. It was the President himself who gave the order: No travel. What is happening is a shoot-out between Congress and the Executive over money. Technically, as of 12:01 A.M. on November 21, 1981, it became illegal for the federal government to spend *any* money, so that travel, when government funds are involved, is—proscribed.

George is telling me how *awful* he feels, what *stratagems* he has considered in order to be able to get here, how one after another he had to *discard* them. George's voice is always relaxed, but there was no doubting the authenticity of his concern. He asks, How would it be if he got Jeane Kirkpatrick to take his place? He had no idea whether the UN ambassador could disengage from whatever she was undoubtedly up to, but he'd certainly give it a try.

Yes yes, I said; and then he eased over to the subject of my son.

We had never spoken about Christopher before, and what he said, which left me purring with pride and gratitude, easily made up for the crisis. George told me he would be in New York two and a half weeks from today, on December 11, and had reserved the entire afternoon, from lunch on, during which, in expiation of our convulsion at today's lunch, he would do anything we asked of him. I told him that was swell of him, but that such a thing as we had got together for today takes a couple of months to arrange, and could not be put together again in a fortnight. He would keep the afternoon *anyway*, he said, just in case; and would ring me back as soon as he reached Kirkpatrick.

So I called Bill Rusher, and Helen located Rob Sennott, our advertising director, and we patched together a summit. There are three alternatives, I said. One is to cancel the lunch altogether. A second is to call all the guests and tell them George Bush isn't going to be there, but they're welcome anyway. The third is to call nobody, to hope for

Jeane Kirkpatrick, and to put on a show of our own if she didn't come — and rely on the presumed good nature of busy people who understand that such things do happen. Even though the New York *Times* says such things (the United States government running out of money) *don't* as a matter of fact routinely happen. (This, the reasons apart, is the first time in history. Never mind.)

Rob tells us that several of the guests (they are all presidents, or board chairmen) are flying in from out of town and it was already too late to reach them. Bill injects that if half of them pulled out and Mrs. Kirkpatrick *did* come, the thing would be rather embarrassing, and I agree. So, I say, let's just go with it. They agree; and I can tell that Rob, who has done all the work, is pretty disappointed.

I completed the column . . . "The bishops have been very active of late. The Ordinary of Charleston having outlawed capital punishment, perhaps he will proceed to outlaw murder. But the bishops are stirring, and their involvement in public policy saddens. One recalls the late Willi Schlamm, who defined scientists as men who first build the Brooklyn Bridge, then buy it."

I started to leave, but Pat put down the telephone to tell me I must look again at the seating. I tell her merely to substitute "X" for Bush, and leave all the others where they were. Jerry is waiting and I told him I wish the Vice-President had relied on him, rather than *Air Force Two*. By the time I got to the office, word had come in. Mrs. Kirkpatrick, with great gallantry, would cancel her lunch and attend ours. I am to brief her on what is expected of her, via her Number Two, because she has gone to the floor of the General Assembly, no doubt to give one of those brilliant speeches nobody ever listens to. I tell Number Two that she is expected, at our functions, to speak for ten minutes after lunch, and then to answer questions for fifteen, and that we guarantee the lunch will be over at 2:30.

But now we have an issue of *National Review* to put out.

We sit around the long black table, which has been here forever. We are in the library-conference room, about twelve of us. Everyone concerned with the editorial end of *NR*'s operations. Each of us has in front of him a copy of last week's issue, and we turn its pages one by one, and anyone who has any comments makes them: about an editorial, cartoon, story, criticism; about the typography, the makeup. We laugh a lot at these sessions. Sometimes the laughter is—exponential!, as Mr. Woods would in this case permit me to say. I think. Jeff will make an amusing comment about somebody or something, more often than not a Democrat, Bill Rusher will see him and raise, and Joe Sobran will double the pot.

We go through the issue, and then Bill Rusher lists, with great panache, his fortnightly suggestions, complaints, whatever—distributing his document file between me and Priscilla. He speaks first because, traditionally, he then leaves the room, to attend to his own affairs.

Priscilla is next (now that Jim Burnham is no longer here), and she goes down the list of subjects that need editorial or polemical attention. I write these down, composing the master list, while others scratch Priscilla's items from theirs, where there are coincidences. Inevitably she adduces topics others had also listed to bring up, but no longer need to do so.

So it goes, with a little cross-table discussion, though not much; because, generally, the subjects are familiar, the orientation steady. The counterclockwise referendum completed, those who are not writing editorials rise and leave, I make the assignments to the writers, and we disperse to our typewriters.

Not, today, to my own typewriter, to begin the editorial work. Frances has accumulated what she calls date requests, dating back to noon Friday, since which time we have not spoken. Henry Kissinger is having a dinner for the French ambassador on January 11. We look at the calendar—the day is or is not clear, depending on what time I need to leave for Dallas. She will explain to Chris Vick, Henry's Frances. The Chilean National TV wants an interview (nix). The Council on Foreign Relations asks if I will preside at a meeting at which my friend Lewis Lehrman, a candidate for governor of New York State, will talk about the gold standard (yes). Dan Shockett of something called *Cigar* asks if I will serve as a member of a cigar-tasting panel. All that's involved is that they will send three cigars which I can smoke at my leisure, returning comments (certainly). A Mr. Ed Cullen wants to discuss movie and TV rights for my novels. That's been going on for five years, but I refer them now to Richmond Crinkley, sometime Washington editor of *National Review*, now executive director of the Vivian Beaumont Theater at Lincoln Center, who is interested in getting a movie made out of *Saving the Queen*. Timothy Leary called, but didn't leave a return number (that often happens). CBS Cable TV wants an interview for their program "Signature." Frances's note says: "I said you would appear to talk about your new book, out in January, since you did not like being interviewed on the 'what do you like for breakfast basis'" (exactly). Swiss Broadcasting wants to ask me questions about Reagan's speech Wednesday (nix). Lecture requests (the usual). Betty Prashker of Doubleday says the Book-of-the-Month Club needs a date for a luncheon (we find one). The BOM has selected *Marco Polo* as a *Dual* Main Selection. (I have persuaded Doubleday, in its promotional literature, simply to refer to *Marco Polo* as "A Main Selection of the Book-of-the-Month Club," which is accurate, with emphasis on the indefinite article. I have always been convinced that there are people out there who believe that a "Dual" Main

Selection means that the book is only half as good as a just plain "Main" Selection.) My hosts at Vail in April say if I want to arrive a day earlier than my lecture, I can ski, as their guest. Frances points out I'll be traveling away from a Tulane engagement Friday night, so I might as well accept, unless I want to go New Orleans-New York-Denver in thirty-six hours (OK). But now we *do* have to leave.

At noon exactly, Jerry took Bill Rusher and me up for the luncheon, because when businessmen are invited to lunch someone *always* arrives early. This will be I think our twelfth such lunch, predecessors having featured Spiro Agnew, Milton Friedman, Ronald Reagan, Henry Kissinger, William Simon, James Buckley, Barry Goldwater, Frank Shakespeare, and a few other divinities. The idea is to invite very important and acute businessmen, share a lunch, let them visit with someone in the public eye, and hope that their advertising departments will get an amiable memo about *National Review*, which sometimes happens, usually doesn't. The guest of honor is not asked to pitch in any way for us, and seldom does, though the circuitry of bright men doesn't need many traffic switches.

And sure enough, although we got there at 12:20, two guests had already arrived. A few minutes later I greeted with great pleasure Eastern Air Lines President Frank Borman, ex-astronaut moon-man, who is (along with George Bush) one of the twenty-six members of Hillbillies, our little club in the Bohemian Grove.

I cherish an experience last summer with Frank. I put in a call to him, and it went like this:

"Frank, I'm making last-minute revisions of a novel I wrote this winter. It's about the U-2. Do you mind if I ask you a couple of questions?"

"Fire away. Only I'm not an expert on the U-2. But I know people who are."

"Well, when I read two books about the U-2 they

didn't of course give the speed at which it travels, but I made some deductions based on general inferences, and I figured it traveled at Mach .9, so I made my calculations about my hero's flight from Tokyo to Alma-Ata based on that speed. Do you happen to know if my guess was correct?"

"Well, I'll need to find out 1) if it's classified. 2) What the speed is—I don't happen to know. Can I call you back? Five minutes, maybe ten?"

"Of course, and thanks loads."

Five minutes later.

"Bill? Hi, Frank. 1) It *is* classified. 2) The speed is Mach .7."

I thanked him hugely; and now reminded him of the wonderful context in which he had framed his answer, and we said, jocularly, the usual things about the folly of classifying material obviously known to the Russians.

Our guests were now practically all there, in the smaller red library room, most of them known to each other, and of course the word had circulated instantly that the guest of honor wouldn't be there, but there wasn't, really, any sense of resentment, because by now the radio and the early afternoon papers had made it very clear that *no one* was to travel *anywhere*, and obviously they understood: the Vice-President had to stand out as the exemplar.

Then Jeane Kirkpatrick came—handsome, composed, energetic, charming—bringing with her, by prearrangement, Ambassador Charles Lichenstein, her assistant. I had known Chuck at Yale since even before I knew Pat, and we all exchanged greetings, and I told Jeane what a sweetheart she was, and promised to tell the Third World about her.

We were seated and, if I may say so, no chief of state or prodigal prince ate better that day than we did, thanks primarily to Pat, but also to Julian, and Gloria. And during lunch I was able to give Jeane a little additional briefing on the forthcoming drill, not that she needed it. On her right, Walter Wriston, head of Citibank, began questioning her, with his distinctive intelligence, and soon at our table she was answering everyone's questions.

After lunch we went into the living room for coffee and liqueurs (no one, I noticed, took a liqueur), and after a moment or two I introduced Mrs. Kirkpatrick, easy enough for me to do so enthusiastically, enthusiastic as I am about her.

I served a hitch (28th General Assembly, 1973) as the U.S. public member at the UN, assigned primarily to the Third Committee, which deals with human rights. When, last May, I read Jeane Kirkpatrick's speech on human rights, as delivered to the Council on Foreign Relations, I was, simply, ecstatic. I had begun my column: "In a single speech, delivered in early March . . . in New York, Jeane Kirkpatrick . . . shed more light on the subject of human rights and national policy than all the candlepower of the UN Human Rights Commission has shed in a generation. Her statement has liberating force. Such is said about those few statements that cause the scales to fall from one's eyes, even as the epiphany befell St. Paul. Mrs. Kirkpatrick talked about four distinctions 'crucial' to a consideration of human rights and national policy. They are worth memorizing . . ." (The distinctions: 1) between "ideas and institutions," 2) between "rights and goals," 3) between "intention and consequence," 4) between "personal morality and political morality.")

She spoke now like a professor turned advocate; her own evolution exactly. She specified at two points that particular things she was about to say were off the record.

In the ten minutes she had, she made shrewd use of the time, dealing directly with points of interest and concluding with the (requisite) business about how, notwithstanding its frustrations, the UN was a necessary institution—which conclusion it would be very difficult for a resident ambassador at the UN *not* to arrive at. During the question period she sprang to life. She had been recently in the news for doing something absolutely unheard of: she had sent out several dozen letters to ambassadors ostensibly friendly to the United States, asking why they had voted against the United States in one of those virulent anti-American UN-related resolutions implying our vassalization of Puerto Rico or whatever. Apparently it had never occurred to anyone publicly to ask the jolly ambassador you see two or three times a day and who enjoys U.S. favors just *why* he joined in denouncing America in general terms.

How had they reacted? someone wanted to know; and she replied that, surprisingly, she had had replies to three quarters of her letters, that half had been conciliatory, only one quarter hostile. She believes very strongly that an American presence in the United Nations has got to be forthright. In this respect she is much like Moynihan, though the styles are different. One cannot imagine Mrs. Kirkpatrick, after a vote denouncing Zionism as racism, rushing across the room and embracing the Israeli ambassador; although the substitution would almost certainly be pleasing to the Israeli ambassador.

It was 2:30, and I thanked her, thanked my guests, and say that whatever inconvenience was suffered, it was good to be alive on the day that the government spent no money. Everyone, on the way out, shook hands with me, Bill Rusher, Rob Sennott, and Mrs. K., thanking her most sincerely. The *NR* contingent got into the car and we returned to the office, whence I wire George: "I CAN'T THANK YOU ENOUGH BOTH FOR YOUR CONCERN AND FOR YOUR FURNISHING THE U.N. COBRA. SINCE DECEMBER 11 IS TOO SOON TO PUT TOGETHER THE KIND OF PEOPLE YOU DESERVE I'LL

TAKE YOU UP ON YOUR KIND OPTION TO DO IT ALL AGAIN IN
THE SPRING. SO MANY THANKS AND IF YOU RUN OUT OF
MONEY AGAIN WALTER WRISTON PROMISED TO HELP OUT.
WARMEST REGARDS."

Back in the office, I assembled my own column for *National Review*, "Notes and Asides," which comprises letters received from people saying interesting things, requiring, in some cases, a published retort, which I compose. Then I pluck out the editorials that have been written, and go over them. They are in the dumbwaiter that descends to Priscilla. There is left an hour, reserved by Frances for necessary work on the sailing book, whose proposed jacket, and jacket copy, I didn't like. I designed the jacket for *Airborne*, and whereas I meant that it should convey to the reader that the sea is at the heart of the book, I didn't want it to be thought a "sailing book," which it is not. So is it with *Atlantic High*. I had subconsciously been in search for over a year now for a subtitle. For *Airborne* I used "A Sentimental Journey." The motives were in part preemptive. I didn't want reviewers to think to one-up me by saying, "This is pretty sentimental stuff." Actually, they were kind. I have decided in *Atlantic High* to append "A Celebration," and Sam, and Alex Gotfryd, Doubleday's art director, and Christopher Little, whose photographs are an integral part of the book, like the idea. Christopher, a superb young professional, is coming in for today's cover session. He has a painter friend who will attempt to transcribe our instructions. Almost an hour went into this, and suddenly it's 6:15.

Jerry took Priscilla and me to Sixty-eighth and Park Avenue, where Mother lives when she isn't in Connecticut or South Carolina. The heart always beats almost audibly at the prospect of seeing her when one gives the telltale buzz on the buzzer (dash dot-dash dash) and Big Mary, in her white nurse's uniform, opens the door. Mother is seated at the far end of a card table in the living room, dressed, as ever, as if to receive ambassadors. Always there are the pearls, and the touch of lace, and the familiar scent, the dress, the high-heeled shoes. She smiles that smile of fresh ardor, eyes wide open; at eighty-seven she can look like a girl, expressions to match—joy, benevolence, serenity. We kiss and greet Mother's pizza companions, because indeed she is having a pizza dinner with three grandchildren. With her are Allie and John, siblings in their twenties, and Claude, Reid's son, who at twenty-two retains his Spanish accent, having spent his first twelve years in Madrid. Mother does not follow conversations, though she will pronounce on them, in a vaguely attenuated way, so that, though we are ostensibly addressing Mother, in fact we are conversing among ourselves. We learn from John that he is tremendously excited at the prospect of *The Wall Street Journal*'s running one of his rock reviews, from Claude that he loves the art school he is attending, from Allie that CBS is treating her fairly. I went and checked the spinet Mother used to play but, really, can't now, though every now and again we essay a duet. Mary brought Priscilla and me a glass of chablis. Mother beamed, and occasionally commented on, oh, how cold it was in Paris yesterday.

A year ago, in Mexico, visiting my old retired nurse, who was with us thirty-five years, I put in a call to Mother, so that she and Felipa could speak for the first time over the telephone since Felipa's retirement in 1952. Mother was twenty-two, Felipa twenty-eight when Mother's aunt, for whom Felipa worked as laundress, so to speak "gave" Felipa to Mother for her wedding; and Felipa (and, subsequently, her two sisters) went with us everywhere. Now Felipa, whose mind at ninety-three hasn't wandered at all, was reminiscing with Mother, over the phone to New York, how Mother used to look when she came back from her New Orleans high school to visit from time to time with her aunt in the late afternoon. The conversation, by participants, was about events in the year 1910!—a strange feeling for someone not even born until a generation later. Mother regularly captured by her beneficent fantasies, had replied most distinctly over the telephone that she happened to be *in* Mexico, that she had in hand gifts for Felipa and her two sisters, and that she would bring them around the *very next day*. I had warned Felipa about Mother's absentmindedness, and now Felipa handled the problem with exemplary diplomacy: How *nice*, she said, it would be to see the señora again.

I winked at Pitts and we got up to go. Every time I leave her, I wonder whether it will be for the last time. With help from Mary, Mother saw us to the elevator, and we embraced.

The editors dine at our place on Seventy-third Street the night of the fortnightly editorial meetings, the evening before we go to press. Usually we have guests, but not tonight; it was just Joe Sobran and Priscilla, Jeff Hart and Rick—Bill Rusher couldn't make it. There is great harmony at work, I feel: that graduating congruity of intellect and affection that matures when people are happily in professional and personal contact with one another. Oh, there are disturbances all right, and they reach you, and one does what one can. But *National Review* is a good place to work; after all, Priscilla is there. And then there is enough bite in the product to prevent the fungoid growth of tapioca, which can kill a journal. It matters that one should understand exactly what is meant by "bite." We suffer no lycanthropic compulsions at *NR*. We do not fancy ourselves out preying on victims preferably guilty, but if the biological appetite is not satisfied, then—however regrettably—innocent. I suppose it could be said that, like wolves, we have biological needs that require satisfaction: if there were nothing to complain about, there would be no *National*

Review. On the other hand, if there were nothing to complain about, there would be no post-Adamite mankind. But complaint is profanation in the absence of gratitude. There is much to complain about in America, but that awful keening noise one unhappily gets so used to makes no way for the bells, and these have rung for America, are still ringing for America, and for this we are *obliged* to be grateful. To be otherwise is wrong reason, and a poetical invitation to true national tribulation. I must remember to pray more often, because providence has given us the means to make the struggle, and in this respect we are singularly blessed in this country, and in this room.

After dinner there is some general conversation, but Pat, worn out by the Vice-President's non-party, has excused herself. My colleagues leave early, and, upstairs, I find that Pat is already asleep, the television blaring. I turn it off, and so risk waking her. I undress. The chair by my bed is stacked high with books and magazines. But I am tired, and settle for the blaring headline of the evening paper. There is a story that the Stamford *Advocate* has fired the roommate of Kathy Boudin, because the publisher didn't believe her story about not knowing that Ms. Boudin was a fugitive from justice. The Stamford *Advocate* is owned now by the Los Angeles *Times*. It was a suggestion from the then-editor of the Stamford *Advocate*, made to Harry, that caused Harry to call me in 1962 and propose that I write a newspaper column.

But my mind is wandering now, so I turn off the light.

Weariness, Bill—you cannot yet know literally what it means. I wish no time would come when you do know, but the balance of experience is against it. One day, long hence, you will know true weariness and will say: "That was it."

Letter from Whittaker Chambers,
April 9, 1961.

INDEX

LIST OF PHOTOGRAPHS